JEWISH LEADERSHIP DURING THE NAZI ERA:
PATTERNS OF BEHAVIOR IN THE FREE WORLD

Edited by

RANDOLPH L. BRAHAM

Social Science Monographs
and
Institute for Holocaust Studies of
The City University of New York
Distributed by Columbia University Press, New York

1985

EAST EUROPEAN MONOGRAPHS, NO. CLXXV

Copyright © 1985 by Randolph L. Braham
Library of Congress Card Catalog Number 84-52081
ISBN 0-88033-067-8

Printed in the United States of America

CONTENTS

Holocaust Studies Series

Randolph L. Braham, Editor
The Institute for Holocaust Studies
The Graduate School and University Center
The City University of New York

Previously published books in the Series:
Perspectives on the Holocaust, 1982
Contemporary Views on the Holocaust, 1983
Genocide and Retribution, 1983
*The Hungarian Jewish Catastrophe. A
Selected and Annotated Bibliography,* 1984

The Holocaust Studies Series is published in cooperation with
the Institute for Holocaust Studies. These books are out-
growths of lectures, conferences, and research projects sponsored by the Institute. It is the purpose of the series to subject
the events and circumstances of the Holocaust to scrutiny by a
variety of academics who bring different scholarly disciplines
to the study. The first three books in the Series were published
by Kluwer-Nijhoff Publishing of Boston.

PREFACE

Some of the most agonizing questions relating to the Holocaust concern the attitudes and reactions of the Jewish leaders, both in Nazi-occupied Europe and in the free world. During the first few decades of the post-World War II era, attention was focused primarily on the wartime role and behavior of the Jewish Councils *(Judenräte)* in the countries subjugated by the Third Reich. The number of books and articles dealing with the Jewish Councils has increased at a relatively high rate in recent years. Many of these were the fruit of conferences held in several prestigious centers of learning and research. While a considerable number of these works are partisan in nature, with their authors obviously resolved to condemn or defend the Councils, several deal with them in a scholarly and balanced manner. The authors of these works clearly endeavored to explore and analyze many of the controversial questions relating to the Councils, including the issues of collaboration, effectiveness of leadership, and involvement in rescue and resistance operations. They did so with dedication to objectivity and the pursuit of truth based on currently available evidence.

Many of the studies on the Jewish Councils were part of larger monographs dealing with the fate that befell the local or national Jewish communities with which they were associated. These constituted—and continue to constitute—an integral part of the scholarly efforts centering on the victims. A few evaluations were incorporated in larger studies dealing with the perpetrators and their accomplices. In these studies, the Councils were evaluated primarily in terms of their cooperation with or resistance to the oppressors. Comparatively little, if any, attention was paid to the Councils in the studies dealing with the position of the "onlookers" during the Holocaust, currently one of the areas under intense scrutiny. On the other hand, an increasing number of the studies dealing with the wartime attitudes and reactions of the free world, including the Allies, neutral powers, the

Vatican, and such international organizations and institutions as the International Red Cross and the Christian Churches, devote considerable attention to the positions taken by the national and international Jewish organizations and their leaders during the Holocaust.

No independent study has yet appeared on the patterns of Jewish leadership in the free world during the Nazi era. Many contemporary Jewish leaders, both lay and religious, motivated by the best of intentions, continue to argue against the investigation of this sensitive topic, using a variety of reasons: the proximity of events, the lack of adequate preparatory work, the unavailability of many archival sources, the impossibility of objective analysis, the possible detraction from the guilt of the Nazis and their accomplices, and the harm that might be caused to the Jewish community—to cite just a few. But similar arguments were also advanced against the studies dealing with the Jewish Councils, a much more explosive topic in light of the many accusations of collaboration that were raised against these leadership groups in the immediate postwar period. The issues relating to the wartime positions of the Jewish leaders in the free world are indeed sensitive, but not impervious to scholarly investigation.

The issue of the wartime positions of the Jewish leaders in the free world is especially sensitive in view of the accusations that have been leveled against them by many Jewish leaders in Nazi-dominated Europe as well as by the anti-establishment Jewish leadership groups in the free world itself. Spokesmen for the latter groups as well as many Holocaust survivors continue to raise searching questions in this respect. They often portray the Jewish leaders of the free world as part of a "conspiracy of silence" that enabled the Nazis and their accomplices to carry out their sinister designs against the European Jews with virtual impunity. They also accuse them—especially the Zionists among them—of having sacrificed the immediate needs of rescue for the requirements of a future Jewish state. Some examples will illustrate this point of view. A few months after the alleged Hitler Order on the Final Solution was made public, Chaim Greenberg, the editor of the *Yiddisher Kempfer,* launched a scathing attack on the American Jewish leadership for its "bankrupt" response to the Nazis' plan for the extermination of European Jewry. In the February 1943 issue of his paper he stated *inter alia:*

> The basic fact is evident to any Jew who has the courage to look at the situation as it is: American Jewry has not done—and has made no effort to do—its elementary duty toward the millions of Jews who are captive and doomed to die in Europe.

The leaders of the Jewish National Committee of Poland, representing the fighting Jews in that German-occupied country—apparently upset over the perceived failure of Rabbi Stephen S. Wise, Nahum Goldman, and the leaders of the American Joint Distribution Committee to react positively to their specific suggestions for help advanced on March 17, 1943—wrote a scathing letter to Ignacy Schwarzbart, one of the two Jewish representatives in the Polish Government-in-Exile in London, that not only condemned the Nazis but also berated the Jewish leaders of the free world. It was dated November 15, 1943—i.e., about six months after the crushing of the Warsaw Ghetto Uprising.

> The blood of 3,000,000 Polish Jews will take revenge not only against the Nazi murderers, but against those indifferent elements which have contented themselves merely with words but have done nothing to rescue from the hands of the beasts a people doomed to extermination. This we can . . . never forget or forgive.

About half a year later, Rabbi Michael Dov Weissmandel, a leading member of the Bratislava Relief and Rescue Committee, was even more caustic about the perceived indifference of the Jewish leaders of the free world. Seeing the apathy while the Jews of Hungary were being deported when Allied victory was clearly in sight and the secrets of Auschwitz had been fully revealed, he reproached the Jewish leaders of the West in a letter addressed to the *Hehalutz* in Geneva:

> And you, you Jewish brethren in all the free countries, and you, government leaders in all countries, how can you be silent in the face of these murders in which some six million Jews have been killed up to now and in which thousands are still being killed every day! With devastated hearts the murdered Jews are screaming at you and about you, you cruel ones, you murderers, because of your cruel silence and your folding your hands in inaction, because you have the ability to refuse to allow—and to prevent—these events at this time.

The alleged conspiracy of silence has been the subject of an increasing number of books and articles in recent years. Many of these dealt specifically with the alleged inaction and indifference of the Allies, mostly the Western Allies. Others were devoted to other groups of "onlookers": the neutral powers, the Vatican, and several governmental and nongovernmental organizations, including the International Red Cross. Still other writings, accusatory and polemical, dealt with the perceived inaction of the Jewish communal leaders in the free world. The primary objective of these appears to have been the indictment of individual Jewish leaders, groups, and organizations, usually from a particular political perspective.

It was partially in reaction to the appearance of an ever larger number of subjective works that the leaders of the Jack P. Eisner Institute for Holocaust Studies and of the Center for Jewish Studies of the Graduate School and University Center of The City University of New York decided to make possible an in-depth, objective, and systematic investigation of the attitudes and reactions of the Jewish leaders of the free world during the Nazi era. Toward this end they organized the first international conference devoted to this chapter of the Holocaust. Held on November 9–10, 1981, the conference focused attention on the four largest Jewish communities in the free world: the United States, Great Britain, Palestine, and Switzerland. While the goal of the conference was to pursue the approximation of truth on the basis of the currently available evidence, the organizers were nevertheless convinced that the findings of the conference could in no way detract from the culpability of those who must bear ultimate responsibility for the Holocaust: The Nazis and their accomplices in all parts of German-dominated Europe. Partial responsibility must also be borne by the onlookers: the local Christian populations that were mostly passive in face of the tragedy of their Jewish neighbors, but also the Vatican, the Allied Powers and the neutral countries— the homelands of the Jewish leaders of the free world. For it was partially because of their indifference to the plight of the Jews that the Nazis and their accomplices were able to carry out their concerted and singleminded drive for the Final Solution of the Jewish question in Europe.

Notwithstanding the Nazi myth about the unity and power of the Jewish people, a myth fostered by such forgeries as the *Protocols of the Elders of Zion,* the Jews were neither united nor powerful. They were in fact disunited and powerless, not only in Nazi-dominated Europe but to a large extent in the free world as well. The wartime concerns of the Jewish communities outside of the Nazi sphere reflected their particular milieus, varying in terms of their histories and the histories of the host nations. In all of them, the Jewish community was divided along religious, socioeconomic, and political lines. The concerns of the British and American Jews with the war effort were as natural and understandable as the concerns of the Swiss Jews with the preservation of the independence and neutrality of Switzerland or the concerns of the Jewish community of Palestine *(Yishuv)* with the immediate problems of security and the building of a Jewish national state.

This volume, the fourth in the series of Holocaust studies published under the auspices of the Jack P. Eisner Institute for Holocaust Studies, is an outgrowth of the November 1981 conference. The first paper, *The American*

Jewish Leadership and the Holocaust, is by Professor David S. Wyman of the University of Massachusetts, a well-known authority on the subject. He focuses attention not only on the patterns of leadership within the Jewish community, but also on the attitudes and reactions of the leaders of the American government.

The next study is an analytical overview, *Patterns of Jewish Leadership in Great Britain During the Nazi Era,* by Professor Bernard Wasserstein of Brandeis University. Professor Wasserstein demonstrates, among other things, that during the Nazi era the response of Anglo-Jewry to the crisis differed significantly from that of the other major Jewish communities, especially the American one, primarily because of the special characteristics of its communal structure and the unique social and political context within which its leadership operated. The third study is by Professor Bela Vago of the University of Haifa, a recognized authority both on the Holocaust and on East-Central European history. Professor Vago's basic objective in his balanced and dispassionate account, *Some Aspects of the Yishuv Leadership's Activities During the Holocaust,* is to answer a number of provocative questions that have agitated—and continue to agitate—scholars and laypersons alike: Who were the *Yishuv* leaders? What did they know about the realities of the Holocaust and when? How did they react? What were the priorities in their interests and activities? How were their intentions translated into deeds? What objective possibilities of rescue were available to them? How effective were their efforts?

The fourth study is by Gerhart M. Riegner, the Executive Director of the World Jewish Congress. Dr. Riegner's study, *Switzerland and the Leadership of Its Jewish Community During the Second World War,* is an authoritative account based on thorough familiarity with the subject as well as personal experience. Stationed in Geneva during the war, Dr. Riegner was in a unique position to assemble and transmit vital information about the plight of European Jewry in German-dominated Europe, and to observe and evaluate the attitudes and reactions of the Swiss Jewish community's leadership.

The last study in this volume, *Patterns of Jewish Leadership in Latin America During the Holocaust,* is by Haim Avni of the Hebrew University of Jerusalem. A well-known authority on the Jewish communities in the Spanish-speaking world, Professor Avni contributed this study to fill a gap discerned during the 1981 conference. In addition to evaluating the positions of the Jewish leaders of the various Latin American countries during the war, Professor Avni also provides an analytical overview of the basic processes that shaped the infrastructure of the Diaspora in South America.

ACKNOWLEDGMENTS

The publication of this volume was made possible through the cooperation and support of many individuals. I hereby express my sincere thanks, first of all, to the contributors. I would also like to gratefully acknowledge the support of the many officials of the Graduate School and University Center of The City University of New York who recognized the importance of Holocaust studies at this public institution of higher learning. Special thanks in this respect are due to President Harold M. Proshansky, Provost Stanley Waren, and Dean Solomon Goldstein.

Publication of this volume, like many other activities of the Institute for Holocaust Studies, has been made possible by the support of the Holocaust Survivors Memorial Foundation, which is hereby acknowledged with gratitude. I would also like to express my appreciation to all the contributors to the Special Holocaust Research and Publication Fund of the Graduate School and University Center for their generosity.

Randolph L. Braham
February 1984

CONTRIBUTING AUTHORS

Haim Avni is Professor of Contemporary Jewish History at The Hebrew University of Jerusalem. Between 1980 and 1982, he served as Director of the University's Institute of Contemporary Jewry, where he is still in charge of the Division for Latin America, Spain, and Portugal. He is the author of a number of scholarly works, including *Argentina, the "Promised Land." Baron de Hirsch's Colonization Project in the Argentine Republic* (in Hebrew); *Spain. The Jews and Franco* (in English, Hebrew, and Spanish); and *The History of Jewish Immigration to Argentina, 1810–1950* (in Hebrew and Spanish). A recognized authority on the Jewish communities in the Spanish-speaking world, Professor Avni served as departmental editor on Latin American Jewry for the *Encyclopaedia Judaica*.

Gerhart M. Riegner is Secretary-General of the World Jewish Congress, a position has held since 1965. A native of Berlin, Dr. Riegner has been associated with this international Jewish organization since its founding in 1936. During World War II, Dr. Riegner played a particularly important role as head of the organization's Geneva Office, one of the leading centers for information and rescue. Dr. Riegner was instrumental in transmitting to the Western Allies (August 1942) the information about the Nazi plan to bring about the liquidation of European Jewry during the war. During the postwar years, Dr. Riegner worked toward improving Christian-Jewish relations and was one of the founders of the International Jewish Committee for Interreligious Consultations.

Bela Vago is Professor of General History and the holder of the Strochlitz Chair in Holocaust Studies at the University of Haifa, where he also heads the Historical Documentation Center on East-Central Europe. A recognized expert on East-Central European History and on the Holocaust in general and the Romanian chapter in particular, Professor Vago is the author or editor of numerous works, including *The Shadow of the Swastika* and *Jews and*

xiii

Non-Jews in Eastern Europe. His articles have appeared in a variety of professional journals, including the *Journal of Contemporary History, East European Quarterly,* and *Jewish Journal of Sociology.* Professor Vago serves, among other things, as member of the World Council of Yad Vashem and of the Executive Committee of the Historical Society of Israel.

Bernard Wasserstein is Associate Professor of History and Director of the Tauber Institute at Brandeis University. He has held appointments at Oxford, Sheffield, and the Hebrew Univesrity of Jerusalem. Professor Wasserstein's publications include *The British in Palestine; Britain and the Jews of Europe, 1939-1945;* and *Letter and Papers of Chaim Weizmann.* His articles and reviews have appeared in a large number of professional journals, including the *Times Literary Supplement; Jewish Journal of Sociology; Middle Eastern Studies; History; English Historical Review; American Historical Review; Journal of Jewish Studies; Middle East Journal; European Studies Review; Political Studies* and many others.

David S. Wyman is Professor of History and Head of Judaic Studies at the University of Massachusetts. An authority on modern American history and on the Holocaust, Professor Wyman is the author of *Paper Walls. America and the Refugee Crisis, 1938-1941.* His study, "Why Auschwitz Was Never Bombed" (*Commentary,* May 1978), is one of the most authoritative accounts on this subject matter. His *The Abandonment of the Jews* is scheduled to appear toward the end of 1984.

THE AMERICAN JEWISH LEADERSHIP AND THE HOLOCAUST

David S. Wyman

Hopes for Rescue

The best hope for rescuing European Jews during World War II lay in a strong and concerted effort to convince the United States government to undertake a comprehensive rescue program. For American Jews, the obvious approaches were two: contacts by Jewish leaders with high government officials; and a national campaign to publicize the mass killings, with a view to building public pressure for rescue and directing it toward the Roosevelt Administration and Congress. American Jewish leaders, once aware of the Nazi extermination plan, moved in both those directions. But lack of united action severely diminished their impact. Furthermore, the Zionist organizations, the most politically effective of the American Jewish groups, continued throughout the crisis to place first priority on their long-term goal of achieving a Jewish state in Palestine.

During the Holocaust, and since, the American Jewish leadership of that era has been faulted for failing to do what it could and should have done for rescue. Criticism has also been leveled because of the disunity and fighting that racked organized American Jewry and hobbled the rescue efforts that were made.[1] One of the sharpest rebukes is Hayim Greenberg's bleak and

---

I want to acknowledge the friendship, help, and encouragement given over several years time by two of my former students, Aaron Berman and Eliyho Matzozky. They have generously shared with me documentary findings of vital importance to this study. And each has contributed hours of discussion of the issues involved.

For a list of abbreviations, please see the last page of this chapter.

1

scathing article entitled "Bankrupt," which appeared—in Yiddish—in the midst of the crisis—in February 1943. Greenberg, a leading Labor Zionist, charged that "American Jewry has not done—and has made no effort to do—its elementary duty toward the millions of Jews who are captive and doomed to die in Europe!" He was especially dismayed that "the chief organizations of American Jewry . . . could not in this dire hour, unequalled even in Jewish history, unite for the purpose of seeking ways to forestall the misfortune or at least to reduce its scope; to save those who *perhaps* can still be saved." What, he asked, "has such rescue work to do with political differences?" Actually, as Greenberg conceded in his article, a start had been made, during the last weeks of 1942, toward action, even united action. But it had died out by January 1943.[2]

Soon after Greenberg published his indictment—and possibly partly in response to it—united Jewish action for rescue was rekindled and started to gather momentum. This tardy but promising development was short-lived, however. The Bermuda Conference of late April 1943 mortally wounded it, and the American Jewish Conference, held four months later, extinguished it.

Reactions to Revelations About the Holocaust

Starting in late June 1942 reports of massive killings of Jews reached the British and American news media from authoritative underground sources in Axis Europe. These accounts spoke of 700,000 Jews murdered in Poland alone, and over a million annihilated altogether.[3] The news was relegated to the inner pages of the regular American newspapers, but it dominated the Jewish press and set off calls for immediate steps to urge the Allied governments to act to stem the murder.[4]

In response, the four major defense committees, the American Jewish Congress, the B'nai B'rith, the Jewish Labor Committee, and the American Jewish Committee, joined to sponsor a protest demonstration. On July 21, 1942, 20,000 people crowded Madison Square Garden, while thousands more stood outside, to hear speeches by Rabbi Stephen S. Wise and several other prominent Jews and non-Jews. Messages to the meeting from President Roosevelt and Prime Minister Churchill promised retribution for these Nazi crimes at a future day of reckoning. The mass meeting adopted a declaration urging the United Nations to issue a clear warning of punishment to the perpetrators. But neither the speakers nor the declaration called for actual rescue measures.[5] In the wake of the Madison Square Garden observance, similar mass meetings took place in numerous cities across the United States.[6]

At that time, with the war running heavily against the Allies, and the American Jewish leadership numbed and shocked by the revelations from Europe, practical suggestions for rescue had not yet emerged. It would be several months before specific proposals would be worked out and pressed on the American government.[7]

During that summer and fall additional accounts of Nazi mass murder of Jews reached the United States. Most of them were made public, but received little attention in the news media.[8] The most significant report, however, was kept secret until late November. That was the information relayed in August by Gerhart M. Riegner, secretary of the World Jewish Congress office in Geneva. Riegner's message stated that a reliable source with connections high in the German government reported that a plan was under consideration in Hitler's headquarters to deport all Jews under German control to the East (presumably to Poland) and to exterminate them there. This news made clear the real meaning of the earlier reports of mass slaughter. It also explained the large-scale deportations of Jews, in progress since mid-July, from France and Holland to "an unknown destination" in the East. A policy of genocide was underway.[9]

At Riegner's request the American and British diplomatic missions in Switzerland forwarded the report to their governments, on about August 10. Riegner had also asked that his message be passed on to two leaders of the World Jewish Congress, Rabbi Wise in New York and Samuel Sydney Silverman in London. The British Foreign Office hesitated for a week, then delivered Riegner's dispatch to Silverman. But the State Department deemed the information "fantastic" and decided not to send it to Wise. Near the end of August the message reached Wise anyway—from Silverman, whose telegram to the American Jewish leader somehow was cleared through both the War and State Departments. Shortly afterward, Wise forwarded Riegner's dispatch to Undersecretary of State Sumner Welles. Welles, probably on September 3, asked Wise not to make the information public until the State Department had time to confirm it. Wise agreed.[10]

In the midst of these developments, further terrible news reached New York. On September 3, Jacob Rosenheim, president of the Agudath Israel World Organization, received a telegram from his group's representative in Switzerland, Isaac Sternbuch:

> According to numerous authentical informations from Poland German authorities have recently evacuated Warsaw ghetto and bestially murdered about one hundred thousand Jews. These mass murders are continuing. . . . Similar fate is awaiting the Jews deported to Poland from other occupied territories. . . . Do whatever you can to cause an American reaction to halt these persecutions.

Rosenheim immediately sent copies of Sternbuch's telegram to both President Roosevelt and Eleanor Roosevelt. Neither responded. He also notified Rabbi Wise. Soon afterward, Wise, Rosenheim, and other Jewish leaders met, discussed the two reports, and then asked Welles to check into what had happened at Warsaw. Welles ordered an investigation.[11]

Restrained from releasing the news of extermination to the press, Wise did what he could during September and October to find some way to assist the European Jews. He conferred with Welles several times. He tried in vain to reach President Roosevelt, both through Welles and through Felix Frankfurter, the Associate Justice of the Supreme Court. The Rabbi carried the horrifying reports to the President's Advisory Committee on Political Refugees. He asked Myron C. Taylor, Roosevelt's personal representative to the Vatican, to appeal to the Pope to intervene. He also saw Vice President Henry Wallace, Assistant Secretary of State Dean Acheson, and Secretary of the Interior Harold Ickes. Everyone he approached was sympathetic. No one did anything, except Welles, who promised to seek further information through State Department channels, and Ickes, who tried unsuccessfully to convince Roosevelt to open the Virgin Islands as a temporary haven for 2,000 Jews.[12]

The State Department's lackadaisical inquiry into the authenticity of the Riegner and Sternbuch reports stretched out for nearly three months. Finally, late in November—15 weeks after Riegner's report reached Washington— sufficient additional information had come in to convince Welles. On November 24 he called Wise to Washington, handed him several documents, and said, "I regret to tell you, Dr. Wise, that these confirm and justify your deepest fears." Welles than suggested that Wise release the information.[13]

Almost immediately Wise called a press conference. He told reporters that sources authenticated by the State Department revealed that the Germans had already massacred 2 million Jews. And they were transporting others to Poland from all over the continent to be killed in a campaign aimed at wiping out all the Jews in Nazi Europe. The next day, November 25, Wise met in New York with other Jewish leaders, then held a second press conference where he spoke as representative for several leading American Jewish organizations. He announced that the Jewish groups were convinced, on the basis of State Department documentation, that Hitler had ordered the annihilation of all Jews in German-controlled territory. The purpose in publicizing the information, he stated, was "to win the support of a Christian world so that its leaders may intervene and protest the horrible treatment of Jews in Hitler Europe."[14]

Just as Wise was revealing the annihilation plan to the world, additional crucial evidence of the Nazi genocide was appearing in Jerusalem and London. On November 23 the Jewish press in Palestine published black-bordered reports of systematic extermination recently brought from Poland. In London, on November 24, the Polish Government-in-Exile informed the press that Nazi SS Chief Heinrich Himmler had ordered half of Poland's 3 million Jews killed by the end of 1942 as the first step in their complete destruction.[15]

Thus, after November 24, 1942, it was evident to anyone in the democratic world who cared to know that a hideous and unprecedented extermination program against the Jews was in progress. It should be noted, however, that although the American press published this news, it regularly placed it in its inner pages.[16]

From events traced so far, two observations may be permitted. First, the American Jewish leadership was not inactive in the face of the horrifying information that it received between late June and November 1942. It was, however, held back by the restriction placed on releasing key information. It was also hindered by the difficulty in devising concrete steps that might mitigate the catastrophe.

The second observation concerns Rabbi Wise's acquiescence in Sumner Welles's request that he not release the extermination information until the State Department had checked it. Wise has been criticized on the ground that his silence cost three irretrievable months desperately needed to build pressure on Washington.[17] True, time was already short in September 1942 and the Roosevelt Administration needed strong prodding before it would act. But two points warrant consideration.

For one thing, Wise had no viable choice in the matter. The State Department was responsible for refugee and rescue affairs. Had Wise contravened Welles's request, he would have alienated the department of government whose cooperation was essential in trying to help the European Jews. Secondly, if Wise is to be criticized in this instance, numerous others should be also. The British section of the World Jewish Congress, for instance, had the Riegner report, as well as the British Foreign Office's permission to publicize it. In addition, Wise conveyed the information to several people, including other Jewish leaders, and the members of the President's Advisory Committee on Political Refugees, as well as Felix Frankfurter, Myron C. Taylor, Dean Acheson, Henry Wallace, and Harold Ickes. Any of more than twenty prominent Americans could have called a press conference and broken the news.

6   JEWISH LEADERSHIP DURING NAZI ERA

The Jewish Leaders and the Holocaust: 1942–43

Three months went by from the time the Roosevelt Administration learned of the plan to exterminate the European Jews until that news was made generally available in November 1942. Fourteen *additional* months of mass murder were to pass before the American government, in January 1944, would initiate a program of rescue with the formation of the War Refugee Board. What was the role of the American Jewish leadership in the long struggle to convince the Roosevelt Administration to act? The first several months (from late November 1942 into May 1943) saw hopeful steps toward unity, as the main Jewish leadership took sporadic but important joint action. During this time the Zionists were in the forefront of the campaign. These were the months, in fact, when Zionist responsiveness to the rescue issue reached its peak.

Once freed to release the authenticated news of extermination, Jewish leaders were anxious to spread the information as effectively as they could. They sought to build the public support that would be necessary to move the American and other Allied governments to rescue efforts.[18]

The group that first charted a course of joint action was a temporary and rather loose council of representatives of the major American Jewish organizations. Essentially it was the continuation of a committee of Jewish leaders that had formed around Stephen Wise and Jacob Rosenheim in early September and had met sporadically thereafter to discuss information coming from Europe as well as possible ways to respond to it. It was this group, generally referred to as the "temporary committee," that Wise called together on November 25, the day after his meeting with Welles, to decide on an initial plan of action.[19]

Seven organizations were represented on the temporary committee. Three were pro-Zionist and were led by committed Zionists; they were the American Jewish Congress, the World Jewish Congress, and the Synagogue Council of America. Three were non-Zionist or even anti-Zionist: the American Jewish Committee, the Jewish Labor Committee, and Agudath Israel of America. The other, B'nai B'rith, aimed for neutrality, but its membership was trending toward Zionism and its leadership was pro-Zionist. The temporary committee was a volatile combination; normally relationships among its member groups were characterized by disputes and even sharp conflict. Yet it did achieve a fair amount of cooperation.[20]

At its meeting on November 25, the temporary committee agreed on several actions. Press conferences and other direct efforts to get prominent news coverage for the newly confirmed facts of genocide met with very limited success.[21] But two other projects were more effective, a Day of Mourning and Prayer, held on December 2, and a conference with President Roosevelt on December 8.

The Day of Mourning and Prayer was observed in 29 foreign lands and throughout the United States. In New York, Mayor Fiorello LaGuardia summoned the city to prayer. Several radio stations were silent for two minutes. Over half a million union laborers halted production for ten minutes. (Lest Jews be blamed for slowing the war effort, the time was made up the next day.) At noon a one-hour radio program was broadcast. And special services were held at five o'clock in synagogues throughout the city.[22]

In many other American cities, the Day of Mourning was marked by religious services and local radio programs. Late in the afternoon, NBC broadcast a special quarter-hour memorial service across the nation.[23]

A week later, President Roosevelt met for half an hour with five delegates of the temporary committee: Rabbi Wise, representing the American Jewish Congress and the World Jewish Congress, Henry Monsky of B'nai B'rith, Rabbi Israel Rosenberg of the Union of Orthodox Rabbis, Maurice Wertheim from the American Jewish Committee, and Adolph Held, for the Jewish Labor Committee. Wise, a longtime supporter of Roosevelt, read aloud a two-page letter from the Jewish leaders stressing that "unless action is taken immediately, the Jews of Hitler Europe are doomed." But the only action proposed in the letter was a request that the President "warn the Nazis that they will be held to strict accountability for their crimes" and an appeal for formation of a commission to gather evidence of Nazi atrocities. Wise also handed Roosevelt a twenty-page condensation of the extermination evidence and appealed to him to do everything in his power to bring the news to the world's attention and to stop the mass murder.[24]

The President readily agreed to issue the war crimes warning. He then turned to the group and asked for other recommendations. They had little to add. Held suggested an attempt to get neutral countries to intercede with Germany in behalf of the Jews. The others expressed a few ideas, but these were not recorded. This part of the conversation lasted only one or two minutes. As the delegation left, Roosevelt asked them to prepare the war crimes statement, using as a guide his message to the July 1942 mass meeting in Madison Square Garden. After clearing their version with the President's secretary, the Jewish leaders released it to the press, along with their letter to Roosevelt and the twenty-page summary of the extermination data. Shortly after the White House visit, Wise dissolved the temporary committee, stating that it had completed the tasks it had set for itself.[25]

News reports about the Day of Mourning and the conference with the President focused some public attention on the disastrous situation of the European Jews. And soon after, on December 17, a major burst of publicity about the mass murders accompanied a far more forceful war crimes declaration issued in London by eleven Allied governments, including the United States, Britain, and Russia. (British Jewish leaders played a key role in obtaining the December 17 declaration. American Jews were not involved in that project.)[26] But American Jewish organizations realized that much more public knowledge and sympathy would have to be generated before the American government would commit itself to rescue action.[27]

During December 1942 the American organization most active in trying to build public concern for the European Jews was the Zionist-oriented American Jewish Congress, aided by its affiliate, the World Jewish Congress. The two congresses contributed the bulk of the work that went into the projects of the temporary committee. Directly after the conference with the President, the American Jewish Congress set up a special "planning committee" of its own which soon mapped out an ambitious campaign to arouse public opinion.[28]

The new approach envisioned marches of hundreds of thousands of Jews through the streets of New York and other large cities. Jewish children were to leave their schools to join the processions. Appeals were to go out to Americans of Polish, Czech, Yugoslav, and other national backgrounds to join the processions or hold parallel demonstrations. During the day of the processions, all Jewish stores were to be closed, and a work stoppage was to be arranged through the cooperation of the AFL and the CIO. On the same day, large newspaper advertisements with black borders were to detail the extermination. Radio commentators were to be urged to speak about the massacres. And, as an offshoot of the processions, Jewish mass delegations were to go to Washington to appeal to Congress.[29]

Another project looked toward appeals to the Christian churches to hold Days of Mourning and to explain the facts of the extermination at church services. Additional plans called for enlisting the support of newspaper editors, radio broadcasters, educators' and women's organizations, liberal groups, congressmen, and other political leaders.[30]

The results were microscopic. Christian churches sponsored two or three radio broadcasts, the *Nation* and *New Republic* magazines printed some material, and fifty leading Americans of German descent issued a Christmas Declaration denouncing Hitler's "cold-blooded extermination of the Jews of Europe."[31]

Most of the projects simply evaporated by early 1943. Why? For one thing, cooperation from non-Jews was meager. In addition, some "planning committee" members had reservations about marches and other mass-action projects, fearing they "might make the wrong kind of impression on the non-Jewish community." Probably most important, the American Jewish Congress was trying to do too many things with too few capable people and with resources that were too limited. The planning committee did not work steadily at its task and its leadership was heavily occupied with numerous other matters. Rescue had not taken on an unquenchable urgency.[32]

Throughout December, while trying to publicize the mass murder and arouse the concern of their fellow citizens, American Jews were also searching for practical rescue proposals. One frequent suggestion called for providing havens of refuge for Jews who might succeed in getting out of Nazi territory. England, the United States, and the other Allies should be asked to open their doors. The British should be requested to remove restrictions on refugee immigration to Palestine. The United Nations should encourage neutrals such as Turkey, Switzerland, and Sweden to accept Jewish refugees by agreeing to share the maintenance costs and to move them elsewhere after the war. Food and medical supplies should be sent, under proper safeguards against confiscation, to starving Jews in Nazi-controlled Europe.[33]

In the last weeks of 1942, then, attempts were made to publicize the extermination news, and specific rescue proposals began to appear. American Jewry had at least made a start. But during January and much of February, Jewish organizations were relatively quiescent; the extermination issue received limited public attention. (It was during this interval that Hayim Greenberg voiced his protest against American Jewish passivity.) Two developments in mid-February, however, sparked a quick resurgence of activity.

One was another telegram from Riegner, written this time in collaboration with Richard Lichtheim of the Jewish Agency. It disclosed that the slaughter had intensified. Six thousand Jews were being killed *per day* at a single location in Poland. Vienna had been nearly emptied of Jews and more deportations were going forward from Berlin and Prague. The condition of Jews in Romania was desperate. Of 130,000 Romanian Jews deported to the Transnistria region in 1941, 60,000 were dead. The other 70,000 were destitute, sleeping in unheated rooms, prey to diseases, and dying of starvation. The shocked leadership of the American Jewish Congress released the information to the press on February 14.[34]

The previous day, by coincidence, the *New York Times* reported from London that the Romanian government had offered to remove 70,000 Jews from Transnistria and release them to the Allies. In return, Romania asked to be paid transportation and related expenses of 20,000 *lei* (about $140) per refugee. It was not the offer itself, or the failure of the American and British governments to pursue it, that stirred up the American Jewish leadership. What did was a striking three-quarter-page advertisement that the Committee for a Jewish Army placed in the *New York Times* on February 16.[35]

The Committee for a Jewish Army was one of a half-dozen organizations set up in the United States in the 1940s by a small group of Palestinian Jews who were intent on forwarding the cause of a Jewish state in Palestine. Led by Peter Bergson, these young men were followers of Vladimir Jabotinsky and secretly members of the Palestine underground army, the *Irgun.* The Committee for a Jewish Army worked for the establishment of an independent army of Palestinian Jews and stateless Jewish refugees to fight Hitler alongside the other Allied forces.[36]

Soon after hearing the news of systematic extermination, the Bergson group began to shift its first priority to rescue. As early as December 5, 1942, in an eyecatching newspaper advertisement written by the popular author Pierre van Paassen, the Committee for a Jewish Army recommended formation of a special United States government agency with responsibility for saving European Jews. By February the committee had decided to launch an intensive publicity drive centered on its demand for the establishment of a rescue agency.[37]

The opening gun in this campaign was the army committee's large advertisement reacting to the Romanian government's offer. It appeared in the February 16 *New York Times* under the startling headlines:

> FOR SALE to Humanity   70,000 Jews
> Guaranteed Human Beings at $50 a piece.

(Fifty dollars was the committee's estimate of the value of the 20,000 *lei* price set by the Romanians.) The advertisement, written by Hollywood dramatist Ben Hecht, solicited $50 contributions to help finance the Committee for a Jewish Army's drive to publicize the European Jewish situation and build pressure for government action.[38]

Immediately the established American Jewish organizations and the Jewish press sent up a barrage of protest. They angrily charged the army committee with deliberately and deceptively implying that each $50 contribution would save a Romanian Jew. Undaunted, the committee not only ran a large follow-up advertisement a few days later, but proceeded to reprint Hecht's advertisement in several major newspapers across the nation.[39]

Even before the February denunciations, much of the American Jewish leadership had decried the Committee for a Jewish Army, accusing it of recklessness and sensationalism, as well as gross effrontery in presuming to speak for an American Jewish constituency. Fear now arose that the Bergsonites would move into the vacuum and seize the leadership of the flagging effort for rescue. The lethargy of the previous several weeks rapidly dissolved. Apprised of the army committee's plan to hold a demonstration at Madison Square Garden on March 9, Wise and the American Jewish Congress quickly decided to schedule a March 1 mass meeting at the same location.[40]

The demonstration set off another wave of publicity and activity on the rescue question; 20,000 people jammed Madison Square Garden while 10,000 others stood outside in the winter cold and listened to the speeches through amplifiers. AFL president William Green and several other non-Jewish political, religious, and labor leaders addressed the meeting, as did Stephen Wise and world famous scientist and Zionist spokesman Chaim Weizmann.[41]

Indicative of the progress made since the December conference with Roosevelt was a comprehensive list of specific rescue proposals approved by the mass meeting and forwarded to the President. The 11-point program (in greatly condensed form) called for:

—Approaches to Germany and the satellite governments to allow the Jews to emigrate;

—Swift establishment of havens of refuge by Allied and neutral nations, including acceptance of refugees into the United States, Britain, Latin America, and Palestine;

—Transfer, by the United Nations, of Jewish refugees out of the neutral countries bordering Nazi territory, and encouragement of those countries to allow additional refugees in;

—Organization by the UN, through neutral agencies such as the International Red Cross, of a system for feeding Jews remaining in Axis territory;

—Assumption by the UN of financial responsibility for the overall program; and

—The formation of a UN agency to carry out the program.[42]

The mass meeting and favorable press reaction to it generated enough pressure to force a response of sorts from the Roosevelt Administration. Two days after the demonstration, the State Department released previously secret information indicating that the United States and Britain were planning a diplomatic conference to deal with the refugee problem. The mass meeting's success also hastened steps already underway to revive the temporary committee of top Jewish leaders that had disbanded after the December visit to the White House. This group began to meet again early in March and soon formally organized itself as the Joint Emergency Committee on European Jewish Affairs. (The World Jewish Congress had dropped out; but newly added were the American Emergency Committee for Zionist Affairs, a political action agency representing several Zionist organizations, and the Union of Orthodox Rabbis, a close associate of Agudath Israel. This brought the number of organizations on the committee to eight.) The Committee for a Jewish Army asked to be included, but was rejected.[43]

The Joint Emergency Committee immediately commenced efforts to influence the upcoming British-American refugee conference, set for the third week of April at Bermuda. One early step was to stimulate mass meetings throughout the United States to publicize the Holocaust and to mobilize popular opinion behind the rescue proposals adopted at the March 1 demonstration in New York. During the spring of 1943, 40 such rallies were held in 20 states, sponsored by local Jewish community organizations with help from the Joint Emergency Committee and local branches of its eight constituent bodies. The Synagogue Council of America cooperated by proclaiming a six-week period of mourning and prayer for the European Jews. And convocations of rabbis met in several parts of the nation and sent resolutions to Roosevelt and Churchill urging them to rescue those who could still be saved.[44]

An interesting aspect of the Joint Emergency Committee's campaign to spark the mass meetings was the full collaboration of the American Jewish Committee. Through the years the American Jewish Committee had almost never encouraged mass demonstrations. It wished to keep Jewish issues out of public attention, while quietly working to protect Jewish rights through negotiations with high government officials and other powerful persons. The president of the American Jewish Committee, Judge Joseph Proskauer, had opposed holding the Madison Square Garden meeting. But the dignified manner in which the demonstration was handled convinced him and his administrative committee that similar demonstrations could help influence American opinion "in a decent and decorous way."[45]

A second objective of the Joint Emergency Committee was to induce the United States Congress to go on record in support of rescue action. Despite a quiet but vigorous effort in that direction, the result was nearly useless. In March both houses unanimously approved a resolution concerning Nazi atrocities, but it mentioned the Jews only in passing. It was simply another general condemnation of German war crimes, another call for eventual punishment of those responsible.[46]

Even more discouraging was a meeting that Wise and Proskauer managed to obtain in late March with British Foreign Secretary Anthony Eden, who was then visiting Washington. By that time the Joint Emergency Committee had decided to place its highest priority on just two of the rescue proposals. One called for approaches to Germany and its satellites through neutral channels to obtain release of the Jews. The other asked for organization of a program to feed Nazi victims unable to get out of occupied Europe. If the United States and Britain would agree to these steps, the committee believed, the other proposals could be acted on in a less urgent manner by the intergovernmental rescue agency which, it was hoped, would emerge from the forthcoming Bermuda Conference.[47]

Eden threw cold water on the whole idea, and, in doing so foreshadowed the outcome of the Bermuda Conference. Opening the discussion, Proskauer stressed the request for a declaration calling on Germany to permit Jews to leave occupied Europe. Eden rejected that proposal outright, declaring it "fantastically impossible." The second point, sending food to European Jews, appeared to make no impression on the British leader. To a suggestion that Britain help in removing Jews then in peril in Bulgaria, Eden replied icily that "Turkey does not want any more of your people." Eden would not offer any hope of action, asserting that he could make no decisions without consulting his government.[48]

Eden's response dealt a crushing blow to the American Jewish leadership, as reflected in this description of the reaction of the Joint Emergency Committee when Wise and Proskauer reported back to it:

> Over the entire meeting hung the pall of Mr. Eden's attitude toward helping to save the Jews in occupied Europe. Without expressing it, the people at the meeting felt that there was little use in continuing to agitate for a demand [for action] on the part of the United Nations by the Jews of America.[49]

Based on the encounter with Eden and similar attitudes prevalent in the State Department, members of the Joint Emergency Committee were reasonably convinced that neither the State Department nor the British would seek to map out a real rescue program at Bermuda. If anything significant were to occur at the conference, it would have to come at the insistence of President Roosevelt. Accordingly, Wise telegraphed the White House asking that a few Joint Emergency Committee members be granted the opportunity to talk with the President regarding the fate of millions of European Jews. Although the committee expected to have no trouble seeing Roosevelt, Wise's request got nowhere. The White House simply relayed it to Secretary of State Hull who wrote Wise that such a meeting could not be arranged.[50]

The seven Jewish members of the House of Representatives, led by Emanuel Celler, did succeed in talking with Roosevelt on April 1. But the Jewish congressmen did not press the Joint Emergency Committee's rescue proposals on the President. Celler did, however, ask whether a small delegation of the committee's leaders might be heard at Bermuda. Roosevelt rejected the idea.[51]

Unable to reach the President and excluded from presenting its case at Bermuda, the Joint Emergency Committee decided on a last-ditch attempt to convince the State Department to recommend its rescue proposals to the conference. In a message to Welles, the committee submitted its program (modeled on the Madison Square Garden proposals), along with an appendix of specific suggestions for implementing the plans. The accompanying letter formally requested that a small group from the Joint Emergency Committee be invited to Bermuda to explain the proposals. The message closed with an appeal to Welles, asking him to do all he personally could to influence the conference to urge a meaningful rescue program on the two governments.[52]

When, on the eve of the conference, the Joint Emergency Committee had not received a response, the group met again. Angered at their inability to make effective contact with government policymakers, these leaders of American Jewry briefly considered militant action. But they settled for a press conference intended to expose the State Department's rebuff. It had negligible impact.[53]

Welles never replied to the Joint Emergency Committee's appeal. The only answer came several days later, after the conference had started, from Assistant Secretary of State Breckinridge Long. Long wrote that he had forwarded the committee's material to the American delegation.[54]

The Bermuda Conference was, in fact, no more than a pretense. It was a diplomatic hoax intended to defuse the pressures for rescue that had built up in England and the United States. It accomplished nothing toward rescue, except to recommend a feeble plan for aiding some 2,000 refugees who had reached Spain.[55]

Despite the secrecy that veiled most of the conference's deliberations, enough news slipped out to make clear what had occurred. This information devastated even the small hopes that American Jews had dared hold for the conference. A deep despondency blanketed many segments of American Jewry. As for the Joint Emergency Committee, demoralization set in. It never recovered from the Bermuda Conference's demonstration of the indifference of the two great democracies.[56]

Despite efforts to revive it by Jacob Pat of the Jewish Labor Committee, the Joint Emergency Committee met only three times, and accomplished nothing, during the five months following the Bermuda Conference. The

American Jewish Committee, the Jewish Labor Committee, Agudath Israel, and the Union of Orthodox Rabbis wanted to keep the committee alive; but in the fall of 1943 the Zionist members, led by Wise, succeeded in voting it out of existence. The united front on rescue was finished.[57]

The Position of the Zionists

The Zionist leadership had been in the forefront of the pre-Bermuda attempts to publicize the mass killings and to stir the government into action. Yet during those months, the Zionist movement had continued to devote its main energies to the cause of a Jewish state in Palestine. The American Zionists' overall strategy, initiated many months before the news of extermination became known, aimed at building maximum support in the United States—as rapidly as possible—for a postwar Jewish state in Palestine. The haste arose from the Zionists' perception that the best chance for decades to come to win the Jewish state would arise right after the war. The fluidity in international affairs that would emerge at the end of the war would very likely open the status of Palestine for reconsideration. The Zionist movement had to be ready to wield all the influence it could when the postwar diplomatic settlements were made.[58]

The first essential step toward maximizing American Zionist influence was to reach a consensus among the numerous Zionist factions. This was achieved at the Biltmore Conference in New York in May 1942. There a common policy was adopted that called for the end of the British White Paper (which limited Jewish immigration into Palestine) and the establishment of Palestine as a Jewish commonwealth. (Advocacy of a Jewish commonwealth constituted a fundamental shift. The previous position had accepted indefinite postponement of the statehood goal while concentrating on building up the Jewish community in Palestine.)[59]

Zionism at that time was still a minority movement among American Jews. Thus, immediately after Biltmore, plans went forward for the second step in the overall strategy: lining up American Jewry as a whole behind the Zionist program. The technique chosen was to call all the American Jewish organizations to a conference where they would work out a program for dealing with the postwar problems of world Jewry. American Jews would then be able to present a united front at the peace negotiations. Because the non-Zionist organizations most likely would not respond to a Zionist initiative for such a conference, prominent Zionist leaders, including Chaim Weizmann and Stephen Wise, convinced Henry Monsky, the president of

B'nai B'rith, to issue the invitations. Monsky was popular and respected among American Jews generally and B'nai B'rith was considered neutral on the question of political Zionism. So Monsky's chances of convening the conference were very good. And his personal pro-Zionist views could only help at the conference.[60]

It might be noted that the small meeting at which Monsky agreed to act as convener took place during the first burst of activity following release of the extermination news. It was held December 2, 1942, the Day of Mourning and Prayer. Against that background, an outside observer might have expected the conference under consideration to have dealt first of all with rescue. It did not. When the call for the conference went out, two items were on the agenda: the status and rights of Jews in the postwar world, and the rights of the Jewish people with respect to Palestine.[61]

Through the late spring and summer of 1943, the attention of thousands of American Jews and much of the Jewish press turned to the election of delegates and the other preparations for the convocation, now named the American Jewish Conference. During this time the rescue issue was eclipsed, partly by this rechanneling of Jewish interest and partly because these were the very weeks of despair following the disillusionment of Bermuda. An article in June in a Zionist periodical reflected the shift: "The world at large replies to our protests and prayers and dramatizations only with resolutions and expressions of sympathy—never with deeds." "What can the Jew do now?" asked the writer. He supplied the answer himself: Jews must unite at the American Jewish Conference and demand Jewish postwar rights, especially in Palestine.[62]

Indications are very strong that disillusionment with Bermuda permanently altered the priorities of that part of the Zionist leadership which had previously pressed hard for a government rescue program. Before Bermuda, important Zionists, including Stephen Wise and Nahum Goldmann, had concentrated on two main lines of action: the political Zionist track (which led to the Biltmore Program and on to development of the American Jewish Conference), and the campaign to convince the American government to undertake rescue action. After Bermuda, some effort for rescue continued, but much the greater share of Zionist energies and capabilities went into the American Jewish Conference and the drive which followed to build United States government support for a postwar Jewish state in Palestine.

The American Jewish Conference consisted of 500 delegates. Of the 500 slots, 125 were allotted to the 65 national Jewish organizations who finally participated. The other 375 delegates were chosen by a complex indirect system of local elections which aimed at providing a broadly representative, democratic character to the conference. If any doubt existed that the conference was essentially an effort to prove American Jewish support for the Biltmore Program, it was soon dispelled by the all-out election drive mounted by the several Zionist organizations. Most of them agreed on joint slates of delegates for whom Zionists voted in blocs, thus defeating candidates with less thoroughly organized support. Zionist campaign rhetoric called for election of the maximum number of Zionist candidates, because the significant action at the conference would occur on the Palestine statehood issue and it was essential to show that American Jews were united in supporting that goal.[63]

The Zionists were enormously successful in the elections; an estimated 80 percent of all the delegates were considered "avowed Zionists," and few of the others were outright opponents of Zionism. No one seriously maintained that this outcome proved 80 percent of American Jews supported a full Zionist program. It did seem to show, though, that a majority of America's Jews were by then pro-Zionist, and an even more solid majority of those involved in Jewish organizational life backed the Zionist position.[64]

Some complaints were raised about the representativeness of the elections. But more important dissension arose over the allotment of the 125 delegate slots which went to the various organizations. Both Agudath Israel of America and the Union of Orthodox Rabbis withdrew from the conference before it convened, declaring that they had been granted unfairly small numbers of delegates.[65]

Another factor in the disenchantment of these two ultra-Orthodox, non-Zionist organizations was the continuing failure of the American Jewish Conference's organizing committee to place rescue on the agenda. As far back as January, Agudath Israel had unsuccessfully urged concentration on rescue as well as postwar issues. Only in late July (a month before the conference met), and then only after persistent hammering by the Jewish Labor Committee, was rescue added to the agenda. Even so, the conference's executive committee turned down a Jewish Labor Committee appeal to make the extermination of the European Jews the central issue of the conference, and to prepare an urgent call to the Allied governments for rescue action.[66]

The American Jewish Conference met in New York from August 29 through September 2, 1943. The Palestine issue dominated the proceedings. Convinced of the importance of winning united support for the positions adopted by the conference, Wise, Nahum Goldmann, and a few other leading Zionists planned to press a moderate resolution on Palestine. They recognized that all groups, including the influential American Jewish Committee, could agree on a demand to abolish the White Paper and open Palestine to unlimited Jewish immigration. Though committed to the full Biltmore Platform, these leaders felt that the controversial Jewish commonwealth idea could wait for a later reconvening of the conference.[67]

The moderate plan was swept aside, however, on the evening of August 30 by a stirring pro-statehood address made by Rabbi Abba Hillel Silver, at that time probably the most militant of the front echelon of American Zionist leaders. Silver's speech set off a flood of emotion in the audience and galvanized the delegates into fervent support of the full Biltmore position. Two nights later, with only four negative votes and 19 abstentions, the conference adopted an uncompromising resolution calling for a Jewish commonwealth in Palestine, an immediate end to the White Paper, and unlimited Jewish immigration into Palestine.[68]

The other two issues on the agenda, the rights of Jews in the postwar world and the problem of rescue, were anticlimactic. The delegates showed limited interest in them and passed resolutions of little significance. Before it dispersed, the assembly established an Interim Committee of 55 people elected to carry out the resolutions and attend to other necessary business.[69]

The Zionists had triumphed. A representative assembly that included nearly all segments of American Jewry had overwhelmingly ratified the Biltmore Platform. But the victory came at a price. It led to the disbandment of the Joint Emergency Committee. In many local Jewish communities it reignited old Zionist vs. non-Zionist animosities. It ended all possibility of collaboration with the non-Zionist, ultra-Orthodox groups. And it cut off or weakened the support of other important elements of American Jewry. Not two months after the New York meetings, the American Jewish Committee withdrew from the conference, declaring that it could not support the demand for a Jewish commonwealth. This loss was critical; the American Jewish Committee was too significant a force on the American Jewish scene for the conference to be effective without it. (The American Jewish Committee lacked the broad-based organizational structure needed for most types of political action. But it did have access to high levels in the government and it could raise considerable funds. It applied these strengths to the effort for rescue, but only to a limited extent.)[70] B'nai B'rith and four other organizations supported the conference only partially, holding back on endorsement of the Palestine resolution. And the anti-Zionist Jewish Labor Committee gave only limited cooperation before quitting the conference altogether in December 1944.[71]

Common ground for united activity did exist across the full spectrum of American Jewry. All Jewish groups agreed during World War II on the need for rescue and the need to abolish the White Paper. But unity was impossible when the question of a Jewish state entered the picture. And after the American Jewish Conference, the Zionist leadership insisted that the statehood issue was inseparable from both the White Paper issue and the rescue problem itself. Thus the disagreement over political Zionism stood squarely in the way of any united Jewish rescue effort.[72]

The conference's Interim Committee did not meet until six weeks after the delegates went home, thus losing the interest and momentum built at the New York sessions. When it did convene, in mid-October 1943, it elected as co-chairmen Stephen Wise, Henry Monsky, and Israel Goldstein. It also put the conference on a semi-permanent basis by establishing commissions on postwar Jewish rights, rescue, and Palestine.[73]

In the ensuing months, the Commission on Post-War Reconstruction did little more than issue a few statements concerning restoration of Jewish rights in Europe and a proposed international bill of rights. The activities of the Commission on Rescue were essentially only a relabeling of the limited steps taken by the already existing American Jewish Congress—World Jewish Congress partnership in the area of rescue. About all the Rescue Commission could point to in its year and a half of existence before the war in Europe ended were two mass meetings in New York City. The Commission on Palestine functioned as no more than a rubber stamp for the American Zionist Emergency Council, the political action arm of the leading Zionist organizations.[74]

For the most part, then, the American Jewish Conference served as a means for the American Zionist movement to affix the prestigious label of an apparently broadly representative, democratic Jewish organization onto the activities of already established Zionist committees. As such, the conference could hardly develop as a viable organization. In fact, by mid-1944 its ineffectiveness was obvious and criticism of its virtual inaction reverberated through the Jewish press and at Jewish meetings. The conference's second year was even worse, filled with internal rivalries and conflicts. Weak and ineffectual, the American Jewish Conference limped along until it expired at the end of 1948.[75]

What was the balance sheet on the American Jewish Conference? The main Zionist objective for the conference was achieved. The overwhelming vote on the Palestine resolution offered convincing evidence that the Zionist position had majority support in American Jewry. After August 1943 Zionist leaders could credibly maintain in their publicity and in their governmental contacts that their program represented the broad cross section of American Jewish opinion.[76]

On the debit side, Zionist insistence on committing the conference to a Jewish commonwealth in Palestine, a *postwar* objective, ended the chance for united Jewish action on the immediate issue of rescue, and on the related issue of the White Paper. On those issues consensus existed and Jewish unity was within reach. The American Jewish Conference could have been the instrument of that unity, but by its adoption of the full Zionist program it lost that opportunity.

As for the American Zionist movement, the victory at the American Jewish Conference completed its drive to commit American Jewry to the Biltmore Program. The next objective was to win the backing of the American people and their government. Starting in September 1943, American Zionists poured large amounts of energy into this struggle, and continued to do so throughout the rest of the war and on until the Jewish state was won. Pivotal to this effort was an immensely effective public relations and political action campaign carried out by the American Zionist Emergency Council, which had been revitalized and placed under the dynamic leadership of Abba Hillel Silver at the time the American Jewish Conference met.[77]

An unavoidable conclusion is that during the Holocaust the leadership of American Zionism concentrated its major force on the drive for a future Jewish state in Palestine. It consigned rescue to a distinctly secondary position, especially after the Bermuda Conference of April 1943. Why would Jewish leaders, deeply distressed over the agony of their people in Europe, have permitted *any* issue to take precedence over immediate rescue? No definite answers are possible. But available evidence suggests an explanation.

The Zionist leadership concluded that little hope for rescue existed. Hitler had a stranglehold on the European Jews and the Allied powers showed themselves unwilling even to attempt rescue. A Zionist editorial in September 1943, a survey of the then-closing Jewish year of 5703, mirrored the widespread despair:

> It was during the first few months of that year that the pitiless, horrifying word "extermination" became a commonplace in our vocabulary. . . . It was in that year, too, that all our cries and pleas for life-saving action were shattered against walls of indifference until we began to stifle in the black realization that we are helpless. It was the year of our endless, bottomless helplessness.

Thirty-five years later, in entirely separate interviews, two leaders of the Jewish statehood drive of the 1940s each emphasized the same factor, the feeling of helplessness, the belief that little or nothing could be done.[78]

Although some signs of despair appeared before April 1943, it was the Bermuda Conference that destroyed hope. The brief Jewish effort for government rescue action had failed to break through Washington's "walls of indifference." During that same spring of 1943, however, prospects for the basic Zionist program were rising as the American Jewish Conference movement began to gather momentum. Furthermore, it was essential to press ahead with the statehood campaign because, for a limited time in the war's aftermath, conditions might open for the emergence of the Jewish state. The drive for the state had to be expedited, lest crucial postwar diplomatic decisions take place before Zionist influence could be fully applied.[79]

As limited as Zionist resources were, it seemed reasonable to concentrate them on the possible, rather than to devote them to what appeared to be a nearly hopeless cause. One week after Bermuda, Nahum Goldmann stressed the point at a meeting of the Zionist leadership. Too little manpower was available, he said, both to continue the mass meetings for rescue and to launch a major campaign for the Zionist program. Bermuda convinced him that the emphasis should be on Zionist goals.[80]

Reinforcing the Zionist's choice was their view of Jewish history over the centuries of the Diaspora. Abba Hillel Silver expressed that view in classic fashion in his famous speech to the American Jewish Conference. The chain of disasters that constituted the history of the Dispersion, Silver reminded his listeners, extended far beyond Hitler and the present mass slaughter. It encompassed two thousand years of world hatred and murder of Jews. No end to "this persistent emergency in Jewish life" would come, Silver warned, until Jewish homelessness ceased. And that would occur only with the creation of a Jewish state. The state was the instrument that would at last put a stop to the ceaseless tragedies that dominated Jewish history.[81]

The Zionist leadership, limited in the resources it commanded, faced two momentous obligations. For the immediate need, rescue, the prospects for achievement appeared bleak. For the postwar objective, the Jewish state, the time to press forward seemed at hand and the goal looked attainable. The Zionists made their choice. Events would show, however, that they had misread the signs concerning rescue. Substantially more was possible than they had recognized.

The Bergson Group

Although several American Jewish organizations continued to work for rescue throughout the war, after Bermuda only the Bergson group pushed ahead with a major and concerted campaign for government action. The Committee for a Jewish Army had opened that campaign in February 1943, centering it on the demand for establishment of a rescue agency. On the night of March 9, a week after the American Jewish Congress held its New York mass meeting, the army committee presented Ben Hecht's intensely moving drama *We Will Never Die,* a memorial to the murdered Jews of Europe. The crowd at Madison Square Garden was so huge that an unscheduled repeat performance was given late that night. No formal addresses were made, but the pageant's final passages dealt pointedly with the inertia and silence of the non-Jewish world.[82]

Press and newsreel coverage in New York and across the nation was extensive. With hopes of awakening America to the European Jewish tragedy, the Committee for a Jewish Army made plans to present *We Will Never Die* in dozens of cities across the country. The pageant was actually staged in five other cities, sparking a new round of publicity each time. But after that no other performances took place. The animosity that most of the established Jewish leadership had for the army committee and the Bergson group prevented cooperation with the project. And the American Jewish Congress and some of its allies obstructed the Bergsonites' efforts to finance further performances.[83]

In response to the Bermuda Conference, the attitude of the Bergson group was less one of despair than of anger and determination. Five days after the conference adjourned, the Committee for a Jewish Army published a scathing three-quarter-page advertisement in the *New York Times* labeling the whole proceeding a "cruel mockery." Brushing off a counterattack on the United States Senate floor by Scott Lucas of Illinois, who had been a delegate at Bermuda, the army committee announced its own plans to hold a conference. The new meeting aimed to do what the Bermuda Conference should have done, bring experts together to seek realistic ways to save European Jews.[84]

In July, in New York City, the Bergsonites sponsored the five-day Emergency Conference to Save the Jewish People of Europe. Despite obstruction from several quarters of organized American Jewry, the Committee for a Jewish Army succeeded in assembling an impressive group of participants. Meeting in panels dealing with such topics as transportation, diplomatic negotiations, military affairs, and the role of the church, important specialists hammered out practical rescue projects. Large evening sessions open to the public featured prominent speakers such as Fiorello LaGuardia, Dean Alfange of the American Labor Party, and (by radio) Herbert Hoover. Mention of only a few of the others who were associated with the Emergency

Conference indicates the wide variety of people who sought to do something about the Holocaust: Secretary of the Interior Harold Ickes, Senators Guy Gillette, Edwin Johnson, Elbert Thomas, and William Langer, labor leaders William Green and Philip Murray, and journalists William Randolph Hearst and William Allen White.[85]

The Emergency Conference agreed on a comprehensive set of rescue recommendations, with the strongest emphasis on a proposal for a United States government agency charged specifically with rescuing Jews. It also called for a publicity campaign to make the American people fully aware of the extermination issue. Finally, in order to activate its recommendations, the conference transformed itself into a new organization, the Emergency Committee to Save the Jewish People of Europe. The driving force in the new committee was the Bergson group.[86]

The Emergency Committee immediately began lobbying the Roosevelt Administration in support of its rescue plans, but achieved almost nothing there. It was unable to arrange an interview with the President. Bergson did see Eleanor Roosevelt, from whom he received a very small amount of cooperation. Approaches to the State Department were not productive. Emergency Committee contacts with Secretary of the Treasury Henry Morgenthau Jr. brought out his deep concern about the mass killings. But Morgenthau was not then willing to spearhead a drive from within the Administration to push Roosevelt to act.[87]

Meanwhile, during August and September, the Emergency Committee fired off another round of dramatic newspaper advertisements publicizing the Holocaust and urging formation of a rescue agency. Then in early October it initiated a nationwide petition drive and organized a pilgrimage to the nation's capital by 400 Orthodox rabbis. The rabbis, conspicuous with their beards and long black coats, arrived in Washington three days before Yom Kippur. They marched from Union Station to the Capitol, where they were met on the Capitol steps by Vice President Wallace and a score of congressmen. The rabbis presented a petition urging creation of a rescue agency and calling on the neutral countries, the United Nations, and Palestine to open their gates to the Jews. In mid-afternoon, after offering prayers at the Lincoln Memorial, the rabbis walked to the White House, where five of their number delivered another copy of the petition to a presidential secretary.[88]

The Emergency Committee had tried for weeks to arrange for the President to receive the rabbis' petition personally, but the appeals were repeatedly turned down. On the day of the pilgrimage, the White House informed the press that the President could not see the rabbis "because of the pressure of other business." In reality, Roosevelt had a very light schedule that afternoon. By the time the rabbis arrived he had managed to slip away to Bolling Field to observe the incorporation of a 40-man Yugoslav combat unit into the United States Army Air Force.[89]

The rabbis' pilgrimage received no support whatever from the established Jewish organizations, except the Union of Orthodox Rabbis and the Union of Grand Rabbis. Nor did it generate the amount of publicity that its sponsors had hoped for. But on another front, the halls of Congress, the Emergency Committee's efforts at last began to take hold. Ever since the Emergency Conference, the Bergsonites had been pressing the need for a rescue agency on members of Congress. By November they had organized some powerful backing, especially in the Senate. On November 9, the Emergency Committee made its move. Introduced in the Upper House by Guy Gillette and eleven other senators, and in the House of Representatives by Will Rogers Jr. and Joseph Baldwin, were identical resolutions urging the President to create "a commission of diplomatic, economic, and military experts" to initiate immediate action to save the remaining Jews of Europe.[90]

The Rescue Resolution encountered little difficulty in the Senate Foreign Relations Committee which approved it unanimously. But hearings in the House Foreign Affairs Committee turned up strong opposition from the State Department and from the chairman of the House committee, Congressman Sol Bloom of New York. Bloom, who had been a delegate to the Bermuda Conference, had not forgiven the Bergson group for its advertisement the previous May castigating the conference as a "cruel mockery." Furthermore, he consistently strove to ingratiate himself with the State Department.[91]

None of the established Jewish organizations supported the Rescue Resolution, except for the Union of Orthodox Rabbis. And Zionist leaders, working through the American Jewish Conference, threw roadblocks in its path. Senator Gillette, a dedicated friend of Zionism, spearheaded the drive for the resolution in the Senate. Afterward, describing the behind-the-scenes obstruction by Zionist leaders, Gillette stated: "These people used every effort, every means at their disposal, to block the resolution."[92]

In public, the Zionist leaders were more circumspect. Stephen Wise, testifying for the American Jewish Conference at the House hearings on the resolution, did not recommend its defeat. But he declared it was "inadequate" because it did not spell out a concrete program of action. Most important, said Wise, it failed to call for immediately opening Palestine to Jewish refugees. Four weeks later, in a stinging press release attacking the Bergson group, the American Jewish Conference disparaged the Rescue Resolution, though it stopped short of outright opposition to it.[93]

The resolution had caught the Zionist leaders in a dilemma. They did not dare oppose openly and directly a step for rescue of Jews. But they found it impossible to assist, or even to refrain from interfering with, the project of a group they saw as virtually an enemy. They recognized that success for the resolution would bring prestige, additional public support, and more strength to the Bergsonite faction.[94]

The Zionists' bitter opposition to the Bergsonites arose basically from their fear that the Bergson group might build an effective rival Zionist movement. The Zionists were apprehensive not so much that such a movement could supplant theirs, but that it would draw away badly needed funds and members and disrupt their progress toward realization of the Jewish state.[95]

As 1944 opened, pressures were mounting on the White House. The Senate was poised to act on the Rescue Resolution; almost certainly the vote would be overwhelmingly favorable. And Sol Bloom, in the words of one close observer of the situation, was having "to do everything he can possibly do" to keep his committee from sending the resolution to the House floor. Henry Morgenthau called it "a boiling pot" which was about to pop.[96]

Meanwhile, in an independent sequence of events stretching over the second half of 1943, the Treasury Department had clashed with the State Department on the rescue issue. The Treasury had to struggle for five months to obtain State Department approval for a license to send rescue and relief funds to the World Jewish Congress in Switzerland. In the process Treasury officials discovered that the State Department had consistently stalled and obstructed the rescue possibilities that had come to its attention.[97]

Convinced that the rescue issue had to be removed from the State Department, Treasury staff members (mostly non-Jews) persuaded Morgenthau to take their findings to the President and press him to establish a government rescue agency. Morgenthau did so on January 16, 1944. Roosevelt, fully aware of the growing pressures in Congress, realized that he could no longer sidestep the rescue issue. Morgenthau's disclosures concerning the State Department furnished the necessary last push. On January 22, two days before the Rescue Resolution was to go before the Senate, Roosevelt issued an executive order creating the War Refugee Board.[98]

Two convergent forces were responsible for the emergence of the War Refugee Board, the Treasury Department's pressure on Roosevelt and the long campaign for a rescue agency waged by the Emergency Committee and, earlier, the Committee for a Jewish Army. Spokesmen for the American Jewish Conference publicly denied that the Rescue Resolution had any connection with the President's action. But experienced Washington lobbyists, journalists, and political leaders reported otherwise. Moreover, records now available show that Morgenthau and his staff, the people who were closest to the whole situation, had no doubt whatever that it was the Rescue Resolution that made it possible to force the President to act. Not to be overlooked, however, is the fact that several groups, mostly Jewish, contributed vitally over the months by publicizing the Holocaust and helping to create a limited but essential amount of public concern and political support for rescue action.[99]

The War Refugee Board turned out to be a collaborative effort between the Treasury Department and Jewish organizations in the United States and overseas. It did an important job, helping to save between 100,000 and 200,000 Jewish lives. But it was too little, and far too late. Strong and persistent pressure after the War Refugee Board was formed would have been necessary to have forced the Roosevelt Administration to give the board the support it needed for a maximum rescue effort. That kind of pressure did not materialize, either from the Bergsonites, or the regular Zionists, or others. And rescue never became more than a very low priority in the Roosevelt government.[100]

The Bergsonite Emergency Committee kept on pushing for rescue, but its activities decreased during 1944 and 1945. On the Zionist side, the World Jewish Congress continued to prod the government, but only on a minor scale. The Va'ad ha'Hatzala, the Orthodox rescue committee, expanded its exertions, but it was a very limited operation. A unified and dynamic American Jewish drive for rescue was critically needed after the War Refugee Board emerged, as it had been before. But in 1944 and 1945 unified Jewish action was farther away than ever. And little dynamism seemed to be left in the scattered factions that were still fighting for a full-fledged United States commitment to rescue.[101]

CHAPTER 1 ABBREVIATIONS

AECZA = American Emergency Committee for Zionist Affairs
AJC = American Jewish Committee
AJ Conference = American Jewish Conference
AJHS = American Jewish Historical Society
AJYB = *American Jewish Year Book*
AZEC = American Zionist Emergency Council
CJR = *Contemporary Jewish Record*
CW = *Congress Weekly*
ECSJPE = Emergency Committee to Save the Jewish People of Europe
FRUS = *Foreign Relations of the United States* (diplomatic papers series)
JDC = American Jewish Joint Distribution Committee
JEC = Joint Emergency Committee on European Jewish Affairs
MD = Morgenthau Diaries. (Citations thus: Book/page.)
NP = *New Palestine*
NYT = *New York Times*
PSC = Palestine Statehood Committee
SD = State Department
WJC = World Jewish Congress
WRB = War Refugee Board

Chapter 2

PATTERNS OF JEWISH LEADERSHIP IN GREAT BRITAIN DURING THE NAZI ERA

Bernard Wasserstein

The response of Anglo-Jewry to the crisis of the Nazi period differed significantly from that of other major Jewish communities. The differences arose to a large extent out of the unique social and political context within which the leadership of Anglo-Jewry operated and from the special characteristics of the communal structure. Indeed, the very nature of Jewish leadership in England, as well as its *modus operandi,* diverged fundamentally from the patterns of other major communities. A comparative assessment of the role of Jewish leadership must begin by taking account of the unique social and political culture of Anglo-Jewry.

Perhaps the most salient distinction between Anglo-Jewish and American-Jewish leadership was that in England the Jews did not function politically as an ethnic group. Indeed the whole notion of ethnic politics is alien to English political culture (even today in spite of the large influx since the 1950s of West and East Indian immigrants). There was no organized Jewish vote in England; there were no significant Jewish issues in politics; there was no sense of the Jews as an ethnic lobby. Jewish leaders in England, unlike the U.S.A., could deliver nothing by way of votes, money, or organization to those in high places whom they courted. Probably for this reason Anglo-Jewry did not have leaders who acquired importance in the non-Jewish world simply because they were Jewish leaders: there were no British equivalents of Stephen S. Wise or Abba Hillel Silver, nor of David Ben Gurion or Moshe Shertok.

Jewish leadership in Britain between 1933 and 1945 may be divided into two types. First, there were those who held elected or appointed positions of importance within the Jewish community and who consequently exercised some external representative function. Examples of this type were such figures

29

as Chief Rabbi J. H. Hertz and Professor Selig Brodetsky, President of the Board of Deputies of British Jews from 1939. Second, there were those who derived their internal importance as Jewish leaders from the external prominence they had gained or inherited in the non-Jewish world. Examples of this type included politicians such as Viscount Samuel, former Home Secretary and High Commissioner in Palestine, and businessmen such as Sir Robert Waley Cohen, one of the creators of the Shell Oil company. Although some self-made men were beginning to make their appearance in the Jewish community in this period—for example, Sidney Silverman in politics and Simon Marks in business—the second category still consisted in the main of members of the old-established Anglo-Jewish gentry affectionately portrayed by Chaim Bermant in his amusing book *The Cousinhood*.[1] The difference between the two types was thus also frequently one of social class and this fact gave a special flavor to the internal debates of Jewish leadership in England.

The case of Chaim Weizmann might, at first sight, appear to constitute an exception to the pattern described. But it is not, for his external importance derived not from his role as a leader of Anglo-Jewry but rather from the perception of him by the British political elite as the major representative figure of that mythical unity, "world Jewry." For this reason, although often regarded as the most important Jewish leader resident in Britain in this period, Weizmann cannot properly be regarded as an Anglo-Jewish leader, and a consideration of his very important role falls outside the framework of this analysis. So too does that of émigré Jewish politicians who had found refuge in Britain. Important though their activities were, particularly in the dissemination of news from Europe of Nazi atrocities, they cannot be viewed as part of the Anglo-Jewish leadership.

In its organizational structure the Jewish community in Britain was much more centralized than that of the U.S.A. Leadership was concentrated in one dominant religious institution, the United Synagogue (whose head, the Chief Rabbi, was recognized by many congregations which were not members of the United Synagogue), and one dominant secular body, the Board of Deputies of British Jews, which has had statutory recognition as the representative organ of the community since 1836. In its centralized structure Anglo-Jewish leadership appears closer to the pattern of the *Yishuv* (Jewish community) in Palestine. But such a comparison points immediately to the fundamental weakness of the Anglo-Jewish structure: unlike Palestine, where the central institutions of the *Yishuv* commanded the primary political loyalty of the majority of the community, and where the leadership could mobilize its members (albeit on a voluntary basis) politically and even militarily, the

Anglo-Jewish leadership commanded no such automatic loyalty. In a liberal, assimilationist environment, Jewish loyalties competed with others in the marketplace of political and social solidarities. The ability of Jewish leadership to mobilize the community in Britain was inferior both to that of Palestine and, because of the absence of the ethnic political dimension and because of its much smaller size, to that of the U.S.A.

The special character and structure of Anglo-Jewish leadership helped to determine the ground rules of political action. The weakness in capacity for mobilization meant that the Anglo-Jewish leadership could not operate through institutions characteristic of Palestinian Jewry such as mass political parties, trade unions, and underground military forces, nor through public meetings, propaganda, and ethnic political lobbying after the fashion of American Jewry. However, in the context of British political culture, the inability to mobilize constituted in many ways less of a drawback than might appear. For in spite of the superficial democratization of British politics, concepts such as the "corridors of power," the "establishment," and the "magic circle" still had life and meaning in the 1930s and 1940s. The passion for secrecy which the late Richard Crossman detected in British political life as late as the 1960s was still omnipresent in the earlier period. Decisions of importance were still being taken in Pall Mall clubs rather than in public forums. The effectiveness of political action by the Anglo-Jewish leadership consequently depended less on its ability to mobilize its constituency than in its access to influential quarters; in this its centralized nature (and its deployment of the "notable" category of leaders, those with an external, non-Jewish basis of importance) served the community well. Professor Lewis Namier, who as a historian had such an unerring eye for the real locations of power, betrayed a similar capacity when, in his work for the Zionist Organization during the war, he made a habit of standing in the hall of the Athenaeum Club, ready to waylay any unwary Colonial Office official who might enter. In the British context such buttonholing might be as effective as a monster demonstration in Madison Square Garden in the American.

The effectiveness of the Anglo-Jewish leadership's response to the European Jewish crisis was, as elsewhere, predicated on its information about and understanding of Nazi policy toward the Jews. In the prewar period, when there was free communication between Germany and Britain, information about Nazi atrocities was extensively published both in the general press, most notably the *Manchester Guardian,* and in the *Jewish Chronicle.* The national character of a greater part of the British press and the special position of the *Jewish Chronicle* as a nationally distributed newspaper of the Anglo-Jewish community meant that information about the Jews in Europe was often more readily available to the Anglo-Jewish leadership than was the case in the U.S.A. with its localized and often parochial press, both general and Jewish. From 1933 onward the Board of Deputies published pamphlets containing extracts from reports in such papers as *The Times,* the *Manchester Guardian,* and the *Daily Telegraph* that detailed the persecution of Jews in Germany.[2]

After the outbreak of war, although the free flow of news from Nazi Europe was impeded, it did not dry up. The *Jewish Chronicle,* indeed, published remarkably early and accurate accounts of the stages of Nazi mass murder. On November 10, 1939, it carried the headlines: "Forcible Exodus: Nazis Send Thousands to Lublin: Ghetto-State of 4 Million?" On December 15, 1939: "Mass Murder in Poland: Three Thousand Suicides: Burials Day and Night." On January 12, 1940: "'Annihilating Polish Jewry.' Nazis Boasted Aim: Over 120,000 Victims Already: Nazi Atrocities Confirmed: Mass Slaughter of Polish Jews." On October 24, 1941: Ghastly Pogroms in Ukraine: Thousands of Corpses in River Dniester: 8,000 Slain in Synagogues." On November 7 it reported: "Almost One Third of the Entire Jewish Population of Bessarabia Was Exterminated." On November 14 it reported a ban on all Jewish emigration from territory controlled by Germany. In January 1942 it reported that poison-gas experiments had taken place in the Mauthausen camp. Throughout 1942 the development of the Nazi mechanism of systematic destruction of the Jews continued to be reflected in the *Jewish Chronicle.* On December 11, 1942 the newspaper appeared with a black border and the headline: "Two Million Jews Slaughtered: Most Terrible Massacre of All Time: Appalling Horrors of Nazi Mass Murders." And on May 7, 1943: "Warsaw Ghetto Battle: Jews Went Down Fighting: Nazis Use Tanks."

The archives of the major Jewish organizations reveal the wealth of information available to them from a variety of quarters concerning the Jewish position in Europe. Thus the report of the Joint Foreign Committee of the Board of Deputies and the Anglo-Jewish Association for November–December 1941 stated: "It is reported that after the occupation of Kiev, the Nazi authorities deliberately murdered 52,000 people—Jews and non-Jews."[3] The report for July–August 1942 stated:

An order for the deportation of Jews from the Warsaw Ghetto was issued recently, and daily about seven thousand were being removed to "an unknown destination." There seems to be reason for believing that these deportees are being killed before they reach any destination. The Chairman of the Council of the Warsaw Ghetto, Engineer Cherniakow *(sic),* whom the Gestapo tried to compel to prepare the daily lists of the people to be removed from the ghetto, refused to give them those lists and took his own life rather than comply.[4]

The archives of the British section of the World Jewish Congress contain the reports from Switzerland of Gerhart M. Riegner, including his famous message of August 1942 to Sidney Silverman, Chairman of the British Section, and Stephen S. Wise. Although the British Foreign Office regarded the account of a Nazi plan for total elimination of the Jews as a "rather wild story" it did permit Riegner's message to be communicated to Silverman.[5] The message was succeeded by others, such as Riegner's letter to Silverman of October 3, 1942: "Deportees *(sic)* are going on in an accelerated way from Belgium, France, Holland, Germany and all countries in the East including Poland. There are only two countries where until now these measures are not yet applied, i.e., Italy and Hungary."[6]

Similarly, the Zionist Organization office in London received a stream of reports from Richard Lichtheim, the Zionist representative in Geneva. For example, on September 26, 1942, Lichtheim cabled to London: "All information lately received confirms previous reports about extermination Jews following deportation from various countries to Germany or Poland."[7] And three days later Lichtheim wrote that the "total destruction of the Jewish communities in Belgium and Holland" was nearly complete and that "the most gruesome reports" were coming out of Poland.[8]

Of course it was not merely a matter of information but also of understanding, and in this respect the Anglo-Jewish leadership was in general no more foresighted than Jewish leaders elsewhere. When representatives of the Anglo-Jewish community wrote to the Home Secretary in April 1933 about Jewish refugees from Germany they estimated that the numbers coming to Britain "might be as many as 3,000 to 4,000."[9] By the outbreak of the war the number of arrivals had reached 50,000. Studies recently published have analyzed the process whereby information about Nazi mass murder reached the West during the war, and these have stressed the gap between information and understanding.[10] This gap is evident in the records of the major Jewish organizations. In spite of the massive information at the disposal of the Zionist Organization it is not until November 25, 1942 that the "Extermination of Jews" first appears on the agenda of the meetings of the Zionist political "high command" in London.[11] Indeed, until then the subject is hardly referred to in the minutes of these meetings. With hindsight, it is of course easy to criticize the myopia of these Jewish leaders. In this connection one should bear in mind, however, the stages of development of Nazi policy: there was sporadic persecution from the outset; the Nuremberg

Laws were promulgated in September 1935; the Nazi expansion into Austria and Czechoslovakia in 1938–39 brought hundreds of thousands more Jews under Nazi rule; the concentration of Jews in ghettos began after the outbreak of the war; the slaughter by the *Einsatzgruppen* began after the attack on Russia in June 1941; the Wannsee Conference on "the Final Solution of the Jewish Question" took place on January 20, 1942. What appears in retrospect as a logical progression could not be forecast in advance, as Professor Jacob Katz has pointed out.[12] At any rate such forecasts were not made by any responsible Jewish leaders in Britain.

This tendency, evident until late 1942, to underestimate the nature and dimensions of the problem, did not, however, diminish the speed and energy with which Jewish leaders in Britain applied themselves to the task of rescue and relief. The Anglo-Jewish effort on behalf of German-Jewish, and later European Jewish refugees was characteristically centralized in specialized institutions which drew support from broad sections of the community. Of these the most important were the Central British Fund for German Jewry (later known as the Council for German Jewry), the Jewish Refugees Committee (headed by the merchant banker Otto M. Schiff), and the Academic Assistance Council (supported by many non-Jews) which was concerned with the needs of academic refugees from Nazism. All these organizations were formed in early 1933, shortly after the Nazi seizure of power.

In their proposals to the British Government in April 1933 the Anglo-Jewish leadership (Neville Laski and Lionel Cohen of the Board of Deputies, Leonard Montefiore of the Anglo-Jewish Association, and Otto Schiff) laid down a central principle which was to prove of vital importance in facilitating the entry of Jewish refugees to England. They undertook, on behalf of the community, that "all expense, whether in respect of temporary or permanent accommodation or maintenance will be borne by the Jewish community without ultimate charge to the State."[13] This was a guarantee which was highlighted by the Home Secretary in his report on the subject to the Cabinet Committee on Aliens Restrictions.[14] A Home Office memorandum in September 1935 noted that the guarantee had been "fully implemented."[15] Although the capacity of the community to maintain the guarantee was strained to the limit, particularly after the *Anschluss,* the undertaking was honored until the outbreak of the war in spite of the fact that the number of refugees arriving was more than ten times that originally expected.[16] Without this assurance it is very doubtful if the British government would have admitted such substantial numbers at a time of mass unemployment and considerable public anti-Semitism.

This guarantee could be maintained only on the basis of a massive fund-raising effort. Between 1933 and 1939 the Anglo-Jewish community spent more than £3,000,000 on the reception and maintenance of Jewish refugees in Britain.[17] This was a very large sum for a community of some 330,000. The 50,000 Jewish refugees from the expanded Reich who were admitted to Britain between 1933 and 1939 compared favorably with the figures for other countries: in the same period an estimated 57,000 were admitted to the U.S.A. and 53,000 to Palestine. The comparison with the U.S.A., with a Jewish population more than fourteen times the size of Anglo-Jewry, is particularly revealing.

The achievement of the British community is perhaps best highlighted by the success of the Movement for the Care of Children from Germany in securing the admission of nearly ten thousand children—nine tenths of them Jewish—to Britain in 1938–39. Again, the contrast with the U.S.A. is poignantly revealing. In February 1939 Senator Robert F. Wagner and Representative Edith Nourse Rogers introduced identical bills in the Senate and the House of Representatives which would have permitted over a two-year period the entrance outside the normal immigration quotas of a total of 20,000 German refugee children. But, as has been recorded by David S. Wyman in his book, *Paper Walls,* by June 1939 the Wagner-Rogers Bill had been effectively defeated and its supporters never dared revive it.[18] As A. J. Sherman has pointedly commented:

> One reason for this state of affairs, often obscured by the continuing uproar over immigration to Palestine, was the curiously negative attitude of the American Jewish community to the prospect of any large influx of refugees into the United States, and the resultant refusal of the community's leaders to urge more than token changes in immigration law or procedures.[19]

Whatever explanation may be adduced for the attitude of American Jewish leaders (and it must be recalled that the socio-political context in which they were operating differed radically from that in Britain), there is a clear contrast here with the attitude and achievement of Anglo-Jewry.

However, upon the British entry into the war on September 3, 1939, a new period began in which the capacity of the Anglo-Jewish leadership to influence the British Government over the questions of Jewish refugee admissions or relief was sharply diminished. This was partly a question of finance. After September 1939 the number of Jewish refugees requiring financial assistance greatly increased while the resources available to the Jewish voluntary organizations were, under wartime conditions, inevitably reduced. In 1940 it was agreed that the government would henceforth share the cost of maintenance of destitute refugees on a 50/50 basis. By 1945 the government was paying the entire cost, although by then the expense had been much reduced as refugees had been integrated into the economy.[20] The government recognized that the lapse of the Jewish community's guarantee was, given the changed circumstances, inevitable. But the new arrangement further limited the negotiating power of the Jewish leadership. Henceforth there was little that they might offer to the British government as an inducement toward a more generous policy on the Jewish refugee issue.

For this and other reasons the number of Jewish refugees admitted to Britain after September 3, 1939 showed a dramatic fall from the prewar figures. Although no precise figure is available a reliable estimate is that the net increase in the Jewish refugee population of the country during the war was no more than 10,000. Increasingly during the war it became clear that the government was particularly reluctant to admit Jewish, as against non-Jewish refugees. The figures of those admitted provide an indication of the dramatic change from the prewar period. Before the war some 90 percent of refugees from Nazism admitted to Britain were Jews. During the war more than 80 percent were non-Jews.[21] In the spring of 1940, at the time of the invasion of the Low Countries, the government was said to have plans for the admission of as many as 300,000 Dutch and Belgian refugees.[22] Yet later in the same year, when an appeal was made for the admission of two thousand Jewish refugees from Luxemburg, the request was rejected, a Foreign Office official noting that "They are covered by the Home Office prejudice . . . against people from enemy-occupied territory; and in any case we simply cannot have any more people let into the United Kingdom on merely humanitarian grounds.[23]

Jewish organizations made repeated efforts to persuade the government to relax the rigidity of its immigration policy as applied to Jews. This was particularly so after the United Nations declaration of December 17, 1942, denouncing Nazi mass murder of Jews, a pronouncement which evoked widespread public sympathy in Britain for the Jewish plight. But there was no significant relaxation of the government's policy, for as the Home Secretary, Herbert Morrison, pointed out to a Cabinet Committee on December 31, 1942: "There was considerable anti-Semitism under the surface in this country. If there was any substantial increase in the number of Jewish refugees or if these refugees did not leave this country after the war, we should be in for serious trouble."[24]

The "fifth column" scare of 1940, and the question of the internment of aliens highlighted the changed circumstances brought about by the war, and the constraints upon effective action by Jewish organizations. When the government, in response to a wave of xenophobic panic among the general public, decided in May 1940 to intern most adult enemy aliens, including Jewish refugees, the initial response of the Anglo-Jewish community was remarkably muted. The *Jewish Chronicle,* on May 17, 1940, approved the measure, declaring in an editorial that it could not "be resisted, least of all at this juncture when the very life of the nation is at issue." The chairman of the Defence Committee of the Board of Deputies expressed great concern at the "thoughtless behaviour of so many of them [the refugees] in areas where they are concentrated, namely Golders Green, Hampstead, North London, etc."[25] The passive policy of the Jewish leadership in the first stages of the mass internment policy aroused criticism from a prominent Manchester Jew, Nathan Laski, who complained that the Board had not done enough to counter the injustices of the policy and who wrote to the Board's secretary: "We can no longer put these poor people off by saying the Board of Deputies has it in hand."[26] Laski took matters into his own hands by writing directly to the Prime Minister, with whom he was personally acquainted.[27] The passivity of the Jewish leadership aroused comment even from non-Jews: Sir Andrew McFadyean wrote to Neville Laski on August 29, 1940: "I hear from more than one quarter, in fact I think it was stated in the House, that prominent British Jews have encouraged the Government in their internment policy. This is so shocking that I hesitate to believe it."[28]

The Jewish attitude toward the internment of enemy aliens soon changed. The *Jewish Chronicle* rapidly switched from approval to strong condemnation of the indiscriminate nature of the policy and its several manifest absurdities and injustices. The Jewish Refugees Committee and the Board of Deputies took up such questions as conditions in internment camps, the internment of some Jewish refugees in the same camps as pro-Nazi Germans, the deportation to Australia and Canada of many of the internees, and the physical violence and robbery to which some internees and deportees were subjected. This change of attitude reflected a general public reaction against the earlier "fifth-column" panic and fierce criticism of the mass internment policy in the national press. In the House of Commons Jewish M.P.s such as Sidney Silverman were joined by many non-Jews in their criticism of the policy. As a result, within a few months the majority of the internees had been released and some of those deported were permitted to return to Britain. The episode is revealing of the weakness of the Jewish leadership in Britain in wartime and of its dependence on the support of non-Jews for effective political action.

The sense of desperation and urgency which enveloped the Anglo-Jewish leadership as news of the Nazi horrors was confirmed emerges clearly from the minutes of an emergency meeting convened on December 3, 1942 by the Joint Foreign Committee of the Board of Deputies and the Anglo-Jewish Association. The meeting was attended by representatives of the Jewish Agency, the World Jewish Congress, and the Agudath Israel, as well as by the Chief Rabbi and the Jewish members of the Polish and Czechoslovak governments in London. The purpose of the meeting was stated as being "to consider action to be taken to meet the situation described in the recent reports on the wholesale extermination of the Jewish population in the areas occupied by the Germans." The meeting opened with a statement by the President of the Board of Deputies, Professor Brodetsky, outlining the efforts that were being made to secure a government declaration condemning the atrocities, the approach made to the Archbishop of Canterbury to gain his support, and the work being carried out by the Board in order to enlighten public opinion on the issue. Brodetsky added that "in addition to all the above, it was necessary that the *Jewish Community* itself *should express their sense of horror* and sorrow at what was happening, and express it in such a way that the general community should really be startled out of their complacency."

The discussion which followed was revealing of the inevitable limitations upon effective action. The Chief Rabbi called for "some *manifestation of a religious character—a day of mourning and a Fast* with Services in the Synagogues." It was agreed that "the matter was too urgent to be postponed till a date next year, and that the *Jewish manifestation* should be *more drastic,* and should at least include *the stoppage of all functions such as dances, picture going, wedding ceremonies,* and so forth." Noah Barou of the World Jewish Congress suggested a Jewish demonstration in Trafalgar Square and another suggestion was made of a Jewish procession from Whitechapel to Whitehall. The minutes continued: "These suggestions were discussed, and several opinions were expressed that the organisation of *marches and demonstrations* was full of difficulties, and seemed to be *out of keeping with the general mood of the country."* After further discussion of the point a telephone call was received from Sidney Silverman M.P. who said that he thought a demonstration necessary. Barou warned the meeting that "feeling in the East End ran so high that, if the Executive [of the Board] decided against a demonstration or taking any drastic action, there may be spontaneous outbreaks of feeling which might prove embarrassing."

The conference then moved on to consider what action should be taken to get as many Jews as possible out of Europe. Berl Locker, representing the

Jewish Agency, urged that Jewish and non-Jewish delegations be sent to the Prime Minister and Foreign Secretary; debates should be initiated in both Houses of Parliament; the Pope should be approached as should other neutrals and the International Red Cross; the BBC should be induced to broadcast on the subject in its European services. Other suggestions included an attempt to obtain for Jews in Nazi Europe the status of prisoners of war, the dropping of leaflets over Germany, and efforts to secure release of Jewish children through the Red Cross and neutral countries.[29]

All the Jewish organizations moved fast to put these efforts in motion. The Chief Rabbi proclaimed a "Week of Mourning and Prayer," beginning on Sunday, December 13 with a service in the historic Bevis Marks Synagogue. On December 17 the Women's International Zionist Organization held a mass meeting at the Wigmore Hall. On Sunday December 20 the Board of Deputies held a public meeting, with Brodetsky in the chair and Count Raczynski of the Polish Government-in-Exile, Lord Nathan, Eleanor Rathbone M.P., Professor A. V. Hill M.P., Sidney Silverman M.P., and Berl Locker among the speakers. The British section of the World Jewish Congress held a meeting in the House of Commons. On December 22 a deputation of Jewish leaders, including Brodetsky, James de Rothschild, the Chief Rabbi, Lord Samuel, Sir Robert Waley Cohen, Sir Simon Marks, and others met with Foreign Secretary Eden, and urged various practical steps to save Jewish lives. The Archbishop of Canterbury publicly urged the government to take action to save Jews. An all-party deputation of M.P.s met the Deputy Prime Minister as well as the Foreign, Home, and Colonial Secretaries.[30] Approaches to the Pope, neutrals, the Red Cross, and others were duly made. The BBC was persuaded to make some broadcasts. Leaflets were dropped over Germany and elsewhere. Immediate efforts were made to secure the release of children. The government's declaration denouncing atrocities was made in the House of Commons on December 17, 1942 in reply to a question put by Sidney Silverman M.P. Following the declaration a short, but deeply moving, speech was made by James de Rothschild M.P. Upon the suggestion of a Labour member the House rose for a minute's silence, an unprecedented act. Lloyd George commented to Eden: "I cannot recall a scene like that in all my years in Parliament.[31]

However, the hopes that these efforts, the government's declaration, and the widespread public sympathy might yield some tangible results were soon dashed. Responding to the public concern the British and American governments convened a conference at Bermuda in April 1943 to consider the refugee issue. But, as we now know, the two delegations were hemmed in from the outset with instructions from their governments which reduced their deliberations to a virtual nullity. Efforts by Jewish organizations to secure representation at Bermuda were rejected on the ground that "to admit a Jewish representation would open the door to a request for similar favours from other interested parties."[32] The two governments forebore from publishing the report of the conference, ostensibly in order not to prejudice planned action in favor of refugees, in reality because the conference's decisions were embarrassingly barren of substance.

The failure of the government to translate the declaration of December 17, 1942 into effective action evoked deeply felt responses from Jewish leaders. Eva, Marchioness of Reading, President of the British Section of the World Jewish Congress, wrote direct to Churchill: "In other days I would have come to you in sackcloth and ashes to plead for my people. . . . Some can still be saved if the iron fetters of red tape can be burst asunder."[33] In an uncharacteristically bitter speech in the House of Lords on 23 March 1943 Lord Samuel demanded that a sense of urgency be infused into government policy:

> The declaration of the United Nations was made on December 17. Today is March 23, and, so far as is publicly known, nothing has happened except discussions, conferences and exchanges of notes. We are glad to learn that measures are afoot for securing close cooperation between this country and the United States. But there seems to be a great danger that action is liable to be lost in the sands of diplomatic negotiations. . . . While governments prepare memoranda and exchange notes and hold conferences, week after week, month after month the Nazis go on killing men, women and children.

Pointing to the shortage of labor which existed in Palestine, Lord Samuel conceded that it was by now unlikely that more than a small number of Jews could be expected to escape from Nazi control to contribute to the war effort. But he continued:

> So small is the number that it seems monstrous to refer to difficulties of food supply, in this country of forty-seven million people, or to difficulties of employment, when we know that here also there is a shortage of labour. . . . There is still in this country, however, a rigid refusal to grant visas to any persons who are still in enemy-occupied territory.[34]

Some minor concessions were made by the British government in 1943. The administration of the immigration provisions of the Palestine White Paper of May 1939 were slightly eased; but by now it was virtually impossible for Jews to escape from Nazi Europe. Camps for Jewish refugees were set up in North Africa. The Jewish issue was for a while given a higher priority in war propaganda. Lengthy negotiations led to permission being granted for small numbers of relief parcels to be sent through the economic blockade of Nazi Europe, via Lisbon, to Jewish addressees in occupied territory. Some of these reached their destinations and helped save a few lives, but many were found to be undelivered because the addressees had already been killed.

There were several reasons for the failure of the Anglo-Jewish leaders to make a significant impact on government policy. On the Palestine issue there was the overriding wartime concern of the British defense and foreign policy establishment with the precarious military and supply position in the Middle East and the consequent importance, as they saw it, of avoiding any action in Palestine which might antagonize Arab nationalists there and elsewhere. In Britain itself there was an increased level of public anti-Semitism after the outbreak of the war, noted by many observers, including the Home Intelligence Division of the Ministry of Information. In an interview with a representative of the Board of Deputies in February 1943 the Director of the Division summarized the grounds for the increase "as being due to allegations that the Jews were predominant in the black market and, secondly, to the further allegation that Jews were not doing their full share in the Services."[35] Moreover, whereas the British government had believed, rightly or wrongly, during the First World War that "world Jewry" was a powerful force which was worth courting, this attitude had by now given way to the view that, as one Foreign Office official put it in 1941: "When it comes to the point, the Jews will never hamper us to put the Germans on the throne."[36] Underlying everything was the priority to be accorded to the war effort, encapsulated in Churchill's dictum in October 1943: "Everything for the war, whether controversial or not, and nothing controversial that is not *bona fide* needed for the war."[37] The distasteful decisions to which this often led were regarded as unpleasant necessities of war. A senior Colonial Office official, Sir John Shuckburgh, put it well when he wrote in May 1941: "These are days in which we are brought up against realities and we cannot be deterred by the kind of prewar humanitarianism that prevailed in 1939."[38] This was in a minute supporting the policy of firing on Jewish immigrant ships in order to drive them away from Palestinian ports. Against entrenched attitudes of this kind the pleas of Anglo-Jewish leaders could make little headway.

An overall assessment of the Anglo-Jewish leadership's reaction to the crisis of the Nazi period must be grey rather than black-and-white. There were several negative aspects. There was the general failure to realize until too late the true nature and dimensions of the problem. There was often a paternalist attitude toward the refugees. There was sometimes a shortage of Jewish families willing to take in Jewish child refugees who were therefore sent to non-Jewish families; some of these children were, not surprisingly, left with very bitter feelings toward the Jewish community. There was, in the initial stages of the internments of 1940, far too acquiescent an attitude by the community's leaders—although this soon changed. And, as one distinguished community activist, Professor Norman Bentwich, noted in his memoirs, there was too often "unhelpful competition" between the various Jewish organizations. "We wasted hours protesting, and composing and criticizing memoranda which had no hope of serious attention by the Governments."[39] The differences of outlook among the community's leaders, particularly over Zionism, bubbled under the surface throughout the war. In 1943 they came to a head when the Zionists succeeded in capturing a majority in the Board of Deputies. As the Palestine conflict degenerated into open civil war by 1945, grave strains emerged within the Anglo-Jewish elite. On October 6, 1945, Chief Rabbi Hertz sent a telegram to all synagogues under his jurisdiction calling for "a day of Jewish solidarity with the remnants of European Jewry," and adding that the "Jews of England expect the government to keep faith in regard to Palestine as the only haven of refuge to survivors of Nazi bestiality." The President of the United Synagogue, Sir Robert Waley Cohen, together with a Vice-President, sent a counter-telegram warning that the "last sentence of Chief Rabbi's telegram to your Minister- . . . . may be misinterpreted as advocating introduction of politics into our religious services."[40]

Nevertheless, such strains should not be exaggerated; by and large the community's central institutions showed a remarkable degree of cohesion, particularly by comparison with those of other Jewish communities. Moreover, on the positive side of the ledger must be stressed the speed and efficiency with which the community adapted to the emergency in early 1933 by creating specialized central institutions which, in spite of the enormous pressure of numbers of refugees by 1939, coped until the outbreak of the war without having to default on the community's guarantee to the government that no refugee would fall on the public purse. The declaration of December 1942 and the ensuing public clamor for government help for Jews would not have occurred without the pressure of the organized institutions of Anglo-Jewry. The efforts of the Anglo-Jewish leadership to enlist the active support of broad sections of the political elite and of public opinion were, particularly in late 1942 and early 1943, highly effective.

The prewar record, particularly as measured by the numbers of refugees whose admission to the country was secured, was impressive on any comparative examination. If during the war the record of achievement was slight, the primary explanation must be sought in the altered circumstances of wartime Britain in which the capacity of the Jewish organizations to exercise real influence on the government was minimal. Of course, in retrospect, against the background of the full magnitude of the horrors as we now know them, all that was done was too little and too late. But seen in context the Anglo-Jewish leadership's achievement compares favorably with that of any other major Jewish community. And if the results, particularly during the war, were disappointing, it must be said that this was not for want of trying.

In recent years it has become increasingly fashionable to criticize the Jewish leadership of the war years for supposed sins of omission and a general over-passivity. In the case of Anglo-Jewry, at least, this accusation has little basis in reality. The admonitive words of Ahad Ha-am are apposite here:

Nothing is more dangerous for a nation or for an individual than to plead guilty to imaginary sins. Where the sin is real, the gates of repentance are not locked, and by honest endeavour the sinner can purify himself. But when a man has been persuaded to suspect himself without cause, how will he be able to purify himself in his own eyes?[41]

Chapter 3

SOME ASPECTS OF THE *YISHUV* LEADERSHIP'S ACTIVITIES DURING THE HOLOCAUST

Bela Vago

Talking about such a delicate, and also unrewarding topic—the attitude and the activity of the Jewish community of Palestine *(Yishuv)* during the Holocaust—one cannot refrain from seeking certain methodological schemes in order to facilitate the researcher's task.

This paper centers around a few basic questions. Among them: who were the leaders, who knew what, when, and how in the Yishuv leadership about reality in Europe; how did they react; what was the scale of priorities of their interests and activities; how were their intentions translated into deeds; what were the objective possibilities of lending a helping hand and of rescuing; and to what extent did the leaders succeed in exploiting the objective favorable factors; how effective were their actions?

At the top of the scene were the leaders of the Jewish Agency, of the *Vaad ha'Leumi* (the National Council), of the Zionist Organization, of the *Histadrut* (Trade Union) and of the *Mapai* (Labor) party; in fact there was an overlapping of positions and of the leading roles in all these forums, so that the number of the top leaders can be reduced to six or seven persons. However, the leadership, in its broader sense, included some fifteen persons—most of them, albeit not all of the prominent ones—belonging to the Mapai wing of the Zionist labor movement.

To the inner circle belonged David Ben Gurion, Chaim Weizmann (although he spent most of the war years outside Palestine), Moshe Shertok

---

The Yishuv leaders are identified in this paper by their hebraised names rather than by their former names (thus for example Sharet, Meir instead of Shertok and Meyerson).

I am indebted to three of my graduate students (Mrs. Neima Barzel, Mr. Arie Kohavi and Mr. Arie Steinberg) who helped me in collecting the source material for this paper.

45

(Sharet), Berl Katznelson, and also Yosef Sprintzak, Eliezer Kaplan, Yitzhak Grünbaum, and a few other personalities. It should be made clear that neither Weizmann, nor Grünbaum belonged to the *Mapai-Histadrut* group. The leaders of all other political shades, including those of the Revisionists, the *Agudath Israel,* and the left-socialists, appeared at best on the periphery of the leadership, lacking a real leading role in the Zionist Organization, the Jewish Agency, and other important forums.

This paper will emphasize the attitude of the members of the Executive Committee of the Jewish Agency, since this body saw itself not only as the leading committee of the *Yishuv,* and acted as a kind of government, but also of the Jewish people as a whole.

It should also be kept in mind that there were different phases in the wartime activity of the leadership (following the military and political changes on the map), and that there were marked differences of view even inside the small group of leading personalities. Therefore, besides the attitude or policy of the leadership as a whole regarding the Holocaust, this paper will also follow the personal views, attitudes, and policy of the individual leaders.

Although the schematic division of a leadership's record into positive and negative parts is certainly simplistic, an attempt will be made to draw up a short survey of the credit and debit sides of the balance sheet of the leadership's reaction to the fate of European Jewry during the Holocaust.

Since the most important decisions regarding the *Yishuv's* reaction to the Holocaust were taken at different forums of the Jewish Agency, the *Histadrut,* and the *Mapai,* the archives of these organizations serve as the primary source material for this research.

After the Anschluss the leaders of the Yishuv became more and more involved in elaborating relief and rescue plans—almost always in the framework of *Aliya* (Immigration) projects. A telling example of these endeavors was the grandiose plan to extricate and to ship to Palestine some 10,000 children from Germany and Austria (the drawing up of the plan coincided with the time of the *Kristallnacht.*[1] Important meetings and conferences took place between the Zionist leaders and the British authorities, the former putting pressure on the British government for a positive change in its rigid immigration policy, emphasizing the humanitarian aspects of their demands.[2] The publication of the White Book on May 17, 1939 gave rise to an uproar among the leaders and the whole *Yishuv,* not in the least because of the alarming news from Europe which heralded an unprecedented upsurge of a new type of anti-Jewish persecution.

Most of the Zionist leaders, among them the top figures in *Eretz Israel* (Palestine), had no illusions as to the gravity of the Nazi onslaught in Europe (mainly in Central and Eastern Europe). In April 1938 Weizmann was aware of the fact that "all or most (of the German and Austrian Jews) are thrown into concentration camps, committing suicide, and those who still hold out are subjected to humiliation and torture." It was probably for the first time that a Jewish leader had envisaged the apocalypse of "six million Jews being threatened with extinction."[3] "Part of us will be destroyed—wrote Weizmann with a mixture of pessimism and a peculiar nationalist confidence—and on their bones New Judea may arise! It is all terrible, but it is so."[4]

At about the same time Ben Gurion warned his friends in the *Mapai* leadership that European Jewry was facing a new type of anti-Semitism and persecution, carried out by a totalitarian regime using every modern means for a systematic extermination of the Jewish people.[5]

However, from the critical prewar period (after the Anschluss and before the outbreak of World War II) and later on during the first years of the war a contradiction characterized the awareness (or the apparent awareness) of the impending tragedy, and the facts, the practical reaction of the leaders.

The first important landmark on the international scene where the plight of European Jewry was the only issue, and the first international gathering where the *Yishuv* leadership could have affirmed itself as one of the factors in the relief and rescue activities, was the Evian Conference of July 1938. Although the Jewish Agency was not invited as an interested party, its representatives—in fact the delegates of the *Yishuv*—could participate as observers, and they could have used this rostrum for focusing interest on the necessity of an organized mass exodus meant to preclude a stalemate which physically endangered hundreds of thousands of Jews in Germany and Austria, and in other Central and East European countries. Weizmann and all the other top leaders refused to participate as junior partners, or as mere observers; moreover, they had no confidence in the outcome of the Conference from a Zionist point of view, namely the fostering of the immigration to *Eretz Israel.* Only A. Ruppin, Dov Hos, and Golda Meir participated under the flag of the *Histadrut*—Ruppin reporting mainly about the absorption abilities of Palestine. (Golda Meir later deplored her passivity at the Conference.)[6]

The policy of the *Yishuv* leaders during the Evian Conference regarding the Jewish emigration from the Nazi area was determined by an *Eretz Israel*-centered view, which could be formulated in these terms: If the Conference were to lead to a mass emigration to places other than Palestine, the Zionist leaders were not particularly interested in its work. It was a few months later that, after *Kristallnacht,* Ben Gurion could voice his often quoted words: If he knew that all Jewish children could be saved from Germany by being transferred to England, whereas only half of them could be saved if transferred to *Eretz Israel,* he would choose the second alternative, since the problem, in his opinion, was not only one concerning the children, but a historical issue of the Jewish people.[7] Ben Gurion implied that this dilemma involved the consideration of a national interest, superior to the task of organizing the children's emigration.

During the years of the aggravating ordeal of the Jews in Germany and in former Austria, and after Munich also in "independent" Slovakia and in the Czech Protectorate, and in the period of worsening conditions in Romania and Poland, the *Yishuv's* own problems and interests oversha- dowed in *Eretz Israel* the task of help and rescue; all that happened in Europe was subordinated to the internal necessities and concerns of the *Yishuv.* The principle of *Eretz Israel* as the only place where Jews should find their new home—not merely temporary shelter—and therefore the duty to dedicate every human and material resource to building up the Jewish Homeland, prevailed over other alternative solutions, like financial and material help, diplomatic interventions, and emigration to countries other than Palestine. Moreover, the principle of selective *Aliya* was preferred to the possibility of absorbing every endangered Jew willing to emigrate to Palestine, irrespective of his political views and his usefulness for the *Yishuv.* (In reality a distinction was made between Zionist and non-Zionist elements, between "useful" and "burdensome" immigrants; however, this distinction became devoid of practical consequences partly because of the British immigration policy, but mainly because of the local practice in Europe in the distribution of immigration certificates.)

In the late 1930s the Zionist leadership, and mainly the *Yishuv* leaders, were entangled in a vicious circle and a contradiction which was bound to become insoluble: on the one hand the pretension to represent the whole Jewish people (in reality the Zionist leaders had in mind only European Jewry), and the awareness of the unprecedented danger, coupled with the logical conclusion to help the endangered Jews, and on the other hand the fervent commitment to serve the *Yishuv,* to fight for its progress and to lay down the foundations of the Jewish state. Since obviously the two tasks were seen as a much too heavy burden, the choice of priorities favored the *Yishuv* at the expense of the help and rescue activities on behalf of the Jews in Germany and in other Nazi dominated countries.

In the pessimistic atmosphere of the last two prewar years some of the leading personalities in *Eretz Israel* and on the world Zionist scene voiced strong criticism at the passivity and lack of ability of the *Yishuv* leadership. Zalman Shazar, Rabbi Fischmann and Yosef Sprintzak were among those leading figures who criticized the indifference, or lack of initiative and concrete steps on behalf of the German and Austrian Jews.[8] The opinion of a small minority (including Moshe Schapira, one of the senior officials of the Immigration Department of the Jewish Agency, and of Senator David Werner, the non-Zionist member of the Jewish Agency Executive) that the main task was to help and to extricate the Jews from Austria and also from other countries in the danger area, regardless of the destination of their emigration, was dismissed by the overwhelming majority, including the dominant figures of the leadership.[9] It was Sprintzak who put the finger on the crux of the attitude toward the fate of the Jews in Germany and Austria on the eve of World War II: The concentration of too much interest and energy on the *Yishuv's* own affairs, while neglecting the Jews who were threatened by a major catastrophe in Europe.[10]

Some of the leaders were concerned lest considerable amounts of money should be spent on financing emigration to countries other than Palestine; besides, quite a few, including Grünbaum, expressed their anxiety about the difficulties in the *Yishuv's* labor market: they forecast unemployment in case of mass immigration in a short span of time. When discussing the financial aid to the refugees and to those who still languished in the Nazi dominated territories, the *Yishuv* leaders often objected to the chanelling of large amounts (actually mainly from Western sources) to the refugees and to Central and Eastern Europe, arguing that the money was badly needed for the *Yishuv;* they had little doubt that the money sent to territories under Nazi control was as good as lost, while money spent for the resettlement of the refugees elsewhere than Palestine was detrimental to the Zionist cause.[11] Most of the leaders agreed that, whereas the help lent to the German and Austrian Jews was an unquestioned Zionist duty, attention and effort should not be diverted from the central task—the creation of a National Home, which ultimately was to be the only solution of the Jewish question in Europe.

Although some of the *Yishuv* leaders here and there mentioned the word "annihilation" in connection with the bleak future of European Jewry, in 1938–1939 they could not have been fully conscious of the impending Holocaust, and they continued to devote the debates of the leading *Yishuv* forums to problems which dwarfed in comparison with the relief and rescue tasks.

The task of paving the way for the Jewish state understandably prevailed over all other objectives in the political thinking and practice of Ben Gurion and his top associates; the fostering of the *Aliya* and the opposing of alternative emigration targets was a corollary of this guiding principle. The economic difficulties of the *Yishuv,* unemployment included, and above all the increasing Arab terror, diverted much energy, attention, and time from the fate of European Jewry. While everything that happened in the Nazi sphere of influence concerning the Jews was of great interest and concern to the *Yishuv* leadership, the help and rescue operations were not at the top of the leadership's agenda. The centrality of the *Yishuv's* security problems and the incessant efforts to build up the nucleus of the future state were legitimate preferences in the daily activity of the *Yishuv* leaders; however, some trivial problems, like internal political frictions, the internal struggle in the *Mapai*,[12] personal rivalries, petty, peripheral preoccupations also figured high on the leadership's list of priorities, at the expense of the relief and rescue efforts.

The attitude and the priorities of the *Yishuv* leadership did not change radically after the German attack on Poland; however, the outbreak of war brought a reassessment of their policy toward Great Britain, as they became more ready to join the Allied war efforts against Nazi Germany.

The first alarming news about the setting up of ghettos and concentration camps, about the humiliation, degradation, and spoliation of the Jews in the German occupied part of Poland, and later about the first mass executions, did not arouse the appropriate reaction among the Jewish populations in Palestine, or in the Hebrew press—and not even among the Jewish leaders.

As early as the end of 1940 Berl Katznelson was aware of the fateful impact of the Nazi persecution upon the future of the Jewish people. He was sure that after the war "everything would be different than it had been,"[13] and that every Zionist decision of what should be done had to be anchored in the reality of the destruction of European Jewry.[14] But we have to surmise that voices like his were rather the exception than the rule in the ranks of the leadership.

The problems generated by the growing emigration pressure on the one hand from Germany, Central, and Eastern Europe, and on the other hand by the hostile British immigration policy led to a specific offshoot of the *Yishuv's* rescue activities. A handful of *Yishuv* activists, most of them kibbutz members, set up in 1937 the nucleus of the *Mossad le Aliya Bet* (Center for Illegal Immigration) established as such in 1938 by the *Hagana,* as the main instrument to promote illegal immigration. Few of the top leaders, perhaps only Katznelson and Eliahu Golomb, gave their blessing to the initiative in its incipient phase. Later all the leaders priased the activity of the *Mossad,* which rescued the lives of thousands of Jews just before and throughout the war years. However, the *Mossad* was the result of a grass-roots initiative, and the credit for the implementation and even for the financing of its activity during its first years should be accorded to the small group of barely known, devoted, and courageous activists, rather than to the *Yishuv* leadership.[15] The Revisionists also initiated fruitful rescue operations in Europe, independently from the *Yishuv* leadership.

Information in Palestine about the fate of Polish Jewry, and later about the catastrophe that befell the Jews in other Nazi-occupied territories, was rather scarce. The *Yishuv* press was not well-informed,[16] and not particularly alarmed. This was also true of the *Davar* (Word), which was edited by Katznelson, albeit in name only. The meetings and the debates of the central forums in *Eretz Israel* after September 1939 and during 1940 did not reflect anxious concern about what was going on in Europe, surprisingly enough, not even after the German attack on the Soviet Union. The opening of a new front against millions of Jews failed to lead to dramatic reactions among the *Yishuv* leaders. Their interest remained focused on the *Yishuv's* own specific problems: The setting up of Jewish armed units in the framework of the British Army, the strengthening of the local semi-legal armed forces, and the facing of the real danger threatening from the advancing Axis troops in North Africa.

As the war escalated during 1940 and more information reached the Jewish organizations in *Eretz Israel* and in the West, the *Yishuv* and its representatives abroad stepped up their activities for promoting *Aliya*. Even before the German attack on the Soviet Union, the alerted leaders took the initiative for the extrication of a maximum number of Jews from the critical areas. One example, out of many, was the positive reaction to the anti-Jewish pogroms in Romania during the Legionary (Iron Guard) rebellion against General Ion Antonescu in January 1941.[17]

On February 7, 1941, Weizmann, representing the Jewish Agency, demanded from Churchill the immediate granting of a substantial number of additional immigration certificates for the Romanian Jews.[18] As before, all, or at least most, of these interventions were limited to one form of rescue action only: the fostering of legal and illegal immigration. This policy would continue until the end of 1942.

The imperative of the *Yishuv* to rescue European Jews appeared time and again—but inconsistently—in the debates of the leading forums in *Eretz Israel*. Elyahu Dobkin reassured his audience in October 1941 that the *Yishuv* would not forsake the Diaspora, but—significantly—he made a point of making his determination dependent on the existence of a strong Halutz-movement in the plagued areas.[19] Significantly, in the very same days Eliezer Kaplan raised his voice against diverting the *Yishuv's* financial resources to other purposes than those directly connected with the military efforts against Germany;[20] yet one month later he appealed to his audience to try to alleviate the sufferings of Romanian Jewry.[21] Barely a few days had passed, and the same Kaplan sounded more cautious, warning his associates in the Jewish Agency Executive against taking upon themselves too great a burden by encouraging mass-Aliya from Romania, lest the *Yishuv's* economy should be affected, and lest the immigration of thousands monthly should cause more damage than benefit.[22] At about the same time Grünbaum, who often stood out as an advocate of extremist *Eretz Israel*-centered attitudes, even though he had not started his activity in the country until 1933, sounded as a defeatist and a demoralized leader: he had no plans or advice, and believed that as long as Hitler was in power there could not be even the slightest chances of improving the conditions of the Jews in the Nazi-occupied countries.[23]

Unchecked and summary information about the mass executions in Eastern Europe reached the *Yishuv* leadership in the summer of 1942. (Most reliable were the reports sent from the Geneva representatives of the *Yishuv.*) The Executive of the Zionist Organization in Jerusalem and other leading forums soul-searchingly pondered the trustworthiness of the sad news. The leaders were "not inclined to accept all the statements [about the extermination] at their face value," and "had great doubts as to the accuracy of all the facts reported."[24] But in August and September 1942 they had already been informed about "gruesome details" and were inclined to draw the correct conclusions.[25] At the beginning of October 1942—before the first eyewitnesses had arrived in Palestine—Grünbaum and other leading personalities received confirmation from Richard Lichtheim, the Jewish Agency representative in Geneva, that "the deliberate destruction of the Jewish communities in Poland [was] not only contemplated but already [was] on its way"; further, the *Yishuv* leaders were informed about Jewish interventions in England, in the United States, and in the Vatican "to try to save at least the Jewish communities in the semi-independent states" (i.e., Romania, Hungary, Italy, and Bulgaria), and about actions taken on behalf of Slovak Jewry. Lichtheim concluded in an apologetic tone, that it was his "painful duty" to tell what he knew. "The tragedy is too great for words."[26]

After the arrival of the first group of Palestine citizens from Nazi Europe— they had been exchanged for Germans on November 26, 1942—Sharet cabled to London the news about the "progressive annihilation" of the Jews in Central Europe, the "mass slaughter" in Warsaw, "fearful tortures" in Treblinka and elsewhere, and—a piece of information passed to the West for the first time by a *Yishuv* leader—about "harrowing details . . . of people thrown into flames [in a specially constructed *crematorium* [or] locked up [in] *poison gas chambers*" (italics added).[27]

This time Sharet asked J. Linton, one of the World Jewish Congress leaders in London, "to make utmost efforts [to] ensure widest publication in authoritative press. Emphasize these [are] no atrocity tales but accounts [of] eyewitnesses who were fully cross examined."[28] (Eliyahu Dobkin was slapped in the face by one of the women eyewitnesses because he was skeptical and doubted the veracity of her account.)[29]

Weizmann, residing in London and often visiting the United States, was up to date with the information which had reached not only several Jewish organizations, operating in the West (first of all the World Jewish Congress), but some of the governments in exile as well. Through him, too, the *Yishuv* leadership was kept up-to-date, or got confirmation of some news which had not reached Palestine through the West (e.g., via Istanbul.) We can conclude that in the summer and autumn of 1942 the *Yishuv* leadership had a more or less accurate picture about reality in Nazi-occupied Europe, while in November of the same year it was in possession of first-hand information about the process of extermination, including news about the crematoria and the use of gas.

In February 1943 Weizmann wrote to Lord Halifax that "The news which *continues* to reach us of the *annihilation* of European Jewry remains horribly beyond description"[30] (italics added). On February 16 Weizmann got the news about the liquidation of the Warsaw ghetto, and foresaw the elimination of the ghettos in Eastern Europe. He noted: "It is lamentably clear that Hitler is seeking even in the moment of the downfall and perhaps because of it, to exterminate the Jews of Europe." He was soliciting England's help, this time in rescuing 70,000 Romanian Jews deported to Transnistria, who allegedly were to be allowed by the Romanian government to leave the country.[31]

The *Yishuv* leaders were pressuring the British government during 1943 for more visas, for interceding in Ankara on behalf of the refugees who were likely to leave the Nazi occupied territories in transit through Turkey, and they initiated some steps which could free tens of thousands of Jews from Romania, Bulgaria, and other parts of southeastern Europe.[32] However, these interventions were limited almost without exception to plans for extricating Jews from the Nazi grip and shipping them to Palestine. While these efforts were reasonable, feasible, and motivated by the Zionist fervor of the *Yishuv* leaders, other rescue possibilities were overlooked, or misjudged; thus, for example, plans to enable tens of thousands to flee to Western neutral countries were not considered. The infusion of material help, and enlisting— by bribes—the cooperation of the local Fascist authorities (for example in Slovakia) would have been more realistic than the much more complicated and uncertain *Aliya* plans. Without the intention of diminishing the importance of the rescue efforts by the *Yishuv* leaders at that time, a survey of the problems which preoccupied the leadership in 1943 could raise the question whether it was not only cognizant of the facts—they often mentioned the term of "annihilation"—but was also fully aware of the real priorities, or if it was able to distinguish between the main task it had to fulfill and the secondary, local assignments and concerns.

At about the time when the first groups of eyewitnesses reached Palestine, Slovakia became an invaluable source of information about the major tragedy that was starting to take its course in Poland. The Bratislava Jewish leadership obtained accurate first-hand information about the fate of Polish Jewry and those deported to the East.[33] From Bratislava information reached Jewish Agency and *Histadrut* officials based in Switzerland, who kept the *Yishuv* leadership informed about events in Poland and Slovakia, and pressured the leaders for prompt material and political help. Although some money reached Slovakia, and even Poland, via Bratislava (mainly from Western sources) the amounts were insufficient. Lichtheim could complain in the second half of 1942 that even his advice that the *Yishuv* leadership (and first of all the Jewish Agency Executive) should mobilize the Western mass media for the denunciation of the persecution in Slovakia, Croatia, and Romania, and of course, of the crimes committed on Polish territory, was not heeded. It should be made clear that by the time the *Yishuv* leadership was being bombarded by warnings and demands from Geneva, the imminent danger which threatened the *Yishuv* had been lifted by the positive change in the military situation in the Middle East and Africa (e.g., El Alamein, the Allied invasion of French North Africa), but a radical change in the *Yishuv* leadership's attitude was still not detectable. Presumably after the shock-treatment of the report by the first group of eyewitnesses in mid-November 1942, at long last, in mid-December 1942, a rescue committee was set up in *Eretz Israel,* which was renamed and reorganized on a broader political basis in January 1943, and which took a third and final shape in October 1943, when the Unified Rescue Committee of the Jewish Agency was created.[34] The Committee worked out plans for rescue operations and for the raising of the necessary financial means. But again, this time too, two different views clashed, although not overtly, on the surface; one trend favored the raising of funds and the mobilization of the *Yishuv* primarily for the creation of a material and military infrastructure in *Eretz Israel,* joining the Allies' military efforts and thus helping the remnants of European Jewry, and also preparing the *Yishuv* for the postwar era; others saw in the rescue activity, in its literal sense, the first and foremost duty of the *Yishuv.* As a matter of fact, the rescue committees, in their different organizational forms, lacked autonomy and executive power, and the various rescue operations during 1943 and 1944 were subordinated to the specific interests of the *Yishuv*, as seen and interpreted by Ben Gurion, Sharet, and Weizmann; therefore their activity should not be overestimated.

As in the case of the *Mossad*, during 1942 and 1943 a new and very efficient rescue organization emerged without the direct involvement of the inner circle of the leadership. In Istanbul a group of Jewish Agency delegates and representatives of several political parties and kibbutz movements from the *Yishuv* succeeded in creating a kind of rescue center, or representative body dedicated to the help and rescue efforts.[35] Geneva remained an important liaison center between the *Yishuv* and the free world on one side, and the Jews in the Nazi-occupied territories on the other; but while the *Yishuv* representatives in Switzerland acted on their own, without constituting a bureau, or a unified delegation, a unified and representative delegation came into being in Istanbul, where, besides the Jewish Agency, the *Histadrut* and the *Mapai*, other political forces, including the General Zionists, the Agudath Israel, and the Revisionists, were also instrumental in coordinating the common rescue efforts.[36] The Istanbul delegation established contacts with Budapest, Bratislava, and other capitals of the Axis satellites, and even with some camps in Poland via Hungary and Slovakia. The delegation gathered valuable information, forwarded it to *Eretz Israel*, sent practical, operational instructions to the Jews under Nazi yoke, and succeeded in injecting great amounts of money for help and rescue operations in Hungary, Slovakia, Romania and, indirectly, even in Poland. The first dispatch of money from Istanbul reached Budapest in December 1942. This important activity did not involve the *Yishuv* leadership directly; irrespective of the question if such an involvement would have been vital, the fact stands that the first short visit to Istanbul by a *Yishuv* leader, Eliezer Kaplan, occurred as late as in March 1943, and it was not until April 1943 that, at last, the patterns of fundraising for the Istanbul-based rescue operations crystallized in *Eretz Israel*. Significantly, the problem which preoccupied Kaplan in Istanbul in the first place was the promotion of the *Aliya*, rather than the transfer of money for rescue *per se*.[37]

The Central Rescue Committee ("The Committee on Behalf of the Jews in Occupied Europe") conceded in March 1943 that it "had not done enough."[38] When concrete actions were suggested, however—for example by Yosef Klarman, the Revisionist member of the Committee, who proposed to organize a protest mass-demonstration in Jerusalem[39]—or when Michael Landau, a former member of the Romanian parliament, requested that the Committee should join the Ottawa Conference alongside the delegations of all the "enslaved peoples,"[40] the proposals were rejected by the majority. No operational, practical steps were taken. The ineffectiveness of the Committee should be deplored, the more so as, for example, the abovementioned meeting also had on its agenda the feasible plan of the shipping of thousands of children from Romania and Bulgaria. Even in this latter objective, which fitted in with the general rescue policy of the Jewish Agency Executive and other leading *Yishuv* forums, nothing tangible was achieved by the Committee during 1943, and not even in 1944, when the chances of emigration from Romania and Bulgaria looked more favorable.

Characteristic of the narrow and *Eretz Israel*-centered conception of the rescue efforts is a confidential paper presented in April or May 1943 by A. Hartglass, a member of the Central Rescue Committee. Hartglass, working closely with Grünbaum, stipulated that his memorandum should be kept secret, even before the non-Zionist members of the Committee.[41] While his analysis and conclusions should not be considered as necessarily expressing the Jewish Agency's or even Grünbaum's views, neither should they be discarded as the extremist theses of a lonely minor figure in the ranks of those active in the rescue efforts; on the contrary, the reasoning, if not the wording, of his conclusions reflected the views of most of the top leaders.

Hartglass advocated the attainment of three practical goals, important from a Zionist viewpoint: (a) to let the world know that only *Eretz Israel* was willing to accept the rescued Jews; (b) to emphasize that it was the Zionists who had initiated the rescue operations; and (c) to convince the survivors, even before the end of the war, that the rescue operations were carried out by the Zionist movements and by the *Yishuv,* and that consequently the way of the survivors should lead to *Eretz Israel.*[42]

Hartglass defended the idea of a rigorous selection in the Zionist rescue work, his guiding principle being the saving of Zionists. Since there were no chances for rescuing and extricating Jewish *masses* from Europe, he advised, all that could be hoped for—through material help and emigration—was the rescue of a few thousand, or at best of some tens of thousands. He therefore advocated that only children ("the best prospective material for the Yishuv"), and members of the Zionist youth movements, as well as some adult Zionist activists, should be helped and rescued by the *Yishuv.*[43] He concluded that his advice was a harsh one, but the lessons of the past e.g., the *Yishuv's* "bitter" experience with the immigrants from Germany, as well as the burning interests of the *Yishuv* and its limited potential for help and rescue operations dictated this solution. Since there were no means even for the rescue of all the "best" one must desist from rescuing the "damaging" elements. The gist of Hartglass' views, having in mind the postwar era in

Palestine was: (a) if possible, to avoid the organized immigration through rescue operations, of non-Zionists; and (b) to extend substantial help to the rescued Zionist "olim" (immigrants) for their rapid integration in the country's economic life.

While this last conclusion could be taken for granted, Hartglass' cold pragmatism versus humanitarian considerations, at a time when the *Yishuv* leadership regarded itself as the representative of European Jewry, could only have caused bitter resentment among the Jewish masses, had his suggestions been made public during the war.[44]

The *Yishuv* representatives in Istanbul were dissatisfied with the top leaders' involvement in the rescue activity in general, and in the Istanbul center's work in particular. Bitter recriminations were made by some of the Istanbul delegates who deplored the absence of top leaders in this vital center for connections with the Jews in Nazi occupied Europe. (Sharet, the second to arrive in Istanbul, after Kaplan, decided to get acquainted with the delegates' work only in the summer of 1943.) The Istanbul delegates claimed that not enough money was put at their disposal, and that the *Yishuv* leadership did not assess its duties in accordance with the dramatic developments and the urgency of the task.

In a letter addressed in August 1943 to the Jewish Agency, to the Rescue Committee, and to the Executive Committee of the *Histadrut,* three delegates (Venia Pomerantz, Menachem Bader, and Zeev Shind) regretted that they had failed to convince the leaders to increase the financial resources for the rescue operations; they warned that the tragedy of European Jewry had not yet reached its peak, and implored the leaders to "leave for a moment" their routine work and "help to rescue before the curtain drops (and covers) everything."[45]

At about the same time, Ben Gurion's presence started being felt more on the rescue scene. From the summer of 1941 and until October 1942 Ben Gurion had spent his time in the United States. No evidence can be found about his possible concern for the fate of European Jews during this period. After his return to *Eretz Israel,* the otherwise very active Ben Gurion seldom participated in the discussions about the help and rescue activities. In the wake of the uproar caused by the first eyewitness reports about the exterminations, the Jewish Agency Executive put on its agenda, for the first time, at its meeting of November 1942, the tragedy of European Jewry in the debate on "political problems." This was the occasion when Ben Gurion took the floor and demanded that interest should be concentrated around two issues: to put an end to the extermination, and to enable the Jewish people to fight against Hitler.[46] These proposals were not too helpful—although the importance of Jewish (*Yishuv*) participation in the anti-Nazi war should not be minimized; warnings, appeals, and demands by Ben Gurion throughout 1943 constantly expressed two essential ideas: (a) the annihilation of European Jewry, which constituted a real danger for the future of Zionism, and (b) the role of the *Yishuv*—its rescue and absorption potential.[47]

An important speech was delivered by Ben Gurion on August 24, 1943, at a meeting of the *Mapai* leadership. Responding to the criticism voiced by the Istanbul delegates (he referred to Venia Pomerantz), he agreed with the necessity and urgency of doing more in the field of help and rescue, but opposed the idea of using the funds of the Keren *Kayemet* (Jewish National Fund) or *Keren Hayessod* (Jewish Investment Fund) for purposes other than their original goals; in a veiled form he even objected to the use of the Jewish Agency's funds for purposes other than the necessities of the *Yishuv* ("The Jewish Agency is an all-Israel organization for the building of *Eretz Israel*"), and hinted that the Joint, the American relief organization, and the World Jewish Congress and similar relief organizations should take over the responsibility for helping and rescuing. Replying to a proposal regarding the necessity of rescue efforts in southeastern Europe, Ben Gurion asked rhetorically: "It is true that sometimes it is more important to rescue a child from Zagreb [than to act for the *Yishuv*], but here are two different things, and whom will it serve to mix them up. . . .why confuse [different] notions?"[48] At the same meeting Sharet also took the floor, and—in spite of the deep impressions that his recent visit in Istanbul had made upon him— he devoted much attention to the problem of the survivors from the viewpoint of the Zionist enterprise: would there be enough survivors who could materialize the Zionist goals?[49] A few days earlier, in a meeting of the Jewish Agency Executive he had analyzed the tragedy of European Jewry from the same angle, namely, that the political future of *Eretz Israel* depended to a great extent on the number and strength of the survivors.[50]

It should be emphasized that reflections and analyses like the above were usually complemented by critical remarks—though not by top leaders— about the lack of concrete acts of the *Yishuv* leadership. Meir Ya'ari, the *Mapam* (Left Labor Party) leader, deplored the inability of the *Yishuv* to raise more money for help and rescue purposes,[51] and David Remez, then Secretary of the *Histadrut*, voicing the same complaint as Ya'ari, suggested that a special "Minister" in the Jewish Agency Executive should be entrusted with the rescue work, and that he should be engaged "day and night only in this activity."[52] Suggestions about how to organize and centralize the rescue work and how to raise more money were not followed by operative resolutions, and in spite of the intense correspondence between Jerusalem (and Tel Aviv) and the Western world, and numerous interventions at the highest governmental and political level in England and in the United States, no new patterns of the rescue activity were initiated during 1943.

On September 1, 1943, on the fourth anniversary of the German attack against Poland, the inner circle of the Zionist leadership, mainly members of the Zionist Executive Committee, held a meeting in Jerusalem. The Chairman of the meeting, Sprintzak, declared the occasion "the day of Polish Jewry"; he surveyed the plight of the largest Jewish community in Europe, and also expressed the leadership's solidarity with the Polish people. However, the interest of the confidential meeting was focused on Sharet's report about his visit in Istanbul and about his political talks in Cairo concerning the future of Palestine.

Sharet reminded his audience that the main aim of his trip to Istanbul was the promotion of the rescue operations through *Aliyah* from the Balkan countries. He informed his associates that he was ready to discuss with them only the problem of immigration from the Balkans, including the transportation and other technical aspects of the *Aliya*, but—in his opinion—the meeting was not supposed to deal with the otherwise "very important and serious problem of the help activity" on behalf of the European Jews. Sharet's priority to deal only with the task of immigration to *Eretz Israel*, postponing the very important, and perhaps more realistic, relief work to a later date, was in contradiction with his praise for the *help-activity* of the *Yishuv* delegates in Istanbul. While criticizing the loose contacts between the *Yishuv* and some Western help and rescue centers, including those in Geneva, he commended the Istanbul group for having established a window enabling the *Yishuv* to have an insight into Nazi-occupied Europe, and for having created important channels operating in both directions for the benefit of the endangered survivors. Sharet described the means by which material help was instrumental in maintaining some labor camps—for example in Slovakia— which turned out to serve as an alternative for deportation to the death camps in Poland, a respite for at least a period of time.[53] Nevertheless, his analysis was not devoid of illusions—characteristic of many *Yishuv* leaders during the whole war period. For example, he was convinced that some of the Nazi forced labor camps had been transformed by the Zionist youths into *Halutz*-training camps, and that the concentration of Jewish masses provided the Zionists with the opportunity to organize educational and mutual relief activity.[54] As most of his fellow-leaders, Sharet saw in some of these alleged phenomena, which had little to do with reality, a positive aspect of the tragedy, adroitly exploited by the Zionists, with far-reaching practical consequences for the future Jewish Homeland.

Sharet demanded an increase in the financial help sent to Europe via Istanbul, and indeed the only practical outcome of his visit in Turkey (and also of the abovementioned marathon meeting in Jerusalem, with the active participation of many top leaders) was the significant increase of the amounts which reached Istanbul during the last months of 1943 and in the first half of 1944. (The money sent to Istanbul was not raised exclusively in *Eretz Israel,* as Sharet intimated in this report and in his later reports.) The meeting, which apparently was intended to be centered on the fate of European Jewry (around Sharet's report), was dedicated mostly to other problems. The central issue analyzed by Sharet was the complex picture of his negotiations with the British over the *Yishuv's* envisaged military participation in the war. Precisely because Sharet saw the *Yishuv* leadership as "the government-in-exile of European Jews,"[55] he demanded that the *Yishuv* participate in the anti-Nazi war, thus contributing to the war efforts and taking revenge for what the Jews were being subjected to in the Nazi occupied territories.

One can not question the importance of the setting up of Jewish fighting units and of all the other political and military problems which preoccupied Sharet and his associates in 1943. But one cannot overlook the salient disproportion, measurable by pages in the stenogram of his report (and of other leaders' speeches), between on the one hand the account of his Istanbul experience and his conclusions concerning the fate of European Jewry, and on the other hand his absorption in some problems related to the *Yishuv* leadership's negotiations with the British authorities. This lack of proportion between the interest devoted to the catastrophe of European Jewry and to the *Yishuv's* security and its political and economic problems was not in the least remedied during 1944, despite the ample flow of more accurate information about the dimensions of the Holocaust and especially about Auschwitz.

At about the same time as three or four leading *Yishuv* figures were visiting Istanbul and becoming more acquainted with the developments in Nazi Europe, yet another offshoot of the *Yishuv's* rescue efforts came to the forefront. Propelled into the limelight only after the war, and mainly after the creation of Israel, volunteer paratroopers, most of them from kibbutzim, arrived in the Mediterranean area and in southeastern Europe. It was a heroic enterprise, involving some outstanding young people, trained secretly by the *Haganah,* and later enrolled in the intelligence branches of the British army. The operation, viewed from the *Yishuv's* angle and from that of the volunteers themselves, was destined to add new dimensions to the rescue activity and to the Jewish resistance. However, the practical results of these missions, though not the moral ones, were not really significant.

Evidence about the aims that the *Yishuv* leaders had in mind when they initiated, or consented to, this facet of the Jewish participation is scarce. However, it is certain that the leaders did not work out a unified plan, based on a general consensus.

In a recorded testimony Joel Palgi, one of the volunteer parachutists, hinted at a lack of clear vision on the part of the *Yishuv* leaders of the general aims of the help and rescue operations, and of organizing resistance.[56] Yona Rosen, another paratrooper, confirmed this testimony.[57] However, years after the recording of his testimony, in his book published in 1977, Palgi quoted various personalities bearing out the fact that the *Yishuv* leaders were divided among themselves as to the scope of the operation. He summed up their views, obviously only partly voiced in his presence, as follows: Elyahu Golomb saw the main target of the paratroopers in "teaching the Jews to fight"; Ben Gurion wanted the Jews to know that *"Eretz Israel* was their land and their stronghold"; while Katznelson urged the volunteers to save Jews, arguing that if there were no survivors in Europe there would be no *Eretz Israel* and no Zionist undertaking.[58] Chaim Mermesh, another paratrooper, recapitulates the order of the day they heard from their leaders: to act on your own judgment and to the best of your ability.[59] Nevertheless, in Kibbutz Hazorea, where the *Haganah* instructed the future paratroopers, they were told by Ben Gurion—as Hermesh recalls—to prepare the Jews in Europe for the hour of liberation. After the war, they would have to help from the outside to open the gates of *Eretz Israel.*[60] Ben Gurion envisaged a stormy mass immigration into Palestine from liberated Europe; the mobilization of the Jews for the mass-*Aliya* was the chief aim of the paratroopers. His words and attitudes were characteristic of the main objective that most of the *Yishuv* leaders had in mind when British Intelligence raised the possibility of sending young Jews of east-central European origin into the occupied territories. Hermesh, and presumably most of his fellow paratroopers, assumed that as soon as they reached Yugoslav territory under Tito's control, and from there the countries of their destination, their task would be the organizing of the local Jewish youth for armed resistance, and also the evacuation of the older people and of children, possibly to Italy.[61]

These unrealistic plans were partially based on inaccurate information, e.g., the rumor that about 5,000 Jews had managed to flee from the Kolozsvár (Cluj) ghetto in late spring 1944. The differing views of the *Yishuv* leaders regarding the assignment of the paratroopers, and the image the volunteers created about conditions in the Nazi-occupied territories, attest to a distorted picture that both the leaders and the paratroopers had about reality in the area. The conditions of the Jews, the mood of the local population, the grip of the military authorities, and other aspects of the unfavorable circumstances were misjudged, and erroneously assessed. Insofar as the emphasis was put on the organizing of armed resistance by the young emissaries, and not on the help and rescue efforts, some of the mentors of the operation, among them Ben Gurion, were out of touch with reality. The few paratroopers who actually reached some of the countries in the area and managed to survive—among them Joel Palgi—had to admit that the pretentious ambition, like armed resistance and escape of *masses* of older people and children to the liberated territories, was unrealistic. The only feasible task of the paratroopers turned out to be to join the local activists, mainly the young underground fighters, and try to help and rescue, guided by the local leaders.[62] At the same time they must have been aware of their very limited resources to contribute, beyond the boost in morale emanating from the very fact of their presence, to the rescue operations initiated and conducted by the local activists.

By the end of 1943 and during 1944, mainly after the German occupation of Hungary on March 19, 1944, a lot of energy from the *Yishuv* went into various actions on behalf of the Balkan and east-central European Jews. The tragedy of Hungarian Jewry shocked the *Yishuv* precisely because it struck at a late phase of the war, when the chances of its survival looked real, and also because of the unprecedented rapidity of its partial liquidation.[63] Efforts were made to increase the number of certificates—not without success.[64] Ben Gurion was briefed more often than before about the rescue operations, and Sharet and Weizmann stepped up their interventions in London, indirectly in Tito's headquarters, and elsewhere in the Allied circles.[65] However, in spite of the intensified *Yishuv* activities, many critical voices were raised against the leadership's performance, even in the midst of the leading circles.

David Remez, the *Histadrut* secretary, confessed that "there is a painful issue, and I presume that all of us are constantly living with the feeling that a great mistake has been made, and is still being made [namely], that we have not put unlimited amounts of money at the disposal of the rescue operations. . . .If the *Yishuv* had raised a loan for ten million Palestine pounds," argued Remez "the *Yishuv* and the Jewish people could have been sure that no opportunity was missed by the leadership to rescue Jewish lives. That has not been done."[66]

Various immigrant organizations, and first of all the one representing the immigrants from Romania, were critical and impatient because of what they considered a lack of awareness and the wrong choice of priorities by the *Yishuv* leadership.[67] The answers were usually apologetic and based on the unquestioned priority of *Eretz Israel* in determining their tasks.

The Joel Brand mission brought an explosive element into this controversy, the more so as the tragedy of Hungarian Jewry had a peculiar Zionist facet. Since the approximately 800,000-strong Hungarian Jewry (including the "racial Jews"—Christians considered as Jews by the Nuremberg-type laws) which had survived until April-May 1944 was counted upon as the last great European reservoir of the future Jewish state, the impending catastrophe shook the optimism and the faith of many personalities in *Eretz Israel.* And then, when it became clear that the Brand mission had failed, bitter recriminations were voiced by Brand himself and by quite a number of Zionists in Hungary, that Sharet, Weizmann, and other leaders were not up to the mark. While Brand's accusations were much exaggerated,[68] Sharet's and the other leaders' explanations were not entirely convincing on this issue,[69] which arouses passions until this very day.

In June–July 1944, Weizmann, Sharet, and Golda Meir were active in urging the Allies to bomb Auschwitz and the railway lines leading to the extermination camps. However, bitter recriminations persisted even in the ranks of the leading personalities.

As one of the then young *Mapai* leaders, Eliezer Livne, recalls, doubts tormented him, and probably many others in the leadership, about whether their preoccupations were the appropriate ones, and if besides the *Yishuv's* political and military buildup, other concerns, like party squabbles, various cultural enterprises, and similar routine activities were indeed the order of the day at a time when the great reservoir of the future state was perishing in Europe.[70]

Berl Katznelson suffered perhaps more than others, torn by the dilemma of priorities, and by his and his associates' inadequate activity. He was among the few who warned against nurturing illusions, and as early as April 1942 took upon himself the ungratifying Cassandra-role of prophesying that the Nazi solution of the Jewish problem was the graveyard.[71] The eminent theoretician of the Labor Movement was short of conceding that the Zionist movement had failed inasmuch as the *Yishuv* faced the prospect of vegetating without its natural *Hinterland,* and he asserted unequivocally that the *Yishuv* was not trying to achieve the maximum attainable. However, even Katznelson did not initiate any practical measures, did little beyond speeches in rather narrow circles, and was deeply committed to a cultural enterprise he initiated in the very critical years of 1943–44.[72] In his case at least, the failure to convert the awareness into actions could be explained by his being outside the inner circle of the executives, and also by his frail health.

Summary and Conclusions

Time and again the question is asked: What could have been more adequate, more efficient, and more vital than the help actually extended?

Let us quote again Eliezer Livne, a close friend of Katznelson, although he did not belong to the top leaders. After being informed about the August 1944 deportation and extermination of the Jews of Lodz, his former hometown, Livne desperately and soul-searchingly exclaimed:

> There was not one Jewish radio station in our country, or in Europe (already liberated in its greater part), operated by the Hagana, the Etzel, or the Lechi, which could have informed the Jews [of Lodz] what they should expect [the deportation to Auschwitz]. No emissary was sent by the [Jewish] underground or by the Army units of Eretz Israel—although heroism and self-sacrifices were not lacking to warn them. . . .No Hebrew pilot was available out of thousands of our brethren who fought in the Allied air forces who we could entrust with the illegal mission of disseminating warning leaflets.[73]

If one refrains from "writing history backwards," and desists from solutions which seem feasible today, but were beyond reach during the Holocaust, the answer to the "what could have been" should, for practical purposes, be limited to two spheres: the financial aid, and the influencing of the Allies and of public opinion in the free world.

The *Yishuv* and its leaders managed to transfer substantial funds to several Nazi-occupied countries, which served to buy Jewish lives, to relieve hunger and distress, and to enable thousands to leave the Nazi-controlled territories. Obviously, as borne out by the dramatic appeals of the local leaders, for example in Slovakia, and confirmed by the *Yishuv's* emissaries, including those in Istanbul, more money could have been of much more help. And the raising of more money was indeed within reach. In point of fact much more money was raised in *Eretz Israel* than the amounts sent to Europe, but it was used for local purposes. The priority in the allocation of the financial resources was one of the weakest points of the *Yishuv* leaders.

The *Yishuv* leaders were not particularly effective in mobilizing American Jewry, nor is there much evidence of their having stimulated Jewish and non-Jewish organizations in the free world for large-scale help and rescue attempts. The leaders had ample opportunities for taking the floor in the allied countries and in other countries of the free world, except in the Soviet Union they also had easy access to the mass media. But evidence is scarce about their awareness of taking full advantage of these possibilities. Yet, such pressures could indeed have been successful, as evidenced for example, by Admiral Miklo's Horthy's shift of attitude in Hungary in July–October, 1944.

A comparison between the deeds of the *Yishuv* leaders and those of the Jewish communities elsewhere in the free world is not unfavorable to the former, and anyhow, the *Yishuv* leaders were committed to fight for two historical tasks—the survival and the strengthening of the *Yishuv*, and the struggle for European Jewry—a dispersion of energy and resources which did not weigh down the shoulders of the Jewish leaders elsewhere. Undoubtedly the *Yishuv* leadership was motivated by a profound sense of solidarity and responsibility, which induced it to undertake efficient and sometimes even vital help and rescue actions—despite the *Yishuv's* limited human and material resources and the specific conditions imposed by the war and by the British domination.

Nevertheless, understanding and explaining cannot change the fact that the *Yishuv* leadership was rather late in grasping the dimensions and the significance of the Holocaust; it was immersed in its own problems at the expense of the attention that the fate of European Jews should have commanded. Its participation in the help and rescue activities was below its capacities and competence, and it failed to fully exploit the given circumstances.

Chapter 4

SWITZERLAND AND THE LEADERSHIP OF ITS JEWISH COMMUNITY DURING THE SECOND WORLD WAR

Gerhart M. Riegner

Switzerland at the Crossroads of Great Powers

A discussion on the attitude of the Swiss Jewish community and its leadership during the World War II must by necessity start with a short description of the position of Switzerland during that period.

This small, picturesque country, in the heart of Europe, is the guardian of the great passageways linking the north and the south of the continent. It prides itself on being the oldest democracy in Europe. It is organized on a federal basis and for centuries has adopted a policy of permanent neutrality in armed conflicts—a neutrality which has been guaranteed by the European powers since the treaties of Vienna in 1815, and which it is committed to defend against any violation.

Economically, the country was very poorly endowed by nature. It possesses practically no raw materials and its only important natural resources are the water sources in the mountains, which allowed it to develop

---

This paper is limited to the attitude of the Swiss authorities and of the leadership of the Jewish community of Switzerland before and during the Second World War and does not deal with the activities of representatives of international Jewish organizations in Switzerland.

I am indebted to my colleague Sidney H. Gruber for his assistance in researching the archives of the World Jewish Congress and for his valuable suggestions regarding my manuscript. I also wish to express my gratitude to Dr. Willy Guggenheim, Secretary General of the Schweizerischer Israelitischer Gemeindebund, who provided me complete access to its archives. I wish to place on record that this paper owes much to the Report of Prof. Carl Ludwig entitled *The Refugee Policy of Switzerland During the Period from 1933 to 1955,* which he prepared for the Swiss Federal Council for consideration by the Swiss Federal Parliament (Doc. Zu 7347), cited hereafter as the "Ludwig Report."

quite early an important network of electric power stations. It has no access to the high seas and its welfare therefore depends to a great extent on the good will of its neighbors as far as import of food for its inhabitants and the export of goods produced by them are concerned.

In spite of this, it has acquired a high standard of living. But this has not been a gift from heaven. It has been obtained through long centuries of hard labor, by the industry and the energy of the inhabitants who, with the endurance of the peasants of the high mountain valleys, have built up their country and its riches brick by brick and step by step. Their reliability, their energy, the precision of their work have made them some of the best workers of Europe and have helped the development of some of the most modern industries on the continent.

Its prosperity is based on the stability of its institutions—it had not known war since Napoleonic times, with the sole exception of a short internal military expedition in 1847—and on the moderate conservatism of its own population, notably in the rural districts, to which the federal constitution gave considerable weight. With the exception of short periods of tension, labor and management have observed peaceful relations and labor relations have been regulated by collective agreements.

Nevertheless, in the decades before World War II, the country could not feed all its inhabitants. Every year about 50,000 Swiss people left the country and sought work in foreign lands, and these *Auslandschweizer* contributed considerably to the good reputation of Swiss labor and to the establishment of international commercial relations throughout the world.

This whole political system with its permanent neutrality was based on the political equilibrium between the European great powers that surrounded the country, namely Germany, Austria-Hungary, Italy, and France. Slowly this equilibrium broke down, with the disappearance of the Austro-Hungarian empire after World War I and subsequently of the small Austrian republic in 1938. The pact between Hitler and Mussolini for all practical purposes brought the Northern, Eastern, and Southern borders of Switzerland under German influence, and the defeat of France in 1940 eliminated the last independent factor on its borders.

These developments, of course, also had their deep repercussions on the home front and the relationship between the various ethnic and linguistic communities constituting the Confederation. World War I had already put considerable stress on the internal peace between the ethnic groups, as each cultural and linguistic group tended to support the power beyond the border with which it had close cultural ties. It is obvious that this did not help the cohesion and integration of the national community. But, contrary to what had happened during World War I, the political trends and tendencies in the country during World War II worked in the opposite direction. While there definitely existed both in the German and French speaking areas an aggressive fascist and national socialist movement which sought to extend the blessings of the Third Reich to the Confederation, it never represented more than 10 percent of the population. The great majority of the German-speaking population was definitely anti-Nazi and anti-German while suffering acutely from the interruption of the close cultural links. The nearer one went to the German borders, the more anti-German and anti-Axis the population felt, and the same was true of the Italian-speaking part of Switzerland.

A different attitude prevailed in the French-speaking part of Switzerland, where the bourgeoisie was accustomed to look for guidance to the Third Republic and the French Radical Party, with which it had very close ties. The sudden French catastrophe in 1940 created a deep shock for the leading factors in Suisse Romande, which continued to look to France for guidance, and sympathy for Pétain and his policies prevailed for a long time in higher political circles and among the population of French-speaking Switzerland before the cause of the Free French captured their imagination.

The foreign policy of Switzerland was, of course, greatly influenced by these events. Since the coming to power of the Hitler regime in Germany, the Swiss Confederation had been following a very careful policy not to offend its Nazi neighbor. At the same time, Swiss diplomacy made a special effort to maintain and develop close and friendly relations with Fascist Italy. When Nazi Germany encountered great hostility in the League of Nations, Swiss diplomacy did everything it could to prevent the German delegation from feeling completely isolated. The Swiss authorities were quite tolerant with regard to Nazi propaganda in Switzerland up to the murder of *Gauleiter* Gustloff in 1936. But they took a courageous and energetic attitude vis-à-vis the Third Reich after the abduction of a German Jewish refugee, Berthold Jacob, from Swiss territory in 1935, and obtained his extradition by the German authorities.

After the fall of France, the political situation of Switzerland became extremely difficult. Now constituting a small democratic island in the midst of a sea dominated by the Axis forces, it had to use great skill to maintain its independence and its institutions and to resist the constantly mounting pressures from the Axis forces and their ambassadors.

Economically, Switzerland was now practically completely dependent on the Axis powers because there was no other foreign market it could reach. Its industries had the choice of working for the Axis forces or facing large-scale unemployment which might bring with it deep social unrest and as a consequence, perhaps large support for the forces supporting *Anschluss* (Annexation) to the Third Reich.

Switzerland continued its close diplomatic ties with France and tried more and more to develop its relations with the United States. The slogan about the friendship of the "oldest" and the "greatest" democracies in the world was quite popular.

On the other hand, during that whole period Switzerland had no diplomatic relations with the Soviet Union, since Soviet Russia had declared a formal boycott of all relations with Switzerland after the acquital of the murderer of Worowski, the Soviet delegate to the international conference on the straits between Greece and Turkey, held in Lausanne in 1923. The Swiss foreign minister used the platform of the League of Nations repeatedly for determined anti-Russian pronouncements, particularly when Soviet Russia entered the League of Nations in 1934. This policy would cause considerable embarrassment to Switzerland at the end of World War II.

The Swiss Jewish Community

Let me now say a few words about the Swiss Jewish community. The history of Jews in Switzerland is long and not always very happy. The first Jews arrived in the third and fourth centuries with the Roman armies and settled in the cities built by the Romans. There is a long history of expulsions and persecution, particularly in the thirteenth, fourteenth, and fifteenth centuries. The seventeenth century saw the settlement of Jews in two villages of the canton of Aargau—Endingen and Lengnau—and it is from the families settled in those two little villages that the core of Swiss Jewry descends. Later immigration brought Jews from southern Germany and from Alsace-Lorraine; and still later, with the upheavals of World War I, came the beginning of consecutive waves of refugees, including Jews from Czarist Russia and Poland.

The Swiss Jews were one of the last Jewish communities in Central Europe to acquire full equality of rights. It was only after fierce and dramatic fights in the 1860s that the Jews of the canton of Aargau finally achieved their emancipation, and a partial revision of the federal constitution in 1866 eliminated the restrictions on freedom of residence and on equality before the law. These rules were then included in the new constitution of 1874. At the time of these legislative acts about 7,500 Jews lived in the whole of Switzerland.

However, in 1893, a new restriction was imposed on Swiss Jews. By a popular referendum an exceptional article outlawing *shechita* (ritual slaughter) was included in the federal constitution. This prohibition, although eliminated a few years ago from the constitution, exists *de facto* until the present day.

The Jews of Switzerland have always constituted a very tiny minority of the population. During the first half of this century, there were approximately 20,000 souls; the number has remained rather steady since 1910. This means they constitute less than 0.5 percent of the total population. During the period under consideration nearly half the Jews did not possess Swiss nationality. In 1930, 45.5 percent of the Jews were foreigners, in 1941 47.1 percent; this figure fell to less than 40 percent in 1950.

The Jews of Switzerland thus had little influence, playing only a limited role in politics, the press, and in the economy. In parliament there were one or two Jewish members, serving in the Socialist Party and thus most of the time sitting on the opposition benches. In the press Jews were conspicuously absent. In the management of the great financial and industrial institutions Jews were almost never represented. But the Jews constituted an active element in trade and in the professions. They created some private banks of good reputation, some of the enterprises in the clothing industry, and established a number of small watch factories.

Living in a great number of small communities, the largest of which were in Zurich, Basel, and Geneva, the Swiss Jews in 1904 created the Swiss Federation of Jewish Communities, the *Gemeindebund.* Their major task at the beginning was to fight the prohibition of *shechita* and the concern for kosher meat. Slowly, the Federation developed into the representative body of Swiss Jewry.

In the 1930s, the rise of Nazism in Germany and the arrival of the first refugees, the growth of the Nazi-oriented Frontist movement in Switzerland, and the spreading of Frontist anti-Semitic propaganda created new and important tasks for the Federation. Some of its activities during those years are memorable, among them the filing of the defamation case against the circulation of the *Protocols of the Elders of Zion* before the courts in Berne.

It is noteworthy that the financial support granted to the newly arrived refugees and the cost of its fight against anti-Semitic assaults practically exhausted the whole capital of the Federation in 1935.

The Swiss Jewish Community and the Refugees

When war broke out, the Jewish community of Switzerland was thus already embattled in the struggle against the small but aggressive Nazi forces symbolized by the Frontist movement and struggling with the difficult problem of supporting the several thousand Jewish refugees from Germany and Austria who had found asylum in the country.

With the increasing military successes of the German army, the Frontist forces and the Nazi sympathizers became more and more arrogant and benefited fully from the support they received from the agents of the Third Reich.

As to the problem of Jewish refugees, the Swiss Jewish leadership found itself in an extremely difficult position. While Switzerland prided itself as a country of asylum and often stressed the important role it had played, particularly in the nineteenth century, as a land where many European revolutionaries and victims of autocratic oppression had found a haven from persecution, its attitude toward the Jews from Germany, and later Austria and Czechoslovakia, was extremely careful and hesitant and lacked the warm generosity it had shown on other occasions. This careful and hesitant attitude was certainly due to a deep sense of anti-Semitic prejudice prevailing among a considerable part of the population and at the same time to the serious economic and social situation, which was not helpful in encouraging a more generous attitude. While a limited number of German Jewish refugees were admitted in the first years of the Nazi regime, it was clearly stated that Switzerland could only be regarded as a temporary land of asylum and that the refugees had to prepare actively for their emigration overseas. Moreover, it was made clear from the beginning that these people should not become a burden to the state and all costs of maintenance and upkeep therefore had to be covered by the refugees themselves and their friends, or the Jewish community.

An eyewitness, Mrs. Georgine Gerhardt, a non-Jewish member of the *Zentralstelle für Flüchtlingshilfe,* the central body in charge of refugees of all denominations and of all political shades, recalled later a meeting with the Swiss foreign minister Motta in the summer of 1933, in which the latter adopted a sharply negative attitude toward all requests that the Swiss government take a more friendly and understanding attitude toward the refugee problem. "The question was distasteful to him," she reported, "and we did not obtain anything." A Socialist member of parliament, Guido Muller, in one of the great parliamentary debates on the refugee question, summarized the situation as follows: "There is no question in my mind: In the federal rules concerning the entry of non-Aryans, one senses a strong dose of anti-Semitism."

This became especially obvious after the *Anschluss* of Austria in March 1938. The waves of Jewish refugees who presented themselves at the Swiss frontier created great excitement in Swiss police circles. The Swiss authorities protested to the Germans and threatened to require a visa for German nationals wishing to enter Switzerland. This led to secret discussions—which were not even revealed to the Swiss parliament—between the German and Swiss authorities in Berlin and to an agreement whereby the passports of German Jews would henceforth be specially marked, and German Jews had to obtain special visas for entry into Switzerland. The role played in this matter by the head of the Swiss police, Heinrich Rothmund, is well known, and although the Swiss authorities always denied—even in parliamentary debates after World War II—that the initiative in this matter came from them, the diplomatic documents available today do not exonerate the Swiss from a great part of responsibility in this matter. While the head of the Swiss police, at the time of the *Anschluss* and on later occasions, stated that he had only the interests of Swiss Jews at heart and that the admittance of a too large number of foreign Jews would create increased anti-Semitism in Switzerland, the fallacy of this argument is obvious: Jews were simply not desirable in the country.

There exists a very curious document from the time of the *Anschluss:* the head of the Swiss police, Rothmund, in a memorandum to his Minister dated September 15, 1938 argued at that time against the acceptance of the German proposal suggesting the special marking of the passports of German Jews and the limitation of the visa obligation to Jews. The proposal, in his view, made Switzerland dependent on the German authorities and did not cover all cases. In the memorandum he admitted, however, that the Swiss had in previous negotiations with Germany made proposals which were identical with the present one, with the exception of the question of reciprocity.

Then, however, Rothmund went on to state that the introduction of the compulsory visa for Jews would not be understood in foreign countries and the German press would accuse the Swiss of anti-Semitism. "It looks generally," he stated, "that Germany tried with its last proposal to push us toward an attitude of anti-Semitism or at least to make us appear so in the eyes of other countries." And then he went on: "Since the creation of the police for aliens, we have maintained a clear position. The Jews were considered, together with other foreigners as *Überfremdungsfaktor* [an element endangering the Swiss character of the country]. By a systematic and careful effort we succeeded until now to prevent the Jewification of Switzerland (*die Verjudung der Schweiz zu verhindern*). Today we have assumed our part in the care for emigrants and we want to do this in a humane, but also in a strictly orderly way from the point of view of the police for aliens. The Swiss Jews help us in this attempt and consider this to be in their interest."[1]

The last curious remark is ambiguous insofar as it is not clear whether it refers only to the sentence which immediately preceded it or to the whole passage. In the later alternative it constitutes really a statement accusing the Swiss Jews of helping to keep Switzerland *Judenrein* (Jew free).

Later, however, during the secret negotiations in Berlin, Rothmund changed his mind with regard to the German proposal. In Berlin he learned that the Germans, in application of the Nuremberg Laws, now intended to issue specially marked identity cards to Jews and so called non-aryans inside Germany and specially marked passports outside Germany. He now felt suddenly that the proposal was acceptable because it showed that the Germans had themselves a direct interest of their own in marking the documents of Jews—a strange attitude as in this way he was now actively cooperating with the Germans in the implementation of the racial legislation.[2]

This attitude that the Jews were simply not desirable in the country became more and more evident and led finally during the war years to the fateful differentiation in the federal police rules between "political refugees" and "refugees for racial reasons," denying the right of asylum to the latter.[3]

The same attitude was evident even with regard to the treatment of military refugees, as shown by one of the department's circulars of July 1942 containing guidelines on military refugees and providing the following interpretation of Article 13 of the 1907 Hague Convention:

> General rules for admittance can therefore not be established. Every single case is to be decided according to the circumstances.
>
> Generally, however, undesirable elements (Jews, political extremists, people suspected of espionage) should be kept out.[4]

Nevertheless, despite the hesitant and restrictive attitude of the Swiss authorities vis-à-vis the admittance of Jewish refugees from Germany and Austria in the prewar period, at the outbreak of the war, of the approximately 8,000 refugees on Swiss territory, about 5,000 were Jews.

The refugee problem was discussed several times in the Swiss parliament and although individual legislators belonging to various political parties voiced some criticism and advocated a more liberal attitude, there is no doubt that the policy of the federal authorities had the support of the great majority of the parliament and probably of the population.

This did not facilitate the position of the Swiss Jewish leadership. Their position became even more delicate as the financial responsibility they had undertaken with regard to Jewish refugees became an increasingly heavy burden. In spring 1938, they had formally assured the Swiss authorities that the Swiss Jews, with the help of foreign Jewish communities and particularly American Jewry, could finance the assistance to the Jewish refugees and that they would not turn to the state. Their fundraising for this purpose were quite successful. They raised SF 1,700,000 in 1938, about SF 1,100,000 in 1939, approximately SF 700,000 in 1940, and about SF 500,000 in 1941. But the more refugees entered the country, the more difficult the financial situation became, even with the considerable help the Swiss Jews were already receiving from the American Joint Distribution Committee (AJDC). This created an increasingly critical situation: they had to plead with the authorities for the admittance of more refugees without knowing how to cover the expenses and without firm commitments from the American Jews, whose contribution also depended on fundraising income. The great financial contribution that the Swiss Jews themselves made to the refugee problem, however, should be acknowledged. There is no doubt that by their sacrifices they helped to save thousands of Jewish lives.

The Jewish Leadership

Thus, the Swiss Jewish community found itself in an extremely precarious position when the hostilities began in 1939. Those who were entrusted with its leadership at that time[5] included notably the president of the *Gemeinde-bund* (Community Federation), Saly Mayer of St. Gallen, who had taken over the presidency in 1936 from the banker Jules Dreyfus Brodsky (Basel); Saly Braunschweig, the president of the Zurich Jewish community; Georg Guggenheim, its vice-president; Armand Brunschvig, president of the Jewish community of Geneva; and Alfred Götschel, president of the Basel Jewish community. Silvain S. Guggenheim, as president of the *Verband Schweize-rischer Israelitischer Armenpflegen,* in 1943 renamed the *Verband Schweize-rischer Jüdischer Fürsorgen,* directed the activity in favor of Jewish refugees. The work of the *Verband,* which comprised the various local committees for refugees established in the different communities, was carried out under the guidance and general supervision of the SIG, which remained responsible for general policy. Guggenheim thus became one of the most important members of the Board of the *Gemeindebund.* All those leaders were very honorable people, deeply devoted to their cause. Whether they were the best prepared for the quite extraordinary situation to which they were exposed is a question which is not so easily answered.

Their major tasks were, however, quite obvious:

1. To defend the full equality of rights for the Jews in the face of the internal and external pressures;
2. To obtain the admission of the greatest number of Jewish refugees in view of the catastrophe that had overcome the major part of European Jewry;
3. To assure the morale of the members of the Swiss Jewish community in an extraordinarily serious situation.

It was not easy to discharge these functions in a steadily deteriorating atmosphere. The defeat of France in the summer of 1940 created a panic in large sectors of the country and produced considerable population movements. The famous radio speech by the president of the Confederation, Marcel Pilet Golaz, on June 25, 1940, in which he invited the Swiss people more or less to adapt itself to the new order of things, created deep feelings of defeatism. The appeal by General Guisan, the commander-in-chief of the army, on the Rütli on July 25, 1940, in which he declared that "there was no reason to abandon ourselves to defeatism and to doubt our mission" served as a serious check and counterweight to these sentiments.

The Jewish leadership was of course deeply affected by these developments. One observes their mounting concern and their helplessness in the minutes of the SIG Central Committee of the time. There are discussions about the transfer of the secretariat of the *Gemeindebund* to Lausanne, followed by the granting of full powers on this and other matters to a small board. There are expressions of deep anxiety about the future, about the reception of the Frontist leaders by the government, fears of new legislation on naturalization and deprivation of nationality, and of the anti-Semitic utterances in the press.

The leadership tried to take a low-key stand in this difficult situation. This attitude is perhaps best characterized by the following words of Saly Mayer at the Assembly of Delegates in May 1941:

> If we have already been modest in our requests in the past, we have not only remained so, but have become even more modest.
> Our behavior follows the same line Switzerland follows with regard to the outside world, particularly its neighbors.
> We believe the less is said about the Jews, the fewer points of friction are created.[6]

The leadership tried to maintain good relations with the authorities, to deal with the most pressing problems concerning the admittance of refugees with high officials in the Police Department, and to settle the current questions quietly in direct discussions with the Department. This led not only to a certain dependence on the goodwill of the high officials of the Department, but also to a certain secrecy in these relations. This attitude apparently fit in with the character of the president of the *Gemeindebund* who lacked the gift of easy communication, was distrustful of his colleagues, and in the increasingly delicate general situation acted more and more without consultation. This created considerable difficulties in his relations with some of his colleagues, who felt that they were not being kept informed and could not adequately inform the members of their communities. Some of them repeatedly offered to resign.

Swiss Jewry During the War

But the *Gemeindebund* could not remain silent and inactive in the face of several situations which affected the very basis of the legal position of Swiss Jewry.

Thus, for example, it had to intervene strongly in February 1941, when a violently anti-Semitic article appeared in *Heer und Haus* (Army and Home), an official publication of the army, in which, among other things, the Jews were declared "unassimilable" and special statutes for Jews in different cantons were envisaged. Upon the intervention of the *Gemeindebund,* the head of the Military Department (the Minister of Defense) expressed his regrets over the incident and announced that the people responsible for it would be punished and that a correction would be published.

Another example in which the SIG had to act was occasioned by the reply of the Swiss government to a parliamentary written question submitted by National Councillor Paul Graber in 1941, concerning the rights of Swiss Jewish citizens in occupied France whose enterprises had been sequestrated.

In its reply, the Swiss government had stated, *inter alia,* that in occupied France, as in other countries, the Jews were subject to special rules which were considered as part of the *ordre public* (public policy) and therefore also applied to foreign citizens. Thus the Swiss Jews could not claim a treatment different from that accorded to the citizens of the country in question. The government added that nevertheless the Swiss diplomats were trying to assist in defending their interests.

This was an extremely dangerous precedent. It meant that Switzerland accepted that rules relating to *ordre public* in a foreign country had priority over the contractual obligations resulting from treaties between Switzerland and the country in question and from the general rules of international law. Moreover, the governmental reply seemed to accept the applicability of foreign discriminatory laws to Swiss citizens by a foreign country. To accept this without protest meant at the same time the introduction of discrimination between Jewish and non-Jewish Swiss citizens by the Confederation itself.

On the suggestion notably of Professor Paul Guggenheim, a well-known international lawyer, the SIG in December 1941 submitted a memorandum and a very well argued advisory opinion by Professor Guggenheim to the authorities, in which it took strong exception to the written reply by the *Bundesrat* (Federal government). It stated that the concept of *ordre public* could not be opposed to the contractual rights and obligations resulting from the bilateral treaty between France and Switzerland on the reciprocal treatment of nationals and that the acceptance of special treatment of Jewish citizens would be a serious violation of the principle of equality guaranteed by the Swiss constitution.

A preliminary reply by the federal authorities was considered unsatisfactory and after further discussions a solution to this matter was finally found: the authorities recognized that the statement contained in the reply to the parliamentary question was not to be considered as a legal opinion binding for the future, but as a statement of fact reflecting the impossibility of protecting the interests of Jewish citizens in the prevailing situation.

On another occasion, the SIG had to intervene on behalf of 30 Swiss Jewish citizens who had been arrested in occupied France, and who were later released.

The military censorship introduced at the beginning of the war with regard to all publications and strictly exercised in order to maintain political neutrality also created problems for the Jewish community.

The news bulletin published by the press office of the SIG (JUNA) was repeatedly censored by the army authorities. Thus it was prohibited from disseminating the message of the Polish minister in Berne, addressed to the Polish Jewish military internees on the occasion of Rosh Hashana in 1941. On another occasion, the JUNA bulletin was censored because it had circulated an article of the *Glarner Nachrichten* (Glarus News) under the title: *Gehetztes Volk,* which contained very friendly observations on the fate of the Jewish people. Upon appeal, this order was later rescinded.

Moreover, on June 29, 1944, the reproduction of an article by the JUNA on the anti-Jewish persecution in Hungary "Pray for us that we may die soon! The extermination of the Jews of Hungary," containing details on these persecutions, was prohibited by the military censorship.

The Question of Jewish Refugees

Developments in the question of the admittance of refugees led, however, to much more dramatic events. Immediately after the outbreak of hostilities, the Swiss authorities reformulated the rules concerning refugees, notably in the Federal Council decree of October 17, 1939. This decree clearly provided, in Article 9, that foreigners entering Swiss territory illegally could be expelled from the country without any procedure. This clause, however, had not been too rigidly applied. From the beginning of the war until July 31, 1942, a total of 1,200 new refugees had been admitted.

In view of the mounting deportations from Germany, the Central Committee of the SIG in November 1941, on the proposal of Saly Braunschweig, adopted a series of guidelines defining the categories of persons whose admittance the SIG should negotiate with the authorities.[7]

The tragic events of the summer of 1942 led to a constant flow of refugees who presented themselves at the Swiss borders. On August 4, the government was informed, and agreed to a stricter application of Article 9 of the 1939 decree. On August 13, 1942, the head of the Police Department issued a circular which in practice closed the frontier to all Jewish refugees. A clear distinction was made between "political refugees" and "strictly racial refugees," e.g., Jews, and asylum was clearly refused to the latter.

When the adoption of these new rules became known, they provoked an outburst of protest and indignation in the whole Swiss population and also created a deep crisis in the Jewish community.

The new regulations had not been discussed in advance with the leadership of the Jewish community. The president of the SIG invited the head of the Police Department to a meeting of the SIG Central Committee on August 20, 1942, at which the official tried to justify these new regulations. This initiative was later strongly criticized because it could create the impression that the *Gemeindebund* was in agreement with the authorities.

Both Saly Braunschweig and Silvain Guggenheim pleaded with Rothmund not to close the borders to the newcomers. There could be no doubt about the fate threatening those who would be refused. They referred to the many terrifying reports about the deportations and the fate of the deportees. They were convinced that expulsion meant certain death for them and they could not cooperate in denouncing illegal refugees to the authorities.

Rothmund maintained that it was known to him that hundreds of thousands of Jews were in danger and that millions of others felt they were in danger. Switzerland, however, was not able to receive all the refugees from its neighboring countries. It was better to care for those who were already there.

It is strange to note in the minutes that Mayer himself remained completely silent during this discussion.

Information on the terrible fate of the deported people had definitely reached Switzerland during the second half of 1941 and in the first months of 1942, and news about the plan for total extermination had reached Switzerland at the end of July 1942. The Swiss authorities received knowledge of this information during August and September, mainly through the representatives of the Christian churches, to whom all reports on the fate of the Jews were constantly communicated. The Swiss authorities also had their own sources of information about the massacre of whole Jewish populations on the eastern front by spring 1942, when a Swiss sanitary mission returned from the Russian front.

News about the *refoulement* of many Jewish refugees at the Swiss borders and particularly the expulsion of a great number who had already entered the country provoked a deep malaise in the country and many soldiers at the frontiers felt a serious conflict of conscience when called upon to execute the government's orders. I can only briefly mention here the daily fights that the local Jewish refugee committees had to go through with the military authorities in their efforts to help refugees and the conflicts that arose with some of the commanding officers who did not hesitate to deprive some of the Jewish leaders like Armand Brunschvig of their right to visit the camps.

A wave of protest struck the country and those who lived through this period remember with emotion this unique and exhilarating experience. The newspapers from right to left violently criticized the attitude of the government. There was a near unanimous outcry to uphold the principle of the right of asylum and many political, civic, and religious bodies voiced their vehement protest.

A very stormy meeting of the *Zentralstelle für Flüchtlingshilfe*, which was held on August 24, asked at least for certain changes and corrections in the regulations. Many interventions were undertaken with the government and the Minister of Justice and Police, von Steiger. They were not completely without success. On August 23, von Steiger gave instructions that in special cases expulsion should not take place.

The Swiss parliament held a debate on the refugee situation on September 22, and while the three government parties officially supported the policy of the government, the Democratic and Socialist parties clearly supported a more liberal policy. Of the 17 speakers who took part in the debate, nine attacked the government position, among them the following well-known members of parliament: Rittmeyer, Maag, Oeri, Muschg, Bringolf, Meierhans, and Graber. They did not consider that "the lifeboat was full" and that Switzerland had reached the limits of its humanitarian action.

This finally led to new instructions which, while maintaining the fateful distinction between political and racial refugees, provided for the admission of hardship cases: sick people, pregnant women, refugees over 65, unaccompanied children under 16, parents with children under 16, and refugees with close relations in or special links to Switzerland.

These rules were changed further from time to time, not always favorably, but it would lead too far afield to describe here the developments in all their detail. It was only at a later stage in the war, after the breakdown of Fascist Italy, that a more liberal attitude concerning the admittance of refugees came to prevail.

It should, however, also be mentioned that as a result of the pressure in the summer of 1942, the police made some agreements with the churches, as a result of which lists were established periodically, containing names of persons recommended by the church authorities for admission at the frontiers. The Jewish organizations made use of these facilities in order to save additional people. This procedure, however, was distasteful. Every name that was put on the list condemned others who were omitted or forgotten. It was another way of becoming obliged to the police authorities.

One fact, however, was conspicuous: The complete silence of the leadership of the Jewish community during this whole period. Or, as one of the leading members of the *Gemeindebund,* Georg Guggenheim (who at that time belonged to the opposition), said at a meeting of its Central Committee: "The Swiss people were up in arms, but we missed the expression of the official position of the competent organs of the *Gemeindebund."*

One of the private interventions which had been undertaken with von Steiger and had obviously helped in modifying the attitude of the government was that of Paul Dreyfus de Gunzburg, the Basel banker and son of the second president of the SIG, who together with Gertrud Kurz of Berne—a Christian lady with a fantastic record of work in behalf of Jewish refugees and commonly called "the mother of the refugees"—visited the vacationing von Steiger in August 1942 at Mont Pélerin. Years later, in a letter written in connection with the elaboration of the Ludwig Report, Vera Dreyfus de Gunsburg recalled her husband's intervention, adding: "It was an altogether private intervention, which, however, shows very clearly that one had to take such steps without, and indeed despite Saly Mayer."[8]

Intra-Communal Tensions

The events of the summer of 1942 deeply troubled the Jewish community and created a serious crisis of confidence in its leadership. It was particularly in the intellectual circles that a profound malaise manifested itself. Professor Paul Guggenheim again emerged as the spokesman for these circles, but he was by no means alone. Erwin Haymann, Veit Wyler, Jacob Zucker, David Farbstein, Judge Max Gurny, Georg Guggenheim, Benjamin Sagalowitz, the writer of these lines, and others shared his great concern. In a lecture before the Zionist Association of Zurich on October 31, 1942, Professor Guggenheim raised some of the fundamental problems facing Swiss Jewry during the difficult war period and criticized the lack of a clear policy and the political methods used by the *Gemeindebund,* notably its president. He attacked particularly the reliance of the leadership on its good relations with some of the high members of the federal bureaucracy, whatever the results this might produce, and the leadership's complete failure to keep in contact not only with the Jewish community, but with Swiss public opinion and the active political forces in the country. A small minority could defend its basic rights and interests under the prevailing circumstances only by appealing to the deeply entrenched democratic forces in the country, and the failure to inform the public was a grave political mistake.

This malaise manifested itself also within the organs of the *Gemeindebund.* For quite some time the relations among several members of the Board had been deteriorating, due partly to the rather autocratic methods of the president and partly to differences of opinion on some important issues, notably on the work of the defense and press department. Since 1941 several changes had occurred in the composition of the Board and since then some members had offered their resignation. But all attempts to overcome the personal problems and the differences of approach failed, and for several months the Board was deeply divided and unable to function normally; and the Central Committee, in spite of new elections, was not in a position to settle the problem.

Under these circumstances, an extraordinary Assembly of Delegates was called on December 13, 1942. The Assembly heard reports by the presidents of the *Gemeindebund* and the *Verband* about the events and developments since the summer, and for the first time some information was given to a wider Jewish circle on the action that had been taken. Again it was Professor Guggenheim who made himself spokesman for the critics. In an interpellation submitted together with 11 other delegates, he forcefully restated his position and raised in particular the following questions: 1. Why had the SIG not sought contact with Federal Counsellor von Steiger after the negative position taken by Rothmund became known, and why had the initiative been left to a private person? 2. Why had no information been given during the whole period to the Jewish public or to Swiss public opinion and particularly to the members of the federal parliament before the great parliamentary debate? (He felt that the legislators had not clearly understood that deportation meant annihilation and that the *Gemeindebund* had failed to make this absolutely clear to the members of parliament.) 3. What had motivated Rittmeyer, member of the Swiss parliament, to speak in the debate of the *sacro egoismo* (sacred egoism) of Jewish organizations? 4. How did it happen that one repeatedly heard remarks in church circles about the negative and unfriendly attitude toward the refugees on the part of those who directed the policy of the *Gemeindebund?*

At the same time Professor Guggenheim submitted a number of positive suggestions addressed to the Central Committee of the SIG concerning future policy and methods of work. The SIG president and several members of the Board replied to the interpellation. Their most important point was that both the direction of the SIG and of the *Verband* considered that the situation in the summer of 1942 had been a problem for Swiss public opinion and that they should therefore act through the *Schweizerische Zentralstelle für Flüchtlingshilfe* and its president, Briner. It was also stated that since August 20, 1942, there had been no direct contact with the federal authorities and everything had passed through the *Zentralstelle*. They flatly denied the fourth of Guggenheim's questions.

There followed a passionate debate in which a great number of delegates participated. During the last part of the Assembly, organizational and personal problems were discussed. A proposal of the Central Committee to express confidence in the president and the Central Committee was submitted. In view of some opposition and a request to withdraw the proposal, the Central Committee finally agreed to postpone the vote on the proposal to the next Assembly of Delegates.

At the same time a letter from Saly Mayer was read, announcing his irrevocable decision to resign as president from the next Assembly of Delegates.

The next Assembly of Delegates of the SIG took place on March 28, 1943. On this occasion Saly Braunschweig, former vice-president of the SIG and president of the Zurich community, was elected president in place of Saly Mayer. Thus ended a very dramatic chapter in the history of the *Gemeindebund*. At the same time, the SIG Central Committee replied in detail to the various proposals made at the previous Assembly by Professor Guggenheim and accepted a number of them. The Assembly also decided in favor of a revision of the statutes of the SIG, to lead to a democratization of its working methods—a revision which was finally adopted in May 1944.

With the assumption of the presidency by Saly Braunschweig, a new period began. Having served for years as president of the largest Jewish community, that of Zurich, with its democratic traditions introduced under the influence of David Farbstein and others, Braunschweig had a much greater understanding than his predecessor of the political game, of the necessity of working with the political forces, of having recourse to public opinion, and of trying to mobilize its support. His was a much more open and democratic management and he quietly succeeded in overcoming the dissensions and obtaining a broad consensus in the community.

As an ironic epilogue to these developments, it should be noted that, having resigned as president of the *Gemeindebund,* Saly Mayer was appointed by the American Joint Distribution Committee as its representative and entrusted with a great part of its activities in Europe. He thus assumed much more important responsibilities than he had held before.

He did not, however, depart from the *Gemeindebund* scene without writing an effusive letter of thanks to the head of the federal police, Rothmund, in which he expressed his deep appreciation to him and his colleagues for their understanding and helpfulness.[9] In the light of history this letter represents one of the strangest documents in the entire record of this period.

The New Jewish Leadership

Under the new direction of the *Gemeindebund,* relations with the federal government were soon reestablished, so that by the time of the Central Committee session of June 7, 1943, Braunschweig could report in detail on his discussions with Federal Counsellor von Steiger on May 26, 1943. The question of refugees continued to occupy the authorities of the *Gemeindebund* as their first priority. The efforts to have more refugees admitted continued, with varying success. The problems concerning the refugees in the country, the situation in the refugee camps, abuses by camp officials or local military personnel, the problem of the labor service required of refugees, the conditions for liberation from the camps, and the question of uniting families remained on the agenda. Slowly the military situation changed and the repercussions on the political front became evident. In July 1943, the Frontist movement was dissolved. When the Fascist regime in Italy collapsed and the short lived Saló republic emerged, regulations regarding Italian and Yugoslav

Jewish refugees became much more liberal. The fateful distinction between political and racial refugees was ultimately abolished in August 1944. Thus, in the later part of 1944 and in 1945, transports with 2,830 refugees from Bergen-Belsen and Theresienstadt were allowed to enter Switzerland.

The SIG resumed its relations with international Jewish organizations, notably with the World Jewish Congress and the Jewish Agency, which the previous administration had practically suspended for reasons of "neutrality." In June 1943, for the first time the SIG and all its member communities observed a national day of mourning for the Jewish martyrs in occupied Europe. In 1944, also for the first time, the Swiss Jewish community made a public declaration protesting against the anti-Jewish persecutions in Hungary.

Slowly the SIG began to approach the problems of the postwar period. It established a special commission to this effect and published a study, *Jüdische Nachkriegsprobleme* (Jewish Postwar Problems), containing a number of contributions on some of the major problems that world Jewry was to face after the war. At the same time it prepared itself for postwar assistance to the devastated communities.

Switzerland and the Refugees: An Overview

By the end of the war, 6,654 so-called Jewish emigrants (old refugees) and 21,858 Jewish civilian refugees, a total of 28,512 Jews, had found asylum in Switzerland.[10] Compared with the figure of 7,000, which was considered as the maximum tolerable in 1942, this was not a negligible result. It was also not a result with which one could be satisfied, particularly if one thought of the many people who were refused entry at the frontiers and the many thousands more who, because of Swiss policy, gave up all attempts to penetrate Swiss territory. However, there are not many countries that can say that they have saved a greater number.

It is this writer's opinion that with a more liberal attitude, several tens of thousands more could have been saved without any serious consequences to the Swiss population, to its food situation, its labor market, its security problems. This writer is all the more convinced of this as the political situation forced Switzerland to accept at certain moments, and to keep during the whole war, large numbers of military refugees; and at the end of the war it harbored within its frontiers more than 100,000 people in this category— internees, escaped prisoners, deserters, and hospitalized people—and there was never any doubt that they should be admitted.

The Swiss position on the refugees is eloquently reflected in the following quotation from the monumental work on the history of Swiss neutrality by the eminent Swiss historian Edgar Bonjour:

The Swiss boat was not "overcrowded"; it was not "even full" and would have been able, even in politically stormy seas, to take on a far greater number of refugees without sinking. It is true that compared to former periods of Swiss asylum policy, the most recent one was both more variable and more intricate. . . .But as far as the spirit of sacrifice of the authorities or of private persons is concerned, this war period comes off badly when compared with earlier ones. The severe measures taken by the authorities and the inadequately expressed will to help on the part of private persons can be understood in the context of an external political situation periodically fraught with great danger, as well as of a precarious supply situation. However, whether this fact leads one to approve of the official attitude of reserve shown to asylum seekers hotly pursued by certain death, is a question each one has to decide for himself. That some of those looking back refuse to give their approval, is their legitimate right both as citizens and as human beings.[11]

Those who evaluate the activities of the Swiss Jewish leadership during World War II will have to take these observations into consideration. Swiss Jewish leaders did not live in a vacuum. Those who stood the test and those who failed were deeply marked by the events around them. That they tried their best is not in doubt. But finally, we are to be judged by what we achieve.

Chapter 5

PATTERNS OF JEWISH LEADERSHIP IN LATIN AMERICA DURING THE HOLOCAUST

Haim Avni

Latin-American Jewry was a "young" Diaspora community when Hitler came to power in January 1933 and was still young in 1945, when the Nazi regime was defeated and the Holocaust era ended. Nonetheless, the twelve years separating these two events proved decisive for its consolidation.

The Jewish population was augmented by the third and last major wave of immigration; older settlers and newcomers ascended the social ladder as their wealth increased; the map of Jewish communities throughout the continent took on its ultimate shape, and the internal structure of many of these same communities became more coherent and crystalized. All these processes form the background and the basis for the function of the Jewish leadership during the era of the Holocaust.

The first part of this paper will include a review and an analysis of the basic processes which shaped the infrastructure of the Latin-American diaspora before turning to a discussion of the patterns of leadership of the communal and political frameworks as well as of the local branches of international agencies. It will conclude by indicating the spheres in which activities of the Jewish leaders on behalf of the victims of the Holocaust could take place and which still call for further research.

A Diaspora in the Making

In 1918, close to the end of World War I, the *American Jewish Yearbook* published a comprehensive survey of the Jewish communities in Latin

The research on this article has been carried out in the framework of the project "Latin America and the Jewish people during the Holocaust," of the Institute of Contemporary Jewry, the Hebrew University of Jerusalem, which was sponsored in 1981–82 by the Memorial Foundation for Jewish Culture of New York. I am very much obliged to the Tauber Institute of Brandeis University, its Director, Bernard Wasserstein, and to Peter Shaw, fellow of that institute, for their enormous help in the preparation of this article.

87

America. Its author, Harry S. Sandberg, an assistant trade expert at the Pan American Union in Washington, used his institutional contacts with United States officials stationed in the region, as well as his acquaintanceship with prominent Jewish informants, to produce the most complete report on Jewish life and institutions south of Key West and the Rio Grande which had been published until then.[1]

Some 26 years later, as World War II was drawing to its end, another set of estimates regarding the Jewish population in Latin America was published by an official of an American Jewish institution,[2] complementary data simultaneously being compiled by other world Jewish organizations. More than 15 years later, in the early 1960s and in the 1970s, proper demographic research on Latin American Jewry provided us with accurate data concerning the size of the Jewish communities at that time and earlier.[3] Taken together these figures illustrate the demographic growth of the Latin-American communities up to and during the Holocaust Era. (See Appendix A.)

At first glance these figures reveal a substantial increase of the Jewish presence in those countries which already had a significant Jewish population in 1917. The data also indicate that between the end of World War I and the end of World War II additional countries joined the list of those having a considerable Jewish community. But, to better appreciate these facts, one must bear in mind trends that Harry Sandberg discovered toward the end of World War I. After reviewing the situation of the host-societies and of urban life in Latin-America, he observed "despite all the favorable conditions and opportunities one is impressed by two facts: the absence of Jewish women, especially among the Ashkenazic Jews, excepting of course, in the agricultural colonies of Argentina; and the earnestness and frequency with which the men express the hope of returning to their native countries."[4] While the extent of the imbalance between the sexes—in itself a natural phenomenon for every immigrant population—has still to be substantiated by further data, the eagerness to reemigrate from Latin America was nothing new. Before World War I, during the years 1908–1914, some 19.35 percent of the total of Jewish immigrants to Argentina reemigrated; in the same years only 7.14 percent of the Jewish immigrants to the U.S.A. did so.[5]

Reemigration after World War I might have deprived Latin America of some of the recently immigrated Jews but only a very few among them could regard a return to their war-ravaged homes in the dismantled Russian, Austrian, or Turkish empires as a desirable solution for themselves and their families. The constantly stiffening immigration laws in the United States could not encourage reemigration in that direction. Thus, if the predicted return from Latin America did not materialize as a mass movement the Latin continent was not yet attracting masses of Jewish immigrants either. In 1925, when some 5,500 Jewish emigrants found themselves stranded in Poland, Romania, Constantinople and in several European sea ports as a result of the harsh enactment of the new immigration law of 1924, only 273 of them consented to be sent by the (Jewish) United Evacuation Committee to Argentina, and only a slightly larger number went to Brazil.[6]

If many more drifted at that time into Mexico and Cuba, they did so under the mistaken assumption that from these close shores, the "golden gates" of the United States would be more easily attainable.

It was only in 1928 that the combined Jewish emigration agencies HIAS-JCA-Emigdirect—later to become known as HICEM—came to regard Latin America as a preferred destination for Jewish emigrants. At an "Immigration Congress," convened in Buenos Aires on May 27, 1928, and attended by leaders of the three cooperating international organizations, the local community along with representatives of Brazilian Jewry were urged to help Jewish immigrants establish themselves in their countries. At that congress Rabbi Ishaya Rafaelowitch, a leading communal organizer from Rio de Janero, told the Jewish press that until then, whenever consulted, he used to deter people from immigrating to Latin America. Similar warnings were frequently admonished in its *Korrespondenzblatt* (Correspondence Journal) by the Central Office for Jewish Emigration, which was established and maintained by the *Hilfsverein der deutschen Juden* (Aid Association of German Jews) in Berlin. The congress in Buenos Aires was intended to bring about a significant break with that policy. But even at that conference the call for immigration was not unqualified. Only manual laborers such as farmers, artisans and other blue-collar workers, were encouraged to regard Latin America as a prospective new home. All others—merchants and academicians first and foremost—were advised to go elsewhere or even stay out rather than reestablishing themselves in Latin America.[7]

The deep economic crisis which engulfed the countries of the region from 1930 on was the main factor in reversing the tide of Jewish immigration. When, in February 1931, a rumor was spread among the jobless and hungry immigrants in Buenos Aires that the Argentine government was ready to repatriate every immigrant who so desired, hundreds of down-and-out newcomers flocked to the "Hotel de Imigrantes" (the government's hostel for immigrants) demanding that the government make good its "promise." Some 200 Jewish immigrants participated in the raid, refusing to vacate the premises until the Jewish community would provide for their return to Europe. Pressed by the Argentinian immigration officers to take charge of their brethren, the Jewish organizations were forced to raise the necessary funds to help the insurgent immigrants. Thus in November 1932, when the first severe restrictions on immigration were enacted in Argentina, the Jewish organizations were not overly disconcerted. "An unnecessary act," remarked *Di Idische Zeitung* (The Yiddish Paper), one of the two Yiddish dailies published in Buenos Aires, "immigration does not come to Argentina anyhow."[8]

The considerable growth that took place between 1918 and the end of the Holocaust era was, in fact, concentrated in two very limited timespans: the late 1920s and in the latter half of the 1930s. During the Holocaust itself many new communities underwent an initial stage of demographic agglomeration while the more established settlements received their share of new arrivals. The proportion of locally born even in the largest community on the Latin-American continent, namely, Buenos Aires, was quite low: only 38.76 percent of the 120,195 Jews registered in the municipal census in 1936 were born in Argentina. It might well be assumed that a very large number among them were at that time young children and adolescents.[9]

Remarkably small changes in the size of Jewish population occurred between the late 1940s and the 1960s. (See Appendix A.) Immigration was only a minor source for the increase noted in most communities while the teenagers of the 1930s were now parents of the *third* generation of young Latin Americans. It is thus obvious that the years 1933–1945 constitute the decisive period for the demographic consolidation of Latin-American Jewish communities. For some of them—like Ecuador, Bolivia and Paraguay—these years in fact marked the peak of their demographic development.

In the period immediately preceding and encompassing the Holocaust, the socioeconomic situation of Latin American Jewry changed dramatically. "Here it is impossible to say that below this limit begins misery; the limit in itself is already misery"—thus wrote one of the most outstanding social workers, a physician by profession, in October 1930, while describing the degree of poverty prevailing at that time in Buenos Aires. Three years later, in July 1933, the leaders of the local Jewish charities met in order to discuss a problem which had become too conspicuous to be overlooked: the situation of the unemployed, homeless Jewish workers who slept in public parks.[10]

At the other end of Latin America, in Mexico City, in May 1931, a large contingent of Jewish pushcart vendors were evicted from the marketplace. This event, which was accompanied by a vehement anti-Semitic propaganda campaign, terrified the whole community and spelled economic ruin for hundreds of extremely poor breadwinners.[11]

The predominant reality for a very large part of Latin American Jews in the early 1930s was that of an economic stress and want. And yet, as the 1930s drew to a close the situation changed, sometimes dramatically.

The deep depression which hit Argentina and several other countries stimulated the growth of local import-substituting industries. This need was made all the more urgent by the outbreak of World War II, as the Latin American markets were cut off from their traditional European suppliers. The entry of the United States into the war, along with several other nations, further exacerbated the trend. The growing economic nationalism, while mostly anti-British, anti-Yankee and thus anti-liberal and many times also anti-Semitic, provided an ideological justification for the protection of local industry—a policy which lasted even beyond the war years.

These developments primarily benefited the urban trades and occupations in which most of the Jews were to be found. As a result, many of them, across the entire Latin-American continent, experienced a tremendous upsurge in their economic position during the later 1930s and the war years. This situation, in turn, facilitated the social integration of the new refugee-immigrants, most of whom came from the middle classes of highly industrialized countries. New factories were founded by them in countries like Chile, Bolivia, Ecuador, and Colombia, where few if any existed before their arrival and thousands of local non-Jewish workers were employed.

Visitors to Jewish Latin America during the later years of the war brought home the impression that poverty no longer constituted a crucial problem for the Jewish communities and that many who had had recourse to charities and modest loans only a few years earlier had created for themselves a substantially more affluent position. "In Mexico there are already a score or two millionaires in pesos, some of them reputed to be millionaires in United States dollars," thus reported Morris D. Waldman, then the vice chairman of the executive committee of the American Jewish Committee in November 1944, on returning from a three-month visit to seven Latin-American countries. Nathan Bistritzki, the Hebrew writer who spent almost five years working with the Latin-American communities on behalf of the Keren Kayemeth Le-Israel (Jewish National Fund), wrote in his final report "They started with casual and marginal occupations, mainly as peddlars. . . . slowly—and during the World War with a surprising leap—they began to become rich and some even accumulated much wealth."[12]

On the basis of this demographic and economic expansion—a direct result of the persecution of the Jews in Europe and of the circumstances which prevailed in Latin America during the Holocaust Era—the network of Jewish communities developed.

The Communities

The Map

Contrary to what the appearances of highly secularized immigrants might suggest, it was the lack of religious services which provided the starting point for communal life in most Latin American countries. The Brazilian, the Argentinian, the Chilean, the Mexican, the Uruguayan and many other communities count their days of organized existence from the moment the first *Minyan* convened for prayers on the High Holidays. The service of this necessity remained a basic facet of Jewish public life and also a cause of its diversity.

By their very nature, religious institutions are intended to be regional, both as a service for a certain neighborhood in the new country and as a cherished "replica" of the traditions of the "old home." The desire to continue some of the old ways in the new environment found its most natural expression in the synagogue and therefore some of the congregations, which started as institutions of mixed membership, evidenced quite early the departure of the estranged elements. Headed by schismatic leaders they seceded and set up congregations of their own. This was the case of the Moroccan Jews, who separated in 1891 from the Ashkenazi *Congregacion Israelita de la Republica Argentina (CIRA)* in Buenos Aires, and that was what the Ashkenazi Jews did when in 1920 they separated from the "Syrian"-run *Monte Sinai* congregation in Mexico City.

In the early 1930s the religious institutions demarcated the contours of communal life in Latin America. Eastern European Ashkenazim kept aloof from their non-Yiddish-speaking brethren, who in turn were divided into Arabic-speaking-Jews—mainly from Syria- and Ladino-speaking Jews of Turkish and Balkan descent. To further complicate the issue, immigrants from Morocco, now residing in Buenos Aires, segregated themselves from all the aforementioned groups. Similarly, Jews originally from Aleppo had their own congregation, apart from one founded by fellow-Syrian Jews from Damascus. Habits, traditions, and rites divided them. Among the Ashkenazim, who shared a common language, culture, and a more secularized form of Judaism, the differences between Lithuanians, Bessarabians, and Galicians were of much less significance than those between the other groups.

This was the situation in Argentina and in Mexico. Divisions were much less striking in Chile, where close relationships between all the sectors had been established at a very early date. In Peru, where only one Sephardic community existed, communications between it and the Ashkenazic sector were very casual. "This society keeps completely apart and has nothing in common with the Ashkenazim," noted a special envoy of the *HICEM,* Benjamin Mellibowsky, who visited Lima in March 1936 to prepare a detailed report about Peruvian Jewry and the advisability of sending more Jews to Peru. His estimate of Lima's total Jewish population was 900, the Sephardim accounting for some 25 percent.[13]

Other cities scattered across the continent had only one Sephardic community apiece, which in some cases—Venezuela, Panama, and in certain cities in Brazil, and Colombia—exerted a dominant influence on communal life.

This was the basic situation before 1933. But then, with the German immigration of the late 1930s a new segment was added to the Latin-American Jewish amalgam. The newcomers brought with them the German *Gemeinde* (Community) tradition which, much like the Sephardic communities, was mainly synagogue-based but, unlike them, was divided into orthodox, conservative, and liberal rites. All differed radically from the Eastern-European forms of public worship. The creation of new congregations became thus inevitable.

In Argentina, this new sector of Jewish population could count on the help of German-speaking Jews who had already established themselves there. A group of them, who before January 1933, had been happily integrated in the non-Jewish German "colony" in Buenos Aires, found themselves estranged from their fellow countrymen, who enthusiastically embraced Nazism almost immediately after Hitler's rise to power. To replace these social ties, a group of Jews led by Adolfo Hirsh founded an immigrants' welfare society— *Hilfsverein Deutschsprechender Juden* (Aid Association of German-speaking Jews)—even though the HICEM-affiliated and Ashkenazi-run *Soprotimis* had been helping new immigrants for over ten years. Language and mentality barriers brought about the advent of this separate welfare institution; the separate servicing of religious, social and cultural needs followed before long.[14]

The fortune of being helped by earlier established countrymen was not shared by many other German-speaking immigrants elsewhere. The small number of such Jews who had previously immigrated, coupled with their rapid assimilation, accounted for a situation which was symbolized by the extraordinary case of Peru.

When the new refugee-immigrants arrived in Lima they were met by the only survivor of one of the oldest communities on the Latin American continent. Founded in 1869 by immigrants who came mainly from Alsace-

Lorraine, this community had virtually disappeared through intermarriage, emigration, and death. The only member left in the early 1930s kept custody of the communal property, which consisted of the cemetery, and handed it over to the society which the newcomers founded and which they later named "The 1870 Jewish Charitable Society" (*Sociedad de Beneficencia Israelita—1870*) in nominal continuance and in the memory of their predecessors. With that invaluable asset, the recently arrived immigrants acquired a communal status slightly superior to the Sephardi and Ashkenazi Jews of Lima.[15]

In some cities the newcomers could rely on help offered them by the existing Ashkenazi community, while in others the new German-speaking group was for all practical purposes in the majority. This was the case mainly in the Andean capitals of Bolivia and Ecuador, which became the home of considerable Jewish communities thanks to these German-speaking immigrants.[16]

By the end of the Holocaust era, Latin-American Jewry reached its fullest development. Large and diversified communities existed in Buenos Aires, Montevideo, Santiago de Chile, Rio de Janeiro, São Paulo, and Mexico City—where all three branches of the Jewish immigration were represented. There were also minor communities in Caracas, Panama City, and some small towns in Colombia and Brazil dominated by Sephardim, and other communities dominated by the recently arrived central-European immigrants. Language, mentality, and traditions divided them and were conspicuously represented in their synagogues and rites. At that time, the internal structure of the older communities underwent a process of considerable consolidation. Their communal leadership, as it developed between 1933 and 1945, was both the partial cause and a genuine reflection of that process.

The Consolidation

The experience of the *Associación Comunidad Israelita Sefaradi (Acis)* of Buenos Aires, the communal institution of the Ladino-speaking Jews, can serve as a case study of the main issues involved in the development of the older communities during the Holocaust era.[17]

A plethora of organizations and societies, based on differences of origin— Ismir, Istanbul, the Island of Rhodes, etc.—and on separate concentrations in Buenos Aires neighborhoods—Centro, Villa Crespo, Colegiales, etc.— were amalgamating during the 1930s and early 1940s into a unified multi-service community, (See Appendix B.) Although the synagogue remained the central institution of the community, it was now complemented by a modern and comprehensive service-system providing the community with a more efficient institutional basis as well as a broader identity and sense of unity. This change was brought about by the new leadership which, after a series of futile attempts, managed to replace its predecessor, which had administered the organization practically since its inception in 1919.

According to its official statutes the *ACIS* was a voluntary society which was to be governed by a presidium and a council to be elected every two years by its members in a general assembly. Nevertheless, its leader throughout the 1920s and 1930s was Moises Albala. A poorly educated merchant of limited financial resources, he was entirely dedicated to the cause of his community, as he understood it. Endowed with a robust appearance, hearty and open handed manners, he was extremely popular with many members of the community who reelected him, together with some of his closest friends, to the leading positions. Wealthier members of the community, who contributed to its synagogue and welfare funds, stayed away from its leadership; intellectuals—among them David Elnecave, the editor and owner of important Sephardi weekly *La Luz* (The Light)—were able to interfere in communal affairs only from the outside. Thus a combination of a "direct democracy," through general assemblies, along with a *Caudillo* (leader) decided the fate of this community during the first half of the twelve years under consideration, as it did during the preceding decade.

The president elected in 1940, Abraham Chazan, was of a different personality: rich (he was the owner of a factory), scholarly and traditionally educated (he had written an interpretation of the book of Song of Songs) and the possessor of broader Jewish interests (he was a co-founder in 1933 of a Sephardic Zionist Club). The new administration employed as its technical secretary an intellectual: Bechor Issaev, a trained sociologist who lived for a while in Vienna and had the experience of being the secretary of the Jewish community in Sofia, Bulgaria. The new administration managed to unite under its aegis all the welfare and religious organizations which functioned until then independently (see Appendix B). At the same time, membership increased from some 1,000 nominally affiliated, of which only 500 were full dues payers in 1933, to 2,100 in 1941 and 2,304 in 1943, of whom some 90 percent kept their membership dues regularly updated. According to ACIS leadership, these figures corresponded to between 70 and 84 percent of the Ladino-speaking Jews in Buenos Aires. The leaders' declared aim was to reach them all.[18]

In spite of the predominantly religious orientation of the community, both before and after 1940, its leadership did not include a permanent rabbi and spiritual leader. Although in 1929, Rabbi Shabetai Djaen, a well known Sephardi Rabbi from Monastir, Yugoslavia, was appointed, no replacement was nominated for five years after his departure in 1931. In 1936, ACIS appointed a new rabbi, who remained in office until 1942 without however making his mark in the community's history. He was not replaced in the years to come.

At the same time, in face of the German onslaught on the Jewish people and the constantly growing spectre of anti-Semitism in Argentina, the ACIS participated, along with all the other communities, in the formation of a representative umbrella organization. The *Committee Against the Persecution of the Jews in Germany,* which was organized in early 1933, and, after further changes, became in 1935 the *Delegacion de Asociaciones Israelitas Argentinas* (DAIA) (The Delegation of Jewish Argentinian Associations) from its beginnings benefited from an active ACIS delegation. Through it the cooperation of the ACIS members was enlisted in anti-German campaigns, such as the boycott of German products, and in protest meetings.[19]

The most important characteristics of the Ladino-speaking community of Buenos-Aires during the Holocaust era were:

1. A central service—the synagogue—which was needed daily, or was at least highly appreciated by the community, became the cornerstone of a multi-service communal organization;
2. The concentration of services in the areas of religion, welfare, health and partly education under the aegis of one institution, with the exclusion of recreational (and economic) areas. (See Appendix B);
3. A democratically organized association, based on membership and on the idea of mutual help, governed by a leadership, subject to elections, but open to the possible domination of one popular strong man *(caudillo);*
4. The peaceful transfer of leadership from a less advanced to a more modernized group;
5. The low status, and even absence, of religious leadership;
6. Participation in the Jewish struggle of global dimension through a representative umbrella organization.

These characteristics could be used as criteria for the analysis of other communal institutions during the same period. Clearly they would apply to the kindred synagogue-based communities of the Sephardim and partly to the religion-oriented *Kultur-Gemeinde* which the German speaking Jews were organizing at that very time in Buenos Aires and throughout Latin America. Many of them would apply to the largely secularized Eastern European communities as well.

Much like their Ladino-speaking brethren of Buenos Aires, the Ashkenazim too, in the early stages of organization, developed a variety of institutions, there and elsewhere, to serve each of their communal needs individually. Synagogues were to be found among them, however they served primarily the few pious Jews who also maintained them. Welfare organizations were established which, in the case of Buenos Aires, developed into prosperous institutions, like the Jewish Hospital Ezrah, or the Anti-Tuberculosis League. Education was administered by a variety of independent organizations which rarely acquired a central role, as was the case in Mexico City. Such was the fate of cultural and recreational societies. A prominent place among the Ashkenazim was reserved for an area which was completely absent in the ACIS community: the economic associations. Both before and during the Holocaust era, small "loan-banks"—originally organized on a mutual help basis—and peddlers' commercial associations—which usually began as modest cooperatives—developed into solid popular banks and large cooperative institutions.

Each of these varied associations was organized, much like the ACIS, on the basis of individual membership and administered by a leadership elected by its general assembly. This principle applied even to large institutions like the *Hebraica* (the large cultural association in Buenos Aires) or the banks, which by the 1940s served hundreds and even thousands of members. As was the case with ACIS, this "direct democracy" allowed both the emergence of *caudillos* (through an en-bloc presence of their supporters at the general assembly) and orderly shifts of power.[20]

On the surface, it would appear that the atomized nature of Ashkenazic public life derived from a lack of a major communal need, which when institutionalized would have provided a clearly defined center of gravity. And yet, such a need did exist and its organizational impact was constantly increasing during the 1930s and the 1940s. This was the need for a burial place.

Although by and large nonreligious—and in some cases even opposed to religion in principle—the Ashkenazi immigrants to Latin America never jettisoned the obligation to secure a traditional burial place for themselves. The adherence to this very basic religious precept was almost universal and created a heavy demand for the services of an institution which otherwise was quite marginal in a young immigrant community. This phenomenon reached its most extreme expression in the case of the Montivideo Jewish Communists, who although alienated from Jewish traditions and constantly at odds with the other segments of the community, chose to establish a burial place of their own rather than use the general municipal funeral services.

The acquisition of a burial place required many supported affiliates and involved many hardships. The purchase of land, mainly by means of borrowed money, the procuring of the necessary permits, sometimes in the face of opposition by neighbors and politicians as was the case in Buenos Aires, required capable leadership. When it had the skill and the luck to keep a monopoly on such a universally wanted service, it was in command of an important source of communal revenues. The large incomes which the leaders of the Buenos Aires *Hevrah Kadisha Ashkenazit* (The Ashkenazi Burial Society) derived from fees were only a fraction of their actual expenses. Once their debts had been repaid they could then patronize other communal institutions. Thus the burial society emerged as a multi-service organization on its way to becoming a *Kehila* (Community). As such it became an attractive target for a leadership concerned with the community as a whole. Before the Holocaust era was over, the Jewish political parties in Buenos Aires made every effort possible to conquer this previously marginal institution by democratic means, and partly succeeded in doing so.[21]

A similar trend was discernible in other Ashkenazi communities, without, however, the same results. Santiago de Chile, where actually two Ashkenazi burial societies were formed, reveals a reverse tendency. The other communities on the continent can be classified with reference to the above two patterns, depending on the importance of contributions made by the burial society to other services. But even the Buenos Aires burial society, which in 1941 officially changed its name to *Asociacion Mutual Israelita Argentine (AMIA)* (Jewish Argentinian Mutual [Help] Association), did not reach the phase of a united multi-service *Kehila* during the Holocaust era. This would occur only later.

Like the ACIS, the AMIA too participated in the establishment of the umbrella organization. The attack on the Jewish people called for national unity and all the organizations in Argentina—communal, educational, welfare and economic—confederated into one united front—the DAIA. In Chile such an institution was already earlier in existence and it was being established in many other Latin American countries during the Holocaust era. The only exception to this general accord were the Communist-inspired organizations; they organized rivaling popular organizations against anti-Semitism.[22]

Internal strife thus accompanied the effort to defend the Jewish cause almost from its beginning and was propagated by the constantly diversifying political leadership.

The Parties

Political ideals and loyalties made their appearance in Latin America practically with the first immigrants. A group of colonists in one of Baron de Hirsch's settlements greeted Theodor Herzl and the first Zionist Congress in 1897. The second Zionist Congress of 1898 was attended by an Argentinian Zionist delegate. In 1901 a salute was sent to the founding Congress also from Brazil's northeastern region of the Amazon. From that time, Zionism became a fixture in Argentinian and Brazilian Jewish life. The issuance of the Balfour Declaration provided the opportunity for the unveiling of Chilean Zionism. The communal nuclei there were disguised until November 1917 as *Filarmónica Rusa* ("Russian Philharmonic") or *Centro Macedonia* ("Macedonian Center"). In 1919 they proudly congregated in their first local Zionist Congress and founded the *Federación Sionista* (Zionist Federation) as the representative umbrella organization for all Chilean Jews—a unique phenomenon in Latin America and possibly also elsewhere.

In Uruguay, Mexico, and Cuba, where a considerable Jewish presence had been established before the 1930s, immigrant Zionists began to organize and raise money for the Zionist cause almost as soon as they got settled. During the 1920s Latin-American Zionists contributed to Keren Ha-Yesod more than many other Zionists of older, larger, and wealthier communities: Argentina surpassed Holland by a small margin and donated more than twice the sum which Austrian Zionists did; Brazil gave only a little less than France: Chilean Zionists raised more than their Italian and Swiss colleagues; Cuba outdid Turkey, and Mexico equaled Hungary.[23] Moreover during the 1920s Zionists of several Latin-American countries developed a party system which developed further between 1933 and 1945. First and foremost in this process was Argentinian Jewry. We should therefore look into its experience in order to compare it later with that of other communities.

The Argentinian Experience

The original Zionist Federation in Argentina was composed of small groups, whose rivalry was based on personal or other nonideological issues. As early as 1906, and especially from 1920 onward, it was confronted by a dynamic *Poalei Zion* (Workers of Zion) party, which expanded its membership and influence during the 1930s and the 1940s. The tension between these two parties was due not so much to ideological or class differences as to the organizational predominance of the *Federación,* which was actually the General Zionist party. As the first organized party, whose hand was still on top at the time, the Federation was in charge of the two national funds (Keren Ha-Yesod and Keren Ha-Kayemet) and drew its own budget, at least in part, from the former's income; the proletarian Zionists simply claimed their share. The struggle between them was frequently brought to the attention of the central authorities of the World Zionist Organization. The remedy suggested, the formation of a United Local Zionist organization, was slowly and partly being implemented during the war years as both parties were hammered by their common adversaries both on the left and on the right. These were the Leftist Poale Zion on the one hand, and the Revisionists on the other.

The Poale Zion (Left) supporters were attracted to Soviet Russia to the point that they seceded from the Zionist Organization in 1921 and did not return until 1939; symbolically they adopted the spelling of Yiddish which was in use in Russia following a deliberate decision to erase the Hebrew forms from it. Nonetheless they still maintained their Zionist loyalties and tried to reconcile these two rivaling ideologies. Much of the energies of the Leftist Poale Zion were dedicated to the younger generation and they became most influential thanks to the school network they promoted in the early 1930s, which was a cause of their return to the mainstream of communal life. The Revisionist Party, founded in Argentina in 1930, was not integrated in the organizational structure of Argentine Zionists, but subscribed to its fundamental doctrines all the same.

"The formation of the various parties is not based upon the social structure of South American Jewry but is much more an import from Europe, and is thus based on abstract ideology"—so wrote in 1941 A. S. Juris, himself a member of Poale Zion, who as an official delegate of the Zionist movement and a long-time visitor of the Latin American communities was thoroughly acquainted with the Zionist political parties. Nonetheless other differences existed between the parties' membership as did between their leadership as well. "The majority of the members of the Federation are old or belong to a generation bygone," thus testified another emissary of the Zionist movement, Abraham Mibashan, who belonged to the General Zionists.[24] Thus, newly "imported" ideologies and leaders who immigrated in the 1920s might have spurred the interests of the more alert oldtimers as well as some younger, second-generation Argentines, and might have encouraged the leading elements among them to undertake responsibilities in the "younger" parties. Some of the Poalei Zion leaders, both on the right and left flanks of that fragmented party conformed to this pattern as did José Mirelman, the wealthy industrialist and banker, who was the most outstanding leader of the Revisionist Party.

The Jewish agricultural colonies, the socioeconomic element of Argentinian Jewry which marks its uniqueness, provided leaders for almost all Jewish parties and thus corroborated Juris's assertion. It might well be determined that the differences between those who distinguished themselves in the Zionist parties, both as "leftists" and "rightists," and those who were active in the anti-Zionist parties derived from their Jewish experience rather than from their common colonist background.

The Zionist movement in Argentina included some nonpartisan organizations as well. First among them was the local branch of the Women's International Zionists Organization—WIZO—which since its inception in 1926, was engaged in intensive fund-raising campaigns for Palestine, and in educational work for its affiliates. Autonomous, governed by a leadership which rose from the rank-and-file membership in the local chapters, the women of the Zionist movement became, in the words of Nathan Bistritzky, "the model Zionist organization, from the point of view of its administrative capability and of the energy displayed in its day to day activities."[25]

Another nonpartisan Zionist organization was the *Centro Sionista Sefaradi* (Sephardi Zionist Center). Founded in 1933 and nominally affiliated with the Zionist Federation, it served as the meeting place for Zionist activists of all non-Ashkenazi communities. The impetus to work on behalf of Zionist goals was innate in the traditional Judaism common to the members of these communities; Jerusalem, the spiritual and the physical, was its cornerstone. Still, the actual organizational work depended on some individuals who were Zionists before their immigration to Argentina, and wanted to see the Sepharadim taking their appropriate share in the Jewish national movement. Such were David Elnecave, the experienced Ladino journalist from Turkey and Bulgaria, Abraham Moni, the main inspirer of the *Centro,* who came to Buenos Aires after he had been an active Zionist in Istanbul, and Ezra Teubal, the president of the Aleppo community, and one of the richest Jews in Argentina, who served several times as Chairman of the Keren Ha-Yesod Campaign and inspired his fellow Sephardim to increase their donations for Palestine and for the rescue of persecuted Jews. Undoubtedly, the involvement of the non-Ashkenazi communities in Zionism increased during the years of the Holocaust.[26]

A third group of nonpartisan affiliated Zionists were the Central European immigrants. Impressed by their recent experiences under Hitler, many older Zionists found their beliefs reaffirmed, and promptly set up a Zionist milieu for themselves. Other immigrants who were never Zionists found it difficult to reconcile themselves with the loss of their German citizenship. Some were attracted to Zionism but others resisted it without being able, for a while, to provide themselves with any other viable ideology. Leaders, like Hardi Swarsensky, who founded the Zionist inspired *Jüdische Wochenschau* (Jewish Weekly) helped the German-speaking Zionists to organize. Parallel to the Jewish Cultural Association *Jüdische Kultur Gemeinschaft)*, which was shared by all the German-speaking immigrants, German Zionist circles, Bar Kochba associations, and others developed their specific activities. It was only later, at the close of the Holocaust era, that they were slowly drawn into mainstream Argentinian Zionism.

Zionism was not the only political factor in Argentina. Opposed to it were the anti-Zionist proletarian parties: the Bund and the Communists, who did not lag far behind. The first time a Jewish-organized group paraded with its red banners decorated with Yiddish slogans in Hebrew characters was the workers' demonstration of May 1, 1906. Jewish members of the Russian revolutionary movement and Bundists who escaped from the onslaught of the Czarist regime after the failure of the 1905 Revolution, and from the pogroms which ensued, became active in the Argentinian anarchist and socialist parties. In 1909 one of them, Simon Radowitzy, assassinated the Buenos Aires police commander, Colonel Ramon Falcón, in revenge for the assassination of anarchist demonstrators earlier that year.

After the Bolshevik Revolution the lines were drawn and Bundists and Communists established separate parties, although many Bundists joined the Communists. These became part of the Argentinian Communist Party but maintained their Jewish political, cultural, and educational societies. From 1920 onward they intensified their efforts to dominate the principle institutions of the Ashkenazi community.

With the apparent failure of the Zionist enterprise, as manifested by the slow pace of immigration and settlement there and by the 1929 riots, the Communists' drive created a dangerous challenge to the Zionists. Many elections in cultural institutions like the *Hebraca,* in economic corporations like the Jewish banks and peddlers' cooperatives, as well as in communal institutions like the Ashkenazi burial society, stood under the spell of that political conflict. During the 1930s it became even more violent. Biro-Bidjan, the Jewish "land" in the Far Eastern part of the USSR, was presented as a serious alternative to Palestine and an allegedly nonpolitical fund PROCOR (founded in 1924), was being increasingly supported by many well meaning non-Communists. In 1932 and later small groups of emigrants left Argentina to settle in the "promised" Soviet Jewish republic.[27] The Nazi attack on Communism and on the Jewish people in the late 1930s marked the peak of the leftists' influence. With Palestine convulsed in riots (1936-1939) and the capitalist powers' appeasement policy—the Jewish cause seemed to be definitely interwoven with that of the USSR. Liberal and leftist Argentinian parties, allied with the Jewish leftists, seemed to offer sound support for the Jewish cause which the Zionists could not acquire. However, the Molotov-Ribbentrop agreement melted away much of the nonaffiliated support for the leftists and the two years of the Hitler-Stalin pact (August 1939-June 1941) marked a clear decline in their activities. But as soon as the USSR became a member of the Grand Alliance, the prestige of the Jewish Communists was restored. The initial losses of the Red Army and its subsequent victories made a tremendous impression on public opinion. The resulting emotional response and generous donations benefited the leftists' political standing.

The Jewish Communists did not act only through one body. Much of their work was channeled through cultural and welfare organizations, some of which were not even openly connected with their cause. In 1933, they organized the popular defense committee against anti-Semitism, in open competition with the DAIA, and gained the support of some liberal intellectuals. Typical of that situation was the position adopted by one of the two Yiddish dailies, which appeared in Buenos-Aires *Di Presse* (The Press). Owned by its workers and run as a cooperative, it included among its staff members some of the non-Communist leftists along with others who were active members of the Party. *Di Presse* adopted the USSR's system of Yiddish spelling and did not drop it until the 1950s.

Pre-World War I proletarian immigrants and newcomers of the 1920s were not the only elements which provided the Jewish Communists with their membership and activists; some came from the agricultural colonies as well. Estranged from their Jewish environment, and attracted by Argentinian politics, they adopted positions more radical than those accepted by the Socialist Party. While in leading positions, they shared the political work with their Jewish urban comrades who, like some of them, were in the professions or industry. The economic boom boosted many of them into the middle classes without changing their beliefs.

Brazil and Other Republics

Argentina, the largest Latin-American Jewish community, had also the most developed political structure. Brazil, the second largest community, was developing on almost identical lines when the dictatorial regime of President Getulio Vargas forced it to a halt. In August 1938, a governmental decree outlawed any foreign political affiliation. Although its primary purpose was to cut the intensive organizational ties which linked the large German and Italian communities with the Fascist and Nazi regimes, the leaders of the Zionist Federation realized that a policy of pretending that the law did not apply to them might ultimately result in disaster. They preferred to appeal for an official permission to continue their work, presenting themselves as a charitable institution. Their request was not met with favor. Contemporary critics regarded their reaction to the decree as inappropriate and disproportionately severe, the result of a momentary panic.[28] But whether the effort to adapt to the new realities by legal means was justified or not, the results of the new law, as well as of the political atmosphere created by it, were that Jewish political life was forced either to stagnate or go underground. Visible leadership in both cases became a risk.

The situation was further aggravated when the government prohibited the publication of all non-Portuguese newspapers. The Yiddish press in Brazil, along with the German and Italian and others, was doomed. Efforts to obtain a license for a publication of a Jewish paper in Portuguese failed, and then in April 1943, on top of the other hardships, came the difficulty of importing Yiddish papers from Argentina.

Under these circumstances Zionist, as well as anti-Zionist, activities were badly hampered for the duration of the war. Relief and rescue campaigns had to be disguised and their products sent abroad under a variety of ruses. Moreover, for the very appeal to ease these limitations, Brazilian Jewry had to rely, at least partly, on intervention from abroad.[29]

Contrary to the situation in Brazil, Jewish political life in Uruguay took its natural course, developing in a way much similar to Argentina if on a much smaller and more modest scale. "To begin with there is the low economic standard of the Jewish masses in Montevideo. Uruguay has suffered all the mishaps but none of the prosperity which the war has brought to all the other countries of South America." These were the impressions that Baruch Zuckerman brought back from his visit to Uruguay as late as mid-1943, after he had visited Chile, Argentina, and several other republics. The Zionist parties were poorly organized and even the more affluent General Zionists had to be helped in 1940 by Buenos Aires in order to pay the rent of their premises. The Leftists were better organized and strong enough, by democratic means, to conquer the Jewish bank in the late 1930s. Their political downfall in the community was precipitated by the bankruptcy which the bank suffered in 1940 while under their management. The proximity of Buenos Aires made it possible for the local developing leadership to be helped by its more advanced Argentinian counterpart.[30]

Cuba and Mexico, the other sizable communities in Latin America, had an essentially similar political structure to that of Argentina. In Cuba, the political differences among the Zionists were less developed than in Argentina, while the "Reds" were more powerful. The Sepharadim there and in Mexico kept aloof from the Ashkenazi political system, but as was the case in Argentina, there were a few alert leaders, like Victor Mitrani in Mexico, and others, who desperately urged them to organize and participate in Zionist work and in the relief and rescue of their suffering brethren in Europe.[31]

In Mexico, a relatively harmonious political atmosphere prevailed among the Ashkenazim, symbolized until 1941 by its school system. It was in that year that a sensitive equilibrium between Zionists of all shades and Bundists—a harmony which made existence of one large day school possible—erupted into a bitter rift which ended with the establishment of two new, more Zionist-oriented schools. In spite of the quarrels, Bundists and other Leftists were not ostracised and prominent intellectuals of Bundist tendency, including Tuvie Meisel and Avraham Golomb, were to be found in key positions in the otherwise Zionist-dominated community. Extreme leftists were few and far between and their influence was quite limited. Within the Zionist camp, all the factions which were found in Argentina, were also in existence in Mexico by 1940. But there another Zionist party made its appearance in 1939—the Mizrachi—which was vigorously led by the Rabbi of the Ashkenazi community, Shlomo David Rafalin.[32]

A Mizrachi Party was also established in Chile by Rabbi Ilya Maguenzo, but Jewish political life in this country was even less turbulent than in Mexico. Party struggles within the Zionist Federation were never a major issue. Despite the presence of some Leftist-oriented Jews as well as of

Revisionists, their ideas were expressed through journalism or literary organizations rather than through political activities.[33]

An even more nonpolitical atmosphere prevailed in the smaller communities of Venezuela, Peru, Colombia, and Ecuador. Zionism existed there more as a latent feeling, but no political organization was initiated until called for by outside forces. A. S. Juris, the special delegate of the Keren Ha-Yesod, was instrumental in that development, reporting in 1941: "In Bolivia, Peru, Equador, Colombia and Venezuela I founded united Zionist organizations, composed mainly of Poalei Zion and General Zionists. For juridical and tactical reasons these Federations are Departments for Zionist affairs of the communities. This is an ideal form and it means that the community as such considers the work of Zionism as its obligation."[34]

And indeed that was what the leaders of the communities felt and what Morris D. Waldman, the vice chairman of the executive committee of the American Jewish Committee, found out when he visited several countries in Latin American in 1944. "Because of their Eastern-European background they virtually all take Jewish Nationalism for granted. . . . They are virtually all Zionists and they welcomed the privilege of contributing to the Keren Ha-Yesod and the Keren Ha-Kayemet and other Zionist movements." So he reported to his colleagues, in November 1944. "If there is a non-Zionist in these parts he wouldn't dare reveal his views because he would be torn limb from limb" Waldman wrote to John Slawson of the American Jewish Committee in a private letter from Peru.[35]

These remarks—and the very visits themselves—were related to another pattern of Latin American Jewish leadership—the "imported" one.

The International Agencies

Welfare Institutions

Latin-American Jewry benefited from foreign Jewish support almost from its very inception. In 1891 Baron de Hirsch set up his Jewish Colonization Association (JCA) in London and its large settlement project in Argentina virtually opened the Latin-American continent for Jewish mass immigration. From then until the conquest of Paris by Hitler in 1940, the instructions of its leaders, as dispatched from Paris, were executed through JCA's directors in Buenos Aires.

The vital process of building the farmer class, and during the Holocaust era the settling of refugees, was thus led from the outside. No direct participation of local Jewry in the decision-making process was allowed until well after World War II.

Nevertheless, along with its bureaucratic structure and strictly centralized administration in colonization matters, the JCA provided Argentinian Jewry with an important segment of communal leadership. It fostered education, immigrant help, and after 1933 contributed to the counterattack on the anti-Semitic press campaign. Its personnel, both in Buenos Aires and in the provinces, undertook leading positions as individuals—a phenomenon which should be regarded as an indirect contribution of the very presence of the JCA.

In 1903, the JCA started its colonization project in Brazil, which was extended in 1910, and renewed when World War I was over. During the 1930s a new effort was made to expand the Jewish colonies, this time in direct relation to the emergencies caused by the Nazi persecution. Since the 1920s the JCA had been helping urban Brazilian Jewry to consolidate its communal structure by sending there Rabbi Isaia Rafaelovitch. Immigrants' relief work was one of Rabbi Rafaelovitch's main tasks, as it was the JCA's throughout South America from the beginning of the interwar period.

Contrary to its policy in settlement matters, it preferred to carry out the immigration work through local agencies which were encouraged to develop their own activities. When the Holocaust era began, JCA employees, working on behalf of HICEM—the combined immigrants' aid society—were active in Argentina, Brazil, and Uruguay. During the 1930s they expanded their activity to Chile, Peru, and Colombia as well. Local people were called upon in all these communities to assume responsibilities in aiding refugee immigrants; their work was financed and guided, at least partly, from the outside by HICEM.

The increasing tide of refugee immigration to Latin America strained HICEM's financial and administrative resources even before the war broke out. With the Nazi invasion of France, a dramatic change occurred when HICEM's and JCA's central leaders became themselves refugees and had to beg, at least in the case of some of their members, to be admitted as immigrants to Argentina.[36]

On the other edge of the Latin-American continent two other communities were helped in the initial stages of their consolidation by "imported" leadership: Mexico and Cuba. In 1924, when several thousands of immigrants were stranded in Havana and Mexico City on what they believed was their path to the United States, the Emergency Committee on Jewish

Refugees from New York and the B'nai Brith Order, took action to help settle them permanently in these countries. The work was conducted by special American envoys who helped local activists use the funds, which were made available, in order to promote mutual help and relief institutions. A similar action was to be repeated on a minor scale by the American Joint Distribution Committee (JDC) late in the 1930s and during the first years of World War II.[37]

This phenomenon was at that time even more dominant in other countries where Central European Jews arrived. Not too long after Adolfo Hirsch and his colleagues in Buenos Aires had established the *Hilfsverein Deutschsprechender Juden* they turned to the JDC for funds, as did the other nuclei of German-speaking Jews almost all over Latin America. In order to regulate these demands, in March 1939 the JDC sent out two representatives to examine the situation in each country: David Glick, who acted in 1937–1938 as a special delegate of the JDC to Germany to help Jewish emigration, and Friedrich Borchardt, a former director of the *Reichsvertretung der Deutschen Juden* (Reich Representation of German Jews). They traveled to all the South American capitals, checked the activities and accounts of all the existing committees, "refreshed" some of them with new leadership, and advised the JDC headquarters in New York about the kind and amount of help which was needed in each case.[38] Further contacts and agreements with HICEM led to an intensive coordination in the refugee relief work, in which the JDC had a leading role. "The initial efforts of the JDC were largely in the area of direct relief. As the economic conditions of the Jewish refugees improved . . . the program changed with an emphasis on rehabilitation. . . . In line with its traditional policy, the JDC has sought, as far as possible, to utilize existing agencies and facilities. Only when absolutely inevitable did it create new organizations. . . . whether old or new, however, the various agencies have flourished through the impetus given to them by JDC's funds, by frequent consultations with its New York office and more importantly by the extended periodic visits of qualified American social-workers who worked with the committees locally." The author of this report, Louis Sobel, was one of these social workers who in fact stayed in Latin America some eight months. According to the JDC's figures, between 1936 and 1944 it spent some $2.9 million in the countries south of the U.S.A. on a large variety of projects which extended from cash support in most countries, vocational retraining in Havana, and credit cooperative in Quito to youth organizations in Bolivia and Ecuador.[39]

The full impact of JDC's and HICEM's work in Latin America has yet to be investigated, but there is no doubt that this "imported" welfare leadership, which manifested itself through consultations rendered by visiting trained social workers and leaders, fostered local leadership for the welfare organizations. The immediate task of all factors involved was to help the refugees who arrived from the "Holocaust Kingdom."

Political Organizations

The party system of Latin-American Jewry was no less influenced by this "imported" leadership. "Our community is still young, it has not as yet authoritative people to guide it and we lack also close links with the wide Jewish world"—thus wrote in, December 1938, Zeev Nijenson and Jacob Bronfman, the president and the secretary of the Zionist Federation of Argentina, the oldest political organization on the continent. They were asking for a delegate of the World Zionist Organization to come to Argentina for a long visit "to influence and give orientation to our new community."[40] These two leaders were not the only ones to feel the necessity for outside guidelines. Visits by prominent leaders from abroad served as a focal point of local political activity and attention. Some of these visitors stayed long enough to permanently influence the local political scene.

The lack of available material concerning the "leftist" parties compels us to leave open the question of the impact which well known visitors (such as the famous Bundist and later Communist leader Gina Medem, who visited Argentina in 1936), had on the development of their leadership. The Bund and the Leftist Poalei Zion had their own visitors from Poland in 1930, in 1931, and later. The living experience of the major proletarian parties in the Jewish world, which was transmitted on these occasions, must have exerted some influence on their membership as well as upon their leaders. More exact information, however, does exist regarding the Zionist organizations.

The role of A. S. Juris, the Keren Ha-Yesod emissary, in setting up Zionist "departments" has already been noted. He visited Latin America several times after his first visit in 1925 and spent almost the entire war there. Juris crossed the continent from South to North, visited the most remote towns in Colombia, Equador, Venezuela, Uruguay, where Jews were to be found, in many cases inspiring them to set up their local organizations. Leib Jaffe, a highly placed Zionist leader and member of the executive board of Keren Ha-Yesod, was also long-time visitor to Latin America. As early as 1923, when he came back from his first mission to Latin American Jewry, he requested that more should be done to educate and promote local political leadership. He returned to Mexico during the fall of 1941, and then to South

America where he spent most of 1942. In his capacity as senior authority in Zionist circles, Jaffe helped forge unity in Argentina and mitigate personal rivalries in Chile. His meetings with the presidents and ministers of Colombia and Peru brought added prestige to local communal leadership. In all countries he taught Zionist leaders new and improved techniques in fund-raising as well as in attracting members.[41]

Other Zionist leaders who were sent to Latin America acted along similar lines. While their principal effort was dedicated to fund raising, much of their aim was to raise the consciousness of the people, which they did by taking an active part in local politics and conflicts. Nathan Bistrizki, who served Latin America Zionism as a traveling leader from 1941 to 1946, constantly demanded that "imported" leadership should be applied more systematically and widely. He ended his service by drawing up a comprehensive program for that purpose, the most outstanding feature of which was the suggestion to engage envoys for long-term missions.[42]

Abraham Mibashan and Adolfo Arditi actually answered this demand. Mibashan was sent to Argentina in 1936 for 18 months, returned to Jerusalem, and was sent out again in 1939 as a permanent representative of Keren Ha-Yesod. Mibashan served officially in this capacity until September 1947 and was active later in other official Zionist positions. He became a citizen of the Argentine Republic and died in Buenos Aires a well known communal leader. Adolfo Arditi, the main Zionist Sephardi emissary, served the movement in Latin America from 1941 to 1945 and then settled in Mexico, where he became one of the leading intellectuals of the Sephardic community.

The contribution of each one of these "imported" leaders to the development of local political leadership has still to be investigated, but there is no doubt that the history of Zionism in Latin America during the Holocaust era was greatly influenced by them.

While the desirability of a long-term mission as evidenced in the cases of Mibashan and Arditi might be questionable from an Zionist ideological point of view, a similar mission entrusted to another Zionist by the World Jewish Congress (WJC), was not liable to be criticized from that institution's ideological point of view. Jacob Hellman, one of the founders of the WJC and member of its executive, who lived in Palestine, made his mission to Buenos Aires in 1939 a lifelong task. Contrary to the Zionist "imported" leadership, which was called on to serve existing political institutions, his mission was to create a new political organization. This task was facilitated by his long-time affiliation with Poalei Zion, his kinship with the Polish Jewish Diaspora and by the existing good will toward the WJC in the South

American Jewish communities. But his struggle to institutionalize these sympathies in the form of a dominant organization, was liable to conflict with other established institutions. Despite this, Hellman managed to provide the WJC with a foothold in Argentina which, in turn, served as a center of gravity for the Latin-American communities and influenced their political affiliations during World War II and thereafter.[43]

Jacob Hellman was not the only officer of the WJC in Latin America. Kate Knopfmacher, an old-time activist of the WJC from Belgium, who escaped through Spain to the Western Hemisphere, opened in 1941 another office in Mexico City. This office served the whole of Central America and expanded its responsibilities in 1943 to cover Venezuela and Columbia too.[44] Both offices were helped in their work by annual visits by the principal leaders of the WJC. Nahum Goldman, the chairman of its Administrative Committee visited Latin American countries in 1940 and again in 1941. Rabbi Issac Alkalay, former chief Rabbi of Yugoslavia, went there in 1942; Baruch Zuckerman, member of the executive committee and one of the main leaders of Poalei Zion in the U.S.A., worked in Latin America in 1943; professor Arieh Tartakover one of the founders of the WJC traveled there in 1944, and Victor Mitrani, the Sephardi Zionist leader from Mexico, visited Central America several times. Two major conferences were convened during the War, one in Baltimore in November 1941, and the other in Atlantic City in November 1944. Each of these gatherings served as an incentive for the formation of local leaderships and as encouragement for already active leaders.

The immediate task of Jacob Hellman and Kate Knopfmacher, as well as of all the emissaries and affiliates of the WJC, was to direct all the funds that were designated for Latin-American relief and rescue toward the WJC's relief work. This effort brought the WJC into an open conflict with the JDC, which regarded relief to the victims of the War as its exclusive domain since its establishment during World War I. It also infringed upon the Zionist campaigns, which were based on similar motives of rescue and relief through Palestine.[45]

A clash between Leib Jaffe and Nahum Goldman was barely avoided in July 1941 in Mexico when both arrived to conduct their own campaigns there. "The Zionists and I did not like the way Goldman spoke in his speech about Keren Ha-Yesod and the Jewish Congress. He spoke about two equal campaigns. . . . We always knew that we must strengthen the Jewish people, in strengthening them we strengthen Palestine. . . . But Palestine was the crown of all Jewish work. Now we are getting two equal crowns." From the other end of Latin America Mibashan reported that the almost unanimous adherence of the local Zionist leaders to the cause of the World Jewish Congress endangered the primacy of Zionism, and at the same time threatened to draw the Zionist movement into the struggle between the WJC and the JDC.[46]

But these differences between the two international organizations (and between members of the same Zionist party like Jacob Hellman and Leib Jaffe) were easily overcome in face of the strange alliance which was formed between the JDC and the Jewish Communists of Argentina in 1940. In line with their constant opposition to Zionism and to Jewish nationalism, and estranged from the Jewish community because of their support of the Soviet Union even when it was in alliance with Hitler, the Leftists decided to launch a relief and rescue campaign of their own using the slogan of "direct aid." They approached the JDC early in 1940 with the suggestion to transmit their funds to it for relief work in Europe. The JDC, which at Hellman's instigation was denied any influence on, or share in, the united campaign which had been proclaimed in a large conference in December 1939, accepted the Communists' offer. It was thus exposed to the most severe accusation of being direct collaborators with the "Leftist renegades."[47]

The struggle that was waged between the two international Jewish organizations was won in Argentina by the WJC and apparently with great ease. The JDC could count there only on the support of the still marginal German-speaking organizations, the moral adherence of the representatives of the ORT and OSE (the two other international Jewish organizations which had their differences with Jacob Hellman) to the leaders of the HICEM sponsored SOPROTIMIS, and with a small though rich and influential group of important donors, many of whom were members of the Congregacion. The most outstanding of these was the rich industrialist Simon Mirelman. They all accepted the JDC's basic contention that relief work should be regarded as its exclusive domain and that the WJC should content itself with its political activities.

In 1942, long after the JDC's uneasy alliance with the Communists was over, these elements congregated and proclaimed an independent campaign under the leadership of Simon Mirelman. This prestigious and experienced communal figure led the United Zionist campaign on several occasions and was an active participant in communal and national affairs. Although he presented a most serious challenge to Jacob Hellman's authority, his efforts did not undermine the position of the WJC.[48]

The political leadership of the community, united in the DAIA, shared the WJC's fundamental belief that during the Holocaust political action meant rescue which was itself inextricably linked with relief. Consequently the need arose for an independent fund, administered by a democratically elected leadership, as the WJC was believed to be, and allocated according to Jewish national considerations. This support strengthened Jacob Hellman's fund-raising policies. But as his internal correspondence with Baruch Zuckerman and Arieh Tartakover reveals, he recognized the fact that the relief fund—even more than actual rescue work—played a dominant role in consolidating the WJC's position as the representative body of the Jewish people. According to him the WJC owed its central position in Latin-American Jewish life to this fund-raising campaign. Political activity alone would never have done it. His arguments became more emotional and bitter when he found out that Baruch Zuckerman, in the wake of his visit to South America, and in view of the almost universal recognition of the JDC's leading role in the field of relief, was adopting a more conciliatory attitude toward the JDC. According to Hellman, reconciliation was impossible, at least in Latin America.[49]

The conflict between the JDC and the WJC extended throughout Latin America, as the JDC endeavored to organize its followers wherever it could. In 1943 it opened a permanent office in Buenos Aires and sent Jacob Lightman there to serve as its regional co-director. The hope to overcome WJC's supremacy was not lost, at least not with some of the main JDC's supporters in the U.S.A. When Louis Sobel, an emissary of the JDC, suggested in a report on Colombia that some understanding and coordination with the WJC should be sought, Max Gottschalk, the head of HICEM, denounced this suggestion as the product of sheer ignorance and categorically ruled out any collaboration with the WJC. His hope was that JDC and HICEM would discover in Latin America a new and independent leadership which could be encouraged to compete with the WJC-dominated forces.[50]

This hope was shared by another North American agency which began its open involvement in Latin America as the war drew to its close, the American Jewish Committee (AJC).

Its interest in and its activity on behalf of Latin American communities was not new. In May 1931, when anti-Semitic agitation endangered the Jewish community in Mexico, the AJC sent a special agent there who intervened on their behalf and then reported on the situation in detail. The same happened from time to time later and the AJC used its easy access to the State Department officials to help the Jewish communities in their plight. In 1937, the AJC considered establishing a permanent representation in some part of Latin America. Memoranda to that effect were submitted by some experts and gained the initial support of at least some of the Committee's leaders. But such an agency was not brought into existence at that time. It was only later in 1943 that a decision was taken and in April 1944 the AJC was still seeking a suitable Jewish intellectual to serve as its permanent representative. When such a person was found, and all the practical details were straightened out, the war was over. The history of the official work of the AJC in Latin America belongs therefore to the post-Holocaust era.[51]

Nevertheless through its close relationship with the JDC, and with the Jewish Telegraphic agency headed by Jacob Landau, who had served in Mexico since 1943, the AJC was constantly active in Latin-American Jewish affairs. In 1944 it sent the vice chairman of its executive committee, Morris D. Waldman, on an extensive tour to the most important Jewish communities. His findings and suggestions attested to the kind of "imported" leadership which the AJC had indirectly been providing until then and which it intended to provide thereafter openly: "If any good public relations work can be done in these communities it can only be left in the hands of a small number of men, most if not all of whom, are not actively associated with the Central Committee [of the Jewish Communities]. Though some of these men are Zionists they are of the type who are not in sympathy with the tactics of the World Jewish Congress and who could, without much difficulty be persuaded to take part in a group that would cooperate with the American Jewish Committee." A limited, carefully selected leadership, influential by virtue of its own merits (and by implication not by virtue of the support of the masses), and disassociated from the communal umbrella organization— that was the image of the leadership to be promoted by the American Jewish Committee. Its task would not only be to intervene effectively on behalf of the Jewish community but "on the basic theory underlying the work of the American Jewish Committee, that security for Jews can only be guaranteed in a democratic world, fully as much if not greater consideration must be given to the bigger job of reinforcing wherever we can the democratic forces in Latin America."[52]

This was of course a task for Jewish leadership which greatly exceeded what the other Jewish organizations thought proper for that historic moment. The conflict between the international agencies was thus far from being resolved as the Holocaust era drew to a close.

Patterns of Leadership

When Nathan Bistritzky sought ways to improve the local Zionist leadership his main suggestion was to enlarge and broaden the "imported" one. Morris Waldman, too, when outlining the future program for the AJC-sponsored local leaders, concluded by saying: "In order to do the job we must set up some sort of organization" which would include "a general representative who would travel south of the Rio Grande for a good part of the year and spend the necessary time in each of the countries." Three "public relations bodies" were envisaged, in Mexico City, São Paulo and Buenos Aires, which "shall be encouraged to employ professional executives."[53] Both Bistritzky and Waldman were thinking in terms of a paid professional leadership—and that was exactly what the "imported" leadership, whether engaged in political or in welfare activities, was.

This was diametrically opposed to the volunteer-based local leaderships, both communal and the political. All the decision-making positions in the political parties, the communities, the welfare institutions and even in most of the economic corporations were, as a principle, occupied by volunteers. Only technical aids, indispensable low-ranked administrators, were being paid. Issac Kaplan, the energetic and proud director of the agricultural cooperative in Entre Rios, Argentina, and later of the *Fraternidad Agraria* (Agrarian Fraternity), the nationwide confederation of the Jewish agricultural cooperatives, was an outstanding exception to that rule while serving as one of the leaders of the Jewish cooperative movement.[54]

Benjamin Mellibowsky, the long-time secretary of the immigrant aid organization SOPROTIMIS, was a leading personality in his field, second only to such leaders of this institution as Max Glucksman, a wealthy owner of movie houses, and others. But then Mellibowsky was an employee of HICEM and there was much more tolerance toward welfare personnel who, while earning wages, were in decision-making positions, than toward their opposite numbers in the political organizations.[55]

"I decided to quit my job as the secretary of the Zionist organization," thus wrote an embittered young and gifted Zionist activist in Mexico City to his friend, "for one—my salary is too large; for the other—the work is too small." Abraham Mibashan tried hard to broaden his tasks and even change his official appointment in order to avoid his exclusive dependence on Keren Ha-Yesod, which was administrated in Argentina by the local Zionist Federation. Referring to the possibility of expanding Zionist work through full-time activists, he observed "as I see from the attitudes towards myself, it is preferable that such employees should not be known as receiving their wages from the Zionist organization or from its funds. The very fact that he is a paid employee takes away from him the influence which a free independent position would have given him."[56]

The first characteristic of Latin-American Jewish leadership during the Holocaust era which emerges from this analysis so far is the *confrontation between voluntarism and professionalism.* The status of spiritual leadership exemplifies both this and another trait, which could be defined as *the layman republic.*

This study has already demonstrated the low status which the Ladino-speaking community of Buenos Aires assigned to its rabbinate, even when it employed a rabbi. When the Moroccan community of Buenos Aires debated that necessity in 1928, and its opponents argued that no religious authority was needed in a community whose members were accustomed to the nonobservance of the Sabbath and holidays and who served pork even at religious family ceremonies. On the other hand, the Aleppo community of Buenos Aires was strictly observant and vigorously led by its rabbis. The most famous of them, Rabbi Shaul Sithon Dabbah, was, in 1928, the author of a ban *(herem)* on conversions to Judaism in Argentina, which was endorsed by the chief Rabbis of Palestine, Meir Yaacov and Abraham Yitshak Kook, and which is still in effect today. The experience of the ACIS regarding religious leadership was thus flanked on both sides by the more and the less observant communities.[57] Nevertheless, all of them were synagogue-based congregations which regarded religion as the norm for their Jewish identity. One might therefore regard the experiences of these three Buenos Aires communities concerning spiritual leadership as patterns which mark the scale on which the rest of the non-Ashkenazic communities in Latin America could be placed.

Spiritual leadership fared considerably better in the German-speaking congregations. The difference stemmed, on the one hand, from the more central task assigned to the rabbi as a spiritual guide and preacher, rather than as a law interpreter, in the German-Jewish tradition. On the other hand, it was influenced by the availability of ordained rabbis among the refugee-immigrants who came to Latin America directly from leadership positions in Germany or Austria. When Rabbi Egon Löwenstein arrived in 1939 in Chile, Rabbi Israel Lubliner was already serving the Central-European immigrants in Santiago. Nevertheless, he was welcomed, and the B'nai Israel congregation, which was then in its initial phase, served as a home for them both.[58] As in Santiago, so in Buenos Aires, in São Paulo, Rio de Janeiro, and Montevideo—the rabbis, along with their lay colleagues, formed the core of the congregations' builders. However, the consolidation of the new communal organizations was barely achieved when the Holocaust era drew to its close. The impact of the German-speaking rabbis was thus confined at that time mainly to their own communities.

For the East European segment of Latin American Jewry, usually less synagogue-oriented, the issue of religious leadership was ever more complicated. If Rabbi Shlomo David Rafalin of Mexico City, and Ilya Magenzo of Santiago de Chile, distinguished themselves as active guides in religious and in internal political affairs for both the pious and the less observant, they were exceptions to the rule. The position of Rabbi Guillermo Schlesinger, who from 1937 served the oldest congregation of Buenos-Aires—*La Congregacion Israelita de la Republica Argentina* (The Jewish Congregation of the Argentine Republic)—was also unique. Drawing its membership from the more affluent strata of the Western and Eastern European Jews, this congregation adopted the French style of conservative Judaism and accordingly assigned a central role in its life to its rabbi, conferring on him the proud—but largely hollow—title of "Gran Rabino." The CIRA assumed a leadership role in many general communal affairs, of which education was the primary beneficiary. Acting on behalf of this body, Rabbi Schlesinger thus extended the scope of his own congregation to the point of participating several times in delegations dispatched to the authorities in political matters. Nevertheless the remainder of the Ashkenazi community, the East European majority, did not recognize his spiritual leadership, nor did it establish an authoritative rabbinate for itself. Rabbis were regarded as mere servicemen hired for specific ritual functions. Some were employed to supervise ritual slaughtering, but not by a public institution but rather by the butchers and meat tradesmen, who were interested in keeping losses stemming from defects to a minimum. Other employees included lay synagogue leaders and *Hevrah Kadisha* activists, who regarded spiritual leadership as completely secondary to the specific ritual functions which rabbis were called upon to dispense.[59]

Ashkenazi Brazil followed the Argentinian pattern even though it had the benefit of being served by Rabbi Ishaya Refaelovitch, who functioned as a spiritual guide, until 1934. When he left no other rabbi was appointed by the JCA or elected by the community. Uruguay and Peru kept pace with these major communities.

Thus, Latin-American Jewry did not possess a central spiritual leadership, as did British Jewry in its chief rabbinate; nor did rabbis occupy key positions in general, national, or continental organizations—as was the case of some prominent rabbis in the U.S.A. Its central representation was confined almost exclusively to laymen and was organized on a confederative basis which gave an equal vote to every institution.

The presidents of the DAIA in Argentina during the Holocaust era were Nicolas Rapoport (1935-1938), Moshe Kadoche (1938-1943) and Moshe Goldman (1943-1946), two physicians and a lawyer, within the non-Jewish society. Dr. Rapoport, the head of the Jewish Hospital, and Dr. Goldman, a well-known physician, had also the merit of being "Jewish Gauchos," sons of colonists whose childhood in rural Argentina made them thoroughly acquainted with the Argentinian mentality, which to a certain degree they not only adopted, but took great pride in. Moshe Kadoche, the lawyer, member of the old Moroccan community, had also an easy access to Argentinian society and that might have counterbalanced his ignorance of Yiddish and of the way of life that typified Ashkenazi Jews. Taken together, they represented an ever growing segment of the Jewish community but were still much different from most of the leaders of the organizations which were represented in the DAIA.[60]

The search for individuals capable of bridging the gap between the Jewish and host societies, coupled with the necessity of assigning an equal share to Sephardic communities wherever an umbrella organization existed, brought similar individuals in other countries into leadership positions. At the grass-roots level, leadership was obtained or wrangled by representatives of groups or by *caudillos* by means of the ballot in general assemblies. This was the channel for change which occurred either on intergenerational or on political grounds. During the Holocaust it was the way for the parties to assume control of some of the main institutions in the larger communities.

The third characteristic of Latin American Jewish leadership was the transplanted party leaders.

Much of the success of the "imported" political leaders in influencing and guiding their local colleagues was due to their common background. The short time which the Sephardi Zionist leaders spent in Argentina, before becoming the principal activists in the Sephardic Zionist organization, has been noted. Haim Finkelstein arrived in Argentina in 1930 as a young immigrant and almost immediately became a militant activist of the left Poalei-Zion party, on his way to becoming one of its major spokesmen. In Mexico, the much younger community, the brothers Leon and Elias Sourasky, who had immigrated during World War I, by the 1930s were among the most veteran Zionist activists.[61] The same was true for equally young communities and all the more so for the more recently established ones.

Both political differences and political leadership were thus brought into Latin America either by direct immigration of minor activists from the "old home," who ascended to more central positions in the immigrant setting, or by emissaries from abroad who recruited and guided local leaders. A systematic survey of youth organizations, carried out in 1942 in Argentina, indicated that the vast majority of their leaders were foreign-born and educated abroad.[62] If they did not represent the Jewish population of their age group, they nonetheless constituted the politically alert and organized youth of the community and therefore bear evidence to the characteristics of the older political activists.

Another trait of Jewish leadership in Latin America was its quality of a *leadership in ascendance.* Before World War II Latin America was regarded as a remote and unimportant province of World Jewry. This conception disappeared almost as soon as the war broke out. "At this hour, a special duty weighs upon our members and organizations in the countries where possibility for Zionist work does exist. A special place among them is assigned to the South American countries." This was the message sent to Buenos Aires from Jerusalem in October 1939. It coincided with a similar feeling espoused by local leaders. "The American Continent must now mobilize itself . . . and bring the Zionist work to a stage . . . in accord with the fateful situation of World Jewry at large and of Palestine in particular," wrote the Zionists of Mexico headed by Leo Dulzin.[63]

Leadership, resources, and fund-raising energies were invested into Latin America by the international Jewish agencies with much overlapping and disarray. The increasing wealth of the Jews brought tangible results. "Latin America has virtually saved the World Jewish Congress from dissolution. Latin America has furnished the Congress with the major part of its income," reported an angry Morris Waldman to his colleagues, of the AJC. The balance sheet of the WJC said it more calmly with figures: In 1943–44, Latin America gave the WJC $280,383, which formed only 18.5 percent of the total income of the WJC and the American Jewish Congress when taken together; but they formed 87.4 percent of the total receipts outside the United States . . .[64] the incomes of the Zionist national funds also multiplied dramatically.

This financial success also gave rise to an ever-intensifying call to help Latin American Jewry develop and improve its leadership. The predominant atmosphere of *nouveau-riche,* with its psychological and ideological implications, was the starting point for Bistritzky's proposals. Through his, Juris', and other emissaries' activities, part of his suggestions were actually being implemented. As the war drew on, local leadership became more aware of its own importance. This increased as the full tragedy of the Holocaust unfolded and a new position for Latin American Jewry became discernible.

While these changes were happening, the leaders of the communities, the political parties, and the local branches of the international agencies were called upon to do their part in the worldwide Jewish struggle for rescue and survival.

**Jewish Leadership and the Holocaust—
An Agenda for Further Research**

The assault on the Jewish people which started on January 30, 1933, and lasted until May 1945 called for organized Jewish reactions in at least five spheres of activity:

1. The resettlement of hundreds of thousands of refugees;
2. The political struggle against the Nazis and their declared or undeclared allies—the anti-Semites;
3. The extension of economic help to millions of Jews trapped under Nazi rule; and when the systematic and total annihilation had been put into effect;
4. The rescue of small groups or even individuals through diplomatic intervention and ransom;
5. Fund raising.

The fifth area of activity was indispensable for all four: it consisted of an intensive effort to raise the enormous sums of money needed in this tragic struggle which pitted the Jewish people—scattered, divided and organized only in *voluntary* associations—against one of the most powerful states of Europe.

What could Jewish leadership in Latin America have done in each sphere of activity? To what extent did the communities, the political organizations, and the international Jewish agencies use the opportunities of help which Latin America might have offered?

Definite answers to these questions are not available at this stage of our research. Before drawing any conclusions, one must first evaluate the degree to which Latin-American states could have helped the Jews as well as the actual achievements of Jewish leadership. So far only one of these fields—Jewish immigration—has been investigated and this in only one country, Argentina, albeit the most important.[65] With this exception we shall have to content ourselves here with only some preliminary observations as to the nature of Jewish activities related to the Holocaust as undertaken in Latin America.

Resettlement

The eventual importance of Latin America as a haven of refuge for persecuted Jews was dramatically emphasized during the Evian Conference in July 1938; 19 of the 31 countries which participated in that meeting were

Latin-American nations. As Henry Feingold and other scholars have clearly shown, high-ranking American officials repeatedly voiced the expectation that Latin America would bear the lion's share in any activity on behalf of the refugees.[66] Almost three years before Evian, James G. McDonald, the first High Commissioner for Refugees of the League of Nations, tried very hard to pursuade the Latin-American governments to accept small groups of highly trained professionals who were forced to escape from Germany. Accompanied by Professor Samuel Guy Inman, a distinguished authority on Latin American History and politics, he toured the continent from south to north in search of locations for his most skilled protégés. Much of the bitterness which he expressed in his open letter of resignation, written a few months later, resulted from this largely futile effort.[67]

In declining to accept large numbers of refugees, the Latin-American governments argued that their countries had no need for immigrants with an urban and middle-class background. A certain number of rural newcomers, on the other hand, were welcome, particularly if they were destined for agricultural settlement. Brazil explicitly reiterated this point in its law of immigration of 1937 as did Argentina in its respective regulations. Most representatives at the Evian Conference elaborated on this theme eloquently.[68]

To what extent did the Jewish organizations try to use these laws in order to resettle Jewish immigrants who came from a rural background or had been retrained for agriculture? Was anything done either to circumvent these regulations or to challenge them politically?

Schemes for agricultural settlements were proposed and to a certain degree inaugurated in Brazil, Chile, Bolivia, Ecuador, the Dominican Republic, and, on a much smaller scale, in Mexico. Many more projects in these and other countries were presented to the international Jewish agencies, mainly the JDC, the JCA, and HICEM. Several of those projects which were put into practice served as a cover for many more immigrants to come into these countries than the number of those who were actually settled. However, in order to evaluate the achievements of Jewish organizations in the context of the possibilities open to them, each project must be thoroughly examined on its own merits.

In Argentina, where some 40,000 Jewish immigrants managed to enter between 1933 and 1945, only several hundred were brought under the auspices of the JCA as settlers for its colonies. This association possessed at the time large assets in that country both in uncultivated lands and in financial resources. Nevertheless, an extremely cautious financial policy, pursued by its Paris-based Central Administration, coupled with deeply rooted settlement policies, adopted during the pre-Holocaust era, were among the main reasons, for the meager role played by agricultural colonies in Jewish immigration. The difficulties of finding in Central Europe, during the 1930s, genuine agriculturists who would accept the hardships of Argentinian rural life and abide by the rules set by the JCA contributed heavily to this loss of immigration opportunities.[69]

In contrast to the JCA's strictly legal approach to agricultural immigration, the immigrant aid society, SOPROTIMIS, backed by the JCA and partly supported by it through HICEM, adopted a more flexible attitude toward illegal Jewish immigrants. These refugees infiltrated into Argentina by crossing the border illegally from Uruguay, or else they stayed in the country after having entered legally with transit visas, allegedly on their way to Paraguay or Bolivia. They were helped financially as well as in their dealings with the police and immigration authorities. This help can in no way be considered an organized effort to bring in more refugees; nor could it cover, save in a few cases, the very large expenses needed for full legalization. Nonetheless, it provided encouragement to the many thousands who arrived in Argentina on their own and were looking for help. In October 1948, when an amnesty for illegal immigrants was decreed (and affected also those who came after the war, including many Nazis and non-German collaborators), SOPROTIMIS helped to legalize some 10,500 Jewish immigrants.[70]

In contrast to the welfare work undertaken on behalf of the immigrants by SOPROTIMIS and the *Hilfsverein* of the German-speaking Jews, Jewish leadership did very little in the political sphere to effect a change in the immigration regulations. At no time did this issue become a central motive in the activities of the political organizations. This phenomenon became unmistakably apparent when in July 1938, at the very time of the Evian Conference, information leaked out to the effect that new and extremely severe regulations were being prepared by the government. These rumors, in fact, soon became official policy which was immediately and retroactively enforced. The Jewish community and its political umbrella organization, DAIA, remained silent—as did all the political parties. They did not try to organize public protest or even send a delegation to appeal to the President of the Republic or some other highly placed authority.

How can we explain this passivity? Was it caused by a deeply rooted conviction that any such protest would be in vain? Did it originate from a general feeling that the immigration issue was being dealt with appropriately by the welfare organizations? Or was it symptomatic of the little importance attributed, even at that time, to the immigration issues as compared with other areas of anti-Nazi activity? Whatever our conclusion, it did not represent abstention from political activities, including mass gatherings and demonstrations.

Other areas of Jewish activities

Protests against the Nazi persecutions were organized in Argentina and in other Latin American countries in March 1933, coming as a direct response to the newly declared governmental assault on German Jewry. Demonstrations and rallies were held on many more occasions during the twelve years that followed. their immediate purpose was to raise public opinion against Nazi atrocities and they were only a part of a Jewish anti-Nazi and anti-anti-Semitic activities at the local level. In this drive the Jewish leadership in Latin America—as elsewhere—was forced to reckon with the general public's deep-rooted desire to keep their countries out of the European conflict. The strict neutrality observed by the Latin-American governments until 1942—and by those of Chile and Argentina until 1943 and 1944 respectively—greatly hindered any open interference on their part with the Nazi authorities. However, the liberal and democratic traditions of nations like argentina, Chile, Uruguay, or the radical policies of Mexico, provided the Jewish activists with potential allies among the general public. To what extent was the struggle against Nazism in Latin America a success? What were the implications for the Jewish communities of their political alliance with non-Jewish groups, many of which were opposed to the parties in power? Did their campaign against the Nazis and their local collaborators result in precipitating an anti-Jewish backlash? All of these questions must be thoroughly investigated in an attempt to evaluate the political activities undertaken by the Jewish leadership.

In 1942, after Pearl Harbor, most of the Latin American nations severed their diplomatic relations with Germany. Thus, precisely at the time when the Holocaust reached its lethal apex the Latin-American countries lost their ability to directly intervene on behalf of the Jews or, for that matter, in any other area. Even then, however, Chile and Argentina maintained normal relations with the Axis powers. Moreover, other countries, represented in Berlin by Spain or Switzerland, held important assets, material and human, belonging to Germany; the fate of the *Reichsdeutsche* and even of the *Volksdeutsche* in Latin America and of their possessions proved to be an important issue for the Nazis even before the war.[71] These factors might have been used eventually so as to extort some concessions from the Nazis even after the countries involved joined the Allies. Any forthcoming research dealing with the efforts to rescue small groups or even individuals through diplomatic or other means of intervention will have to address itself to this issue.

The efforts to rescue the few during 1943–45 as well as the first rush to help the masses of Nazi victims a decade earlier called for the mobilization of large funds. "Our idea is that . . . any financing of the emergency emigration referred to would be undertaken by private organizations within the respective countries"—thus read the letter which Secretary of State Cordell Hull sent to the governments invited to attend the Evian Conference.[72] Until then, and more so later, the Jewish people had to finance by themselves their struggle for survival. But the Jewish leadership, except for the JCA, could count only on voluntary contributions made by individuals, and these had to be convinced first of the gravity of the threat posed by Nazi Germany to the Jews all over the world before some funds could be collected.

The response of the Jewish public to the fund-raising campaigns depended largely on the ability of the Jewish leadership to comprehend the real situation in due time and to transmit a feeling of emergency to the donors. To what extent did Latin-American Jewish leaders rise to the occasion? To what extent did the sums raised reflect a readiness on the part of the public for real sacrifice? No doubt much of the energies of the Jewish leaders were dedicated to this field of activity. As we have noted, it also generated most of the rivalry and internal struggle among the local and international organizations. Did this adversity ultimately benefit the campaigns' outcome, as some activists argued or did it hamper a major mobilization of the Jewish communities? A proper evaluation of these issues can be provided only in a broad and comparative analysis of the communities' financial priorities as a whole and of the strategies used by the various organizations.

Did Latin American Jewish leadership do its part in the global Jewish struggle for rescue and survival? Did it live up to its potential? As we can see, many issues remain to be resolved before a fair evaluation can be made.

Conclusion

When Hitler came to power, Latin-American Jewry was a remote and underdeveloped branch of World Jewry. During the 1930s as a major outlet for Jewish immigration, it grew in size and number. Then, when war broke out and all the other communities, throughout the world became gradually involved in fighting the Nazis, Latin-American Jewry, living among nations which did not become really belligerent, remained the only community which was spared the hardships of the war.

This unique situation was well understood by many local communal and political leaders who endeavored to reshape their institutions accordingly. No doubt it decisively influenced the attitude of world Jewish leaders toward the Latin American communities. The patterns of Jewish leadership in Latin America were thereby radically influenced at the same time as the self-esteem and awareness of the Jewish leaders regarding their future role in world Jewish life increased.

Ironically, the Holocaust era, which saw the virtual destruction of European Jewry, marked Latin-American Jewry's coming of age.

APPENDIX A

Estimated Jewish Population in Latin America

	1917^a	1943^b	1980^c
South America			
Argentina	110,000	$350,000^d$	242,000
Bolivia	25	5,150	1,000
Brazil	5,000	$110,750^d$	110,000
Chile	500	25,000	25,000
Colombia	80	5,800	7,000
Ecuador	14	3,200	1,000
Paraguay	600	3,000	700
Peru	300	$2,150^e$	5,000
Surinam	1,000	975^f	500
Uruguay	1,700	37,000	40,000
Venezuela	500	1,600	17,000
Central America			
Panama	500	1,350	2,000
Costa Rica	50	600^h	2,500
Nicaragua	50	135	?
El Salvador	60	160	350
Honduras	1	130	?
British Honduras (Belize)	4	?	?
Guatemala	75	895	1,100
Mexico	$/^g$	16,000	35,000
Cuba	1,000	11,450	1,000
Dominican Republic	35	1,035	200
Haiti	50	160	150
Jamaica	1,500	2,220	250
Bermuda	9	?	?
Bahamas	1	?	500
Trinidad	—	450	300
Barbados	few	?	?
Martinique	6	?	?
Curacao	600	650	700^f

[a] Harry O. Sandberg, "The Jews of Latin-America," *American Jewish Yearbook,* (1917–18), 19:45–96.

[b] Louis Sobel, "Jewish Community Life and Organization in Latin America," *The Jewish Social Service Quarterly,* (June 1944) 20(4):180. These figures have been republished in Statistics of the Jews, *American Jewish Yearbook,* (1944–45), 46:500 table VII.

127

APPENDIX A (continued)

[c] U. O. Schmelz and Sergio Della Pergola, "World Jewish Population," *American Jewish Yearbook, 1982,* 82:284 table 4.

[d] A definitely overestimated figure. See U. O. Schmelz and Sergio Della Pergola, *Ha-Demografia shel ha-Yehudim be-Argentina ube-aratzot aherot shel America ha-latinit,* [The Demography of the Jews in Argentina and in Other Countries of Latin America]. Tel Aviv: Hebrew University of Jerusalem and Tel Aviv University, 1974.

[e] *American Jewish Yearbook,* (1944–45) 46:500.

[f] Including the other Netherland's Antilles.

[g] "During the years of peace and order [before the Revolution of 1911–1917] Jewish population esitmated at one time nearly 15,000. . . . At present there are very few Jews left in the country," Sandberg, "Jews of Latin-America," pp. 80–81.

[h] According to CZA (Central Zionist Archives) A346/49, m. Graiver to F. Levinsky, Dec. 15, 1938. The 70 indicated by Sobel and copied in the *American Jewish Yearbook,* 46:500, is an obvious underestimation.

APPENDIX B

ACIS—The Ladino Speaking Community of Buenos Aires: The Evolution of a Communal Organization

Year	ASOCIACION Dpts:	COMUNIDAD Burial Services	ISRAELITA Health Care	SEFARADI	(Reorganized) Welfare	Synagogue	Education (partly)
1941							
1929	Synagogue[l]				Social-Cultural Club[n] Welfare Women Org.[m]		
						Health Care[k]	
1922		Synagogue[j]					
1919				Synagogue[i]	Asociacion Comunidad Israelita Sefaradi Commissions: Burial, Synagogue, School, Welfare		
1917							Burial Society[h]
1914						Tombstone Donors[g] Funeral Society[f] Burial Society[e] Synagogue and Talmud Tora[d]	
1913					Synagogue and Community[c]		
1910							Synagogue[b]
1909						1st Minyan[a]	

APPENDIX B (continued)

ACIS—The Ladino Speaking Community of Buenos Aires: The Evolution of a Communal Organization

Year 1941	ASOCIACION Dpts:	COMUNIDAD Burial Services	ISRAELITA Health Care	SEFARADI	(Reorganized) Welfare	Synagogue	Education (partly)
Originated from					Rhodes	Ismir (Turkey)	Ismir (Turkey)
Neighbor-hood in Buenos-Aires	San Isidro	Once		Flores	Colegiales	Villa Crespo	Centro

a"Kahal Kadosh, La Hermandad Sefaradi."
b"Etz- Hayim," In 1919_2 incorporated in Asociacion Comunidad Israelita Sefaradi—ACIS.
c"Bnei Zion," in existence until 1929.
d"La Hermandad Sefaradi," in 1919 incorporated in ACIS.
e"Hesed Shel Emet," in 1919 incorporated in ACIS.
f"Bikur Holim" (sic!).
g"Ahava Va-Hesed."
h"Hesed Shel Emet," in 1919 incorporated in ACIS.
i"Ahavat Ahim."
jAsociacion Pro-Medicamentos.
k"Bnei Mizrah."
l"Bnei Israel."
m"La Union."
n"Centro Cultural y recreativo—Shalom," Remained independent even after 1941.

NOTES

Chapter 1

1. E.g., Elie Wiesel, *Legends of Our Time,* (New York: Holt, Rinehart, and Winston, 1968), pp. 165-66, 168; Lucy S. Dawidowicz, "Ben Hecht's 'Perfidy,'" *Commentary* (Mar. 1962) 33(3):264; Joseph Tenenbaum, "The Contribution of American Jewry Towards Rescue in the Hitler Period," *Yad Vashem Bulletin* (Apr. 1957) 7(4):4; Nahum Goldmann, "Jewish Heroism in Siege," *In The Dispersion,* Winter 1963/64, p. 6; *JTA News Bulletin,* Nov. 30, 1944, p. 3; Alexander Donat, "Armageddon," *Dissent,* (Spring 1963) 10(2):122.

2. Greenberg's article appeared in *Yiddisher Kemfer,* Feb. 12, 1943. It was reprinted in English in *Midstream* (Mar. 1964) 10(1):5-10. Quotations are from pp. 5 and 6.

3. Lucy S. Dawidowicz, ed., *A Holocaust Reader* (New York: Behrman House, 1976), pp. 291, 316-18; Yehuda Bauer, "When Did They Know?" *Midstream* (Apr. 1968) 14(4):54-55, 57-58; NYT, June 27, 1942, p. 5, June 30, 1942, p. 7; *Boston Globe,* June 26, 1942, p. 12.

4. Re regular newspapers: NYT and *Boston Globe,* as cited in note 3; and, e.g., *Seattle Times,* June 26, 1942, p. 30; NYT, June 27, 1942, p. 5, July 2, 1942, p. 6; *Chicago Tribune,* June 30, 1942, p. 6; *Los Angeles Times,* June 30, 1942, p. 3; *Kansas City Star,* June 29, 1942, p. 8. Re Jewish press: e.g., AJC, "Review of the Yiddish Press" (mimeo.), Week ending July 8, 1942, p. 1, Week ending July 16, 1942, p. 1; CW, (June 26, 1942) 9(24):3, (July 10, 1942) 9(25):3.

5. CW, (July 10, 1942) 9(25):3, (Aug. 14, 1942) 9(26):1, 2, 4; NYT, July 22, 1942, pp. 1, 4; *Opinion,* (Aug. 1942) 12(10):4.

6. CJR, (Oct. 1942) 5(5):520; CW (Aug. 14, 1942) 9(26):15; *Los Angeles Times,* Aug. 19, 1942, 2: 8; AJYB (Philadelphia: Jewish Publication Society, 1943), 45: 192.

7. For instance, *Jewish Frontier,* as late as November 1942 (p. 3), called on the Allied governments "to do whatever may be done to stop the mass murder."

8. E.g., *The Ghetto Speaks,* No. 2, Aug. 5, 1942; *Jewish Frontier,* (Sept. 1942) 9(9):28-29, (Nov. 1942) 9(10): (entire issue); Segal to Hull, Sept. 23, 1942, SD file

131

862.4016/2240; *JTA News Bulletin,* Oct. 6, 1942, 4; NYT, Nov. 25, 1942, 10; CW (Dec. 4, 1942) 9(37):5-7, 9-13.

9. Elting, Memorandum, and enclosed draft telegram, Aug. 8, 1942, SD file 862.4016/2234; *Washington Post,* Aug. 30, 1942, p. 12.

10. Elting, Memorandum, Aug. 8, 1942, Elting to Secy of State, Aug. 10, 1942, SD file 862.4016/2234; Harrison to Secy of State, Aug. 11, 1942, SD file 862.4016/2233; John P. Fox, "The Jewish Factor in British War Crimes Policy in 1942," *English Historical Review,* (Jan. 1977) 92(362):91-93; Easterman to Taylor, Oct. 7, 1942, SD file 740.00116 EW 1939/634; memo by P. O. C. [?], Aug. 13, 1942, Culbertson to Wise, Aug. 13, 1942, Hull to Bern, Aug. 17, 1942, SD file 862.4016/2233; Durbrow, Memorandum, Aug. 13, 1942, SD file 862.4016/2235; Stephen S. Wise, *Challenging Years* (New York: Putnam, 1949), p. 275; Silverman to Wise, Aug. 28, 1942, SD file 740.00116 EW 1939/553; Isaac Lewin, "Telegrams from Hell," *Polityka,* Aug. 9, 1975; Wise to Welles, Sept. 2, 1942, SD file 840.48 Refugees/3080; Carl Hermann Voss, ed., *Stephen S. Wise: Servant of the People* (Philadelphia: Jewish Publication Society, 1970), p. 251. The State Department received the Riegner message on Aug. 11; the British Foreign Office on Aug. 10.

11. Rosenheim to FDR, Sept. 3, 1942, SD file 740.00116 EW 1939/570; Isaac Lewin, "Attempts at Rescuing European Jews with the Help of Polish Diplomatic Missions during World War II," *Polish Review,* (1977) 22(4):5-6; Secy to McDonald to Mrs. Franklin D. Roosevelt, Sept. 4, 1942, James G. McDonald papers, file P43; Lewin, *Polityka,* Aug. 9, 1975; Voss, *Wise: Servant,* p. 249.

12. Voss, *Wise: Servant,* pp. 249-51; Wise to Welles, Sept. 2, 1942, Atherton to Welles, Sept. 3, 1942, SD file 840.48 Refugees/3080; Lewin, *Polish Review,* (1977) 22(4):6; Lewin, *Polityka,* Aug. 9, 1975; MD 688II/223Q; Harold Ickes Diary, 7053-54.

13. Hull to Bern, Sept. 23, 1942, Harrison to Secy of State, Sept. 26 and Nov. 23, 1942, SD files 740.00116 EW 1939/597A, 599, 653; FRUS (1942) 3: 775-76; MD 688II/223Q; Squire to Secy of State, Sept. 28, 1942, with enclosures, and Oct. 29, 1942, SD files 862.4016/2242, 10-2942; NYT, Nov. 25, 1942, p. 10; Wise, *Challenging Years,* pp. 275-76; Gottschalk to Waldman, Nov. 27, 1942, AJC papers, General Record, Germany Nazism 42-43.

14. NYT, Nov. 25, 1942, p. 10, Nov. 26, 1942, p. 16; *NY Herald Tribune,* Nov. 25, 1942, p. 1; *Washington Post,* Nov. 26, 1942, p. 19B.

15. NYT, Nov. 24, 1942, p. 10, Nov. 25, 1942, p. 10.

16. E.g., NYT, Nov. 24, p. 10, Nov. 25, p. 10, Nov. 26, p. 16; *Washington Post,* Nov. 25, p. 6, Nov. 26, p. 19B; *Chicago Tribune,* Nov. 25, p. 4, Nov. 26, p. 4; *Atlanta Constitution,* Nov. 25, p. 20. (All in 1942.)

17. Elie Wiesel, "Telling the Tale," *Dimensions in American Judaism,* (Spring 1968) 2(3):11.

18. *Los Angeles Times,* Nov. 26, 1942, p. 4.

19. Gottschalk to Waldman, Nov. 27, 1942, AJC papers, General Record, Germany Nazism 42-43; NYT, Nov. 24, 1942, p. 10, Nov. 25, 1942, p. 10, Nov. 26,

1942, p. 16; *Bulletin of the World Jewish Congress,* Jan. 1943, p. 1; *PM,* Nov. 26, 1942, p. 12.

20. Gottschalk to Waldman, Nov. 27, 1942, AJC papers, General Record, Germany Nazism 42-43; *PM,* Nov. 26, 1942, 12; Minutes of Meeting of Sub-Committee . . . Nov. 30, 1942, AJC papers, JEC.

21. Gottschalk to Waldman, Nov. 27, 1942, AJC papers, General Record, Germany Nazism 42-43; Minutes of Meeting of Sub-Committee . . . Nov. 30, 1942, AJC papers, JEC; CW, (Dec. 4, 1942) 9(37):15-16, (Dec. 11, 1942) 9(38):8-11. The limited news coverage obtained can be seen, e.g., in *Los Angeles Times,* Nov. 26, 1942, p. 4; *Washington Post,* Nov. 26, 1942, p. 19B; *Boston Herald,* Nov. 26, 1942, p. 46.

22. AJYB 45:193; CW (Dec. 4, 1942) 9(37):16; Minutes of Dec. 2, 1942, Jewish Labor Committee papers (in Yiddish); Minutes of Meeting of Sub-Committee . . . Nov. 30, 1942, AJC papers, JEC.

23. AJYB 45:193; CW (Dec. 18, 1942) 9(39):13; Minutes of Meeting of Sub-Committee . . . Nov. 30, 1942, AJC papers, JEC.

24. NYT, Dec. 9, 1942, p. 20; *National Jewish Monthly,* (Jan. 1943) 57(5):146; [Adolph Held], Report on the Visit to the President [Dec. 8, 1942], Jewish Labor Committee papers, Communications with the White House 1942; Wertheim, Wise, et al. to the President, Dec. 8, 1942, Blue Print for Extermination [Dec. 8, 1942], FDR papers, OF 76-C.

25. [Adolph Held], Report on the Visit to the President [Dec. 8, 1942], Jewish Labor Committee papers, Communications with the White House 1942; MD 688II/243; *Washington Post,* Dec. 9, 1942, p. 18; NYT, Dec. 9, 1942, p. 20; Joint Emergency Committee on European Jewish Affairs, Sept. 28, 1943, AJC papers, JEC.

26. Barou/Easterman to Perlzweig, Dec. 17, 1942, WJC papers, 177A/50; Easternman to Perlzweig, Jan. 15, 1943, WJC papers, U-142#13; Fox, *English Historical Review,* (Jan. 1977) 92(362):98-103; FRUS (1942) 1:66-67.

27. NYT, Dec. 18, 1942, pp. 1, 10, 26; *Kansas City Star,* Dec. 17, 1942, p. 1; *Denver Post,* Dec. 17, 1942, p. 1; Proposals [Dec. 10, 1942], WJC papers, 264/1; *Bulletin of the World Jewish Congress,* Jan. 1943, p. 2.

28. Proposals [Dec. 10, 1942], WJC papers, 264/1; *Bulletin of the World Jewish Congress,* Jan. 1943, p. 2.

29. Proposals [Dec. 10, 1942], WJC papers, 264/1.

30. *Ibid.;* Shultz, Memorandum, Dec. 10, 1942, WJC papers, U-185/3; Planning Committee on the European Situation, Dec. 14, 1942, WJC papers, U-186/A; Activities of the American Jewish Congress and the World Jewish Congress with Respect to the Hitler Program [mid-Jan. 1943], WJC papers, U-185/2.

31. Activities of the American Jewish Congress [mid-Jan. 1943], WJC papers, U-185/2; NYT, Dec. 28, 1942, pp. 5, 13; draft form letter on American Jewish Congress stationery, Dec. 28, 1942, Wise papers, American Jewish Congress, Shultz.

32. Minutes, Special Committee on European Situation, Dec. 14, 1942, WJC

papers, U-185/3; Activities of the American Jewish Congress [mid-Jan. 1943], WJC papers, U-185/2; Greenberg, *Midstream,* (Mar. 1964), 10(1):8-9; Joseph Tenenbaum, *Yad Vashem Bulletin* (Apr. 1957) 7(4):4.

33. *Opinion,* (Jan. 1943) 13(3):5, 16; *Jewish Forum,* (Dec. 1942) 25(12):193; *Christian Century* (Jan. 6, 1943) 60(1):26.

34. Welles to Wise, with enclosure, Feb. 9, 1943, WJC papers, 267/8; MD 688II/99, 688II/223R-S; American Jewish Congress Press Release, Feb. 14, 1943, WJC papers, U-222/3; NYT, Feb. 14, 1943, p. 37.

35. NYT, Feb. 13, 1943, p. 5, Feb. 16, 1943, p. 11; MD 611/275; Welles to Wagner, Mar. 10, 1943, Robert F. Wagner papers, Palestine files, box 2, folder 23; Welles to Davis, Mar. 11, 1943, SD file 840.48 Refugees/3608.

36. *Answer,* (Feb. 1946) 4(2):4ff; interview with Hillel Kook by Natan Cohen, Sept. 26, 1968, pp. 11-16, PSC papers, box 11, folder 33; interview with Peter Bergson (Hillel Kook) by David Wyman, NY, May 5, 1973; NYT, Jan. 5, 1942, p. 13; van Paassen to Daniels, July 31, 1942, Josephus Daniels papers, box 816, folder P; *Jewish Veteran,* (May 1942) 11(9):5.

37. Merlin to Shubow, Mar. 20, 1943, AJHS, American Jewish Congress papers, Uncataloged Box, Committee for a Jewish Army folder; NYT, Dec. 5, 1942, p. 16; *Jewish Review and Observer* (Cleveland), Feb. 19, 1943, PSC papers, reel 18.

38. NYT, Feb. 16, 1943, p. 11.

39. *Opinion,* (Mar. 1943) 13(5):14; NP, (Mar. 5, 1943) 33(9):4; Minutes of Meeting of the Z.O.A. Executive Committee, Feb. 20, 1943, p. 9, Wise papers, Z.O.A. Exec. Comm.; *NY Herald Tribune,* Feb. 22, 1943, p. 16; *Los Angeles Times,* Feb. 22, 1943, p. 8; *Philadelphia Inquirer,* Feb. 23, 1943, 15; *Chicago Daily News,* Feb. 25, 1943, p. 13.

40. *Opinion,* (Apr. 1943) 13(6):7; Planning Committee Meeting Minutes, Dec. 29, 1942, WJC papers, U-185/2; *Jewish Times* (Baltimore), Feb. 12, 1943, *Jewish Chronicle* (Columbus, OH), Feb. 26, 1943, PSC papers, reel 18; *Jewish News* (Detroit), Mar. 12, 1943, PSC papers, scrapbook 13.

41. American Jewish Congress Press Release, Feb. 22, 1943, WJC papers, U-222/3; NYT, Mar. 2, 1943, pp. 1, 4; CW (Mar. 5, 1943) 10(10):15.

42. NYT, Mar. 2, 1943, p. 4; CW (Mar. 5, 1943) 10(10):16.

43. Press response: e.g., NYT, Mar. 3, p. 22; *NY Post,* Mar. 6, p. 21; *NY Sun,* Mar. 3, p. 20; *NY Herald Tribune,* Mar. 7, II:3 (all in 1943). NYT, Mar. 4, 1943, p. 9; MD 688II/247-9; FRUS, 1943, I, 140-44; CW (Mar. 12 1943) 10(11):3-4 LC [Clark, Ottawa], Memorandum, Mar. 4, 1943, SD file 840.48 Refugees/ 3739; Voss, *Wise: Servant,* p. 257; JEC, Sept. 28, 1943, Meeting of JEC, Mar. 15, 1943, Meeting of JEC, Nov. 5, 1943, AJC papers, JEC; Minutes of the Meeting of the Emergency Committee on European Situation, Mar. 6, 1943, AJC papers, Proskauer, Emergency Committee, Memoranda/Materials; Fourth Confidential Report to the Chawerim Nichbodim (1943), Agudas Israel World Organization, p. 5, Fifth Confidential Report to the Chawerim Nichbodim (1943), p. 10, Agudath Israel papers, M. Tress papers, Confidential Reports, box 19;

"Program for the Rescue of Jews," Apr. 14, 1943, WJC papers, 17A/24; Merlin to Ziff, Apr. 23, 1943, PSC papers, box 1, folder 8.

44. Instructions for Organizing Public Meetings [Mar. 1943], Shultz to Trager, Mar. 22, 1943, Trager to Schultz, Epstein, Pat, May 10, 1943, Meeting of the JEC, Mar. 15, 1943, Meeting of the JEC, Mar. 22, 1943, AJC papers, JEC; CW (Mar. 26, 1943) 10(13):13, (Apr. 2) 10(14):16, (Apr. 16) 10(16):16, (Apr. 30) 10(17):2, 21, (May 7) 10(18):13, (May 14) 10(19):2, (May 28) 10(21):2.

45. Instructions for Organizing Public Meetings [Mar. 1943], Waldman to Members of the AJC, Mar. 25, 1943, Levy to Hexter, May 5, 1943, Levy to Galkin, May 5, 1943, with enclosures, Proskauer to Gerstenfeld, Mar. 25, 1943, AJC papers, JEC; Voss, *Wise: Servant,* p. 257.

46. Minutes of the Meeting of the Emergency Committee on European Situation, Mar. 6, 1943, AJC papers, Proskauer, Emergency Committee, Memoranda/Materials; Activities of the American Jewish Congress [mid-Jan. 1943], WJC papers, U-185/2; Shultz to Levy, Feb. 24, 1943, Wagner papers, Palestine files, box 2, folder 23; Rabbi Meyer Berlin, Confidential Memorandum, Feb. 24, 1943, Abba Hillel Silver papers, Manson I-62; Meeting of the JEC, May 15, 1943, AJC papers, JEC; *Congressional Record,* 89: 1570-71, 1723, 1894, 2105, 2184; NYT, Mar. 19, 1943, p. 11.

47. Memorandum Submitted on behalf of the JEC, Mar. 22, 1943, Proskauer and Wise to Taylor, Mar. 22, 1943, SD file 840.48 Refugees/3860; Fourth Confidential Report . . . (1943), p. 2, Agudath Israel papers, Tress papers, box 19; Minute of a Meeting of the Joint Committee on European Affairs, Mar. 29, 1943, Braunstein to Silver, Mar. 23, 1943, Silver papers, Manson I-81, JEC; 58th Meeting of the President's Advisory Committee, Mar. 30, 1943, McDonald papers, file P67; Meeting of the JEC, Mar. 22, 1943, AJC papers, JEC.

48. Minute of a Meeting of the Joint Committee on European Affairs, Mar. 29, 1943, Silver papers, Manson I-81, JEC; Fourth Confidential Report . . . (1943), p. 5, Agudath Israel papers, Tress papers, box 19.

49. Minute of a Meeting of the Joint Committee on European Affairs, Mar. 29, 1943, Silver papers, Manson I-81, JEC.

50. Meeting of the Steering Committee of the JEC, Apr. 2, 1943, Meeting of the JEC, Apr. 10, 1943, AJC papers, JEC; Silverman to Montor, Apr. 7, 1943, Silver to Shulman, Apr. 9, 1943, Silver papers, Manson I-81, JEC; Wise to Early, Apr. 9, 1943, Watson to Secy of State, Apr. 10, 1943, Hull to Wise, Apr. 14, 1943, SD file 740.00116 EW 1939/858.

51. Reports on phone calls from Celler, Mar. 29 and 30, 1943, EMW to Long, Apr. 1, 1943, FDR papers, OF 3186; Meeting of the JEC, Apr. 10, 1943, AJC papers, JEC.

52. Wise to Welles, Apr. 14, 1943, SD file 548.G1/38; "Program for the Rescue of Jews," Apr. 14, 1943, WJC papers, 17A/24; Voss, *Wise: Servant,* pp. 258-59.

53. Meeting of the JEC, Apr. 18, 1943, AJC papers, JEC; NYT, Apr. 19, 1943, p. 4; *PM,* Apr. 19, 1943, pp. 14-15; *Los Angeles Times,* Apr. 19, 1943, A.

54. Long to Wise, Apr. 20, 1943, under cover Wise to Proskauer, Apr. 23, 1943, AJC papers, JEC.

55. Arthur D. Morse, *While Six Million Died: A Chronicle of American Apathy* (New York: Random House, 1967), pp. 50–63; Emigration Figures, under cover Cleveland to Joy, Feb. 7, 1945, Unitarian Service Committee papers, American Friends Service Committee folder; National Catholic Welfare Conference, *Eighth Annual Report ... The Catholic Committee for Refugees* (Washington, 1944), p. 12; "History of the War Refugee Board with Selected Documents," pp. 116-17, 125, WRB papers, box 110; Hayes to Secy of State, Oct. 16, 1944, SD file 840.48 Refugees/10-1644.

56. *Chicago Tribune,* Apr. 18, 1943, p. 12, Apr. 23, p. 9, NYT, Apr. 20, p. 1, Apr. 25, p. 19, *Denver Post,* Apr. 19, p. 3, Apr. 23, p. 7, *San Francisco Examiner,* Apr. 20, p. 10, Apr. 22, p. 11, *Washington Post,* Apr. 30, p. 1, *Seattle Times,* Apr. 19, p. 3; *National Jewish Monthly,* (June 1943) 57(10):314; AJYB, 45: 361; CJR (June 1943) 6(3):278; *Jewish Frontier* (May 1943) 10(5):3; *Opinion* (May 1943) 13(7), 4, (June 1943) 13(8):5; NP (May 7, 1943) 33(13):3; *Jewish Outlook* (May 1943) 7(7):6; CW (May 7, 1943) 10(18):3; Meeting of JEC, May 24, 1943, JEC to Welles, June 1, 1943, AJC papers, JEC; Pat to Schultz, June 24, 1943, Proskauer to Held, June 29, 1943; AJC papers, Proskauer, Emergency Committee 1943; Fourth Confidential Report . . . (1943), p. 5, Fifth Confidential Report . . . (1943), p. 1, Agudath Israel papers, Tress papers, box 19; Rosenheim to McDonald, May 26, 1943, McDonald papers, file P40; Shultz to Wise, Goldmann, Sherman, et al., June 3, 1943, Wise papers, American Jewish Congress, Shultz; Niebuhr, Poling, et al. to The President, Aug. 6, 1943, SD file 840.48 Refugee/4164; NYT, May 2, 1943, p. 17.

57. Pat to Schultz, June 24, 1943, Proskauer to Held, June 29, 1943, AJC papers, Proskauer, Emergency Committee 1943; Meeting of JEC, July 15, 1943; Sept. 24, 1943; Aug. 10, 1943; Nov. 5, 1943; Mar. 15, 1943; May 24, 1943; JEC to Welles, June 1, 1943, AJC papers, JEC; *Conference Record* (AJ Conference), (Feb. 15, 1944) 1(7):6; CW (Nov. 12, 1943) 10(31):20; Fourth Confidential Report . . . (1943), p. 5, Fifth Confidential Report . . . (1943), p. 10, Agudath Israel papers, Tress papers, box 19.

58. Isaac Neustadt-Noy, "The Unending Task: Efforts to Unite American Jewry from the American Jewish Congress to the American Jewish Conference," Ph.D. dissertation, Brandeis University, 1976, pp. 175, 203; Samuel Halperin, *The Political World of American Zionism* (Detroit: Wayne State University Press, 1961), pp. 148, 383, nn. 26, 28; *The Autobiography of Nahum Goldmann* (New York: Holt, Rinehart, and Winston, 1969), p. 222; address by Nahum Goldmann, "Transactions 45th Annual Convention Zionist Organization of America," Oct. 1942, pp. 479-504; Abba Hillel Silver, *Vision and Victory: A Collection of Addresses* (New York: Zionist Organization of America, 1949), pp. 41, 48, 63-64.

59. Goldmann, *Autobiography,* pp. 221-22; Halperin, *Political World,* pp. 210, 220-22, 381, 383 n. 9; Emanuel Neumann, *In the Arena* (New York: Herzl Press, 1976), pp. 168-69, 213; AJYB, 45: 207.

60. Wise to Richards, Dec. 10, 1941, Wise papers, American Jewish Congress; *Reconstructionist* (May 29, 1942) 8(8):4-5; Neumann, *Arena,* pp. 190, 213; Halperin, *Political World,* pp. 147-49, 223, 382 *n.* 16, 383 *n.* 26; Neustadt-Noy, "Unending Task," pp. 148, 175, 203, 383 *n.* 28; Goldmann, *Autobiography,* p. 222; *National Jewish Monthly* (Oct. 1943) 58(2):42.

61. Neustadt-Noy, "Unending Task," pp. 175, 203, 383 *n.* 28; Halperin, *Political World,* pp. 148, 383 *n.* 26; Goldmann, *Autobiography,* p. 222; Alexander Kohanski, ed., *The American Jewish Conference: Its Organization and Proceedings of the First Session, August 29 to September 2, 1943* (New York: AJ Conference, 1944), pp. 15-16, 319, 325, 332-33.

62. AJC, "Review of the Yiddish Press," Weeks ending June 11, 1-3, June 25, 1-2, July 1, 1-2, Aug. 27, 1, and period of July 9-22, 2 (all in 1943); AJ Conference, "Bulletin of Activities and Digest of the Press" (mimeo.), June 18, June 25, July 2, July 9, July 16, Aug. 20 (all in 1943); *Liberal Judaism* (Oct. 1943) 11(6):1; NP (Sept. 10, 1943) 33(18):17; *Jewish Outlook,* (June 1943) 7(8):12.

63. Kohanski, *American Jewish Conference . . . 1943,* pp. 44, 46-47, 334-44; Halperin, *Political World,* 228-30, 383 *n.* 41; Heller to Wise, Jan. 28, 1943, Wise papers, U.S. Government, Anti-Zionism; NP, 33(14, 15, 16), issues of May 21, June 11, and July 16, 1943; *Jewish Outlook* (June 1943) 7(8):7; *Jewish Frontier* (June 1943) 10(6):5, 29; Hadassah Handbook on the American Jewish Conference [1943], Zionist Archives.

64. *Jewish Frontier* (July 1943) 10(7):3; NP (July 16, 1943) 33(16):3, (Aug. 20, 1943) 33(17):issue; Halperin, *Political World,* pp. 152, 230, 232, 249; Neustadt-Noy, "Unending Task," pp. 286-89, 303.

65. AJC, "Review of the Yiddish Press," Weeks ending July 8, p. 1, and Aug. 27, p. 2, and period of July 9-22, pp. 2-3, (all in 1943); AJ Conference, "Bulletin of Activities," June 11, July 23, Aug. 6, 1943; Fourth Confidential Report . . . (1943), pp. 7-8, Fifth Confidential Report . . . (1943), p. 9, Agudath Israel papers, Tress papers, box 19; *American Jewish Conference: A Statement of the Organization of the Conference and a Summary of Resolutions Adopted at the First Session . . . 1943* (New York: AJ Conference [1944]), 10.

66. Fourth Confidential Report . . . (1943), p. 7; Agudath Israel papers, Tress papers, box 19; Kohanski, *American Jewish Conference . . . 1943,* p. 32; Minutes, Executive Committee Meeting American Jewish Conference, July 14-15, 1943, p. 9, Wise papers, AJ Conference 1943-48; Minutes Executive Committee— American Jewish Conference, Aug. 12, 1943, 3-4, Zionist Archives, AJ Conference Minutes of meetings; Neustadt-Noy, "Unending Task," pp. 248, 250; NP (Aug. 20, 1943) 33(17):2; AJC, "Review of the Yiddish Press," Week ending Aug. 27, 1943, p. 2.

67. Halperin, *Political World,* pp. 234, 237-38, 384 *n.* 52; Neustadt-Noy, "Unending Task," pp. 310-14; Neumann, *Arena,* pp. 190-92; AJC, "Review of the Yiddish Press," Week ending Sept. 24, 1943, p. 2.

68. Neumann, *Arena,* p. 191; Halperin, *Political World,* pp. 234, 236; Neustadt-Noy, "Unending Task," pp. 316, 318; Silver, *Vision and Victory,* pp. 13-14; Kohanski, *American Jewish Conference . . . 1943,* pp. 57, 177, 180, 279-80; NP (Sept. 10, 1943) 33(18):2; NYT, Sept. 2, 1943, p. 1; *Statement of the American Jewish Conference on the Withdrawal of the American Jewish Committee* (New York: AJ Conference, 1943), p. 13.

69. Kohanski, *American Jewish Conference . . . 1943,* pp. 61, 115, 125-29, 203-6, 220-21, 370-71; NYT, Aug. 30, 1943, p. 6, Sept. 13, 1943, p. 13; CW (Sept. 24, 1943) 10(27):6; *Liberal Judaism* (Sept. 1943) 11(5):33; *The Day* (NY), Sept. 5, 1943, p. 1; NP (Sept. 10, 1943) 33(18):2; "American Jewish Conference Rescue Committee Sessions Held Aug. 31, Sept. 1, 2," especially pp. 80-93, 148-49, 239-40, AJHS, AJ Conference papers, box 3; CJR (Oct. 1943) 6(5):503.

70. Based on information reported in several parts of my forthcoming book on the American response to the Holocaust. Shown, e.g., in Summary of Position of American Jewish Committee [Nov. 8, 1943], AJC papers, Proskauer, Emergency Committee 1943.

This conclusion is also supported, in general, by Naomi Cohen, *Not Free to Desist: The American Jewish Committee 1906-1966* (Philadelphia: Jewish Publication Society, 1972), pp. 240-49, 536, 552, 555.

71. Meetings of the JEC, Mar. 22, May 15, Sept. 24, Nov. 5 (all in 1943), AJC papers, JEC; Fifth Confidential Report . . . (1943), p. 10, Agudath Israel papers, Tress papers, box 19; Braunstein to Silver, Mar. 23, 1943, Silver papers, Manson I-81, JEC; Pat to American Jewish Conference, Jan. 12, 1944, Silver papers, Manson II-3, AJ Conference; Rauch to Wise, Feb. 2, 1944, Wise papers, U.S. Government, Anti-Zionism; "How Do Communities Respond to the Request for Funds for the American Jewish Conference?" Mar. 20, 1944, American Jewish Conference Press Release, Jan. 10, 1945, AJHS, AJ Conference papers, Published Material, box 6; *Liberal Judaism* (Feb. 1944) 11(10):37, (July 1944) 12(3):28-29; AJYB (Philadelphia: Jewish Publication Society, 1944), 46: 583-87; NYT, Oct. 25, 1943, p. 17; "Conference Record: The Daily Proceedings of the American Jewish Conference" (mimeo.) June 1944, p. 2 (copies in Zionist Archives); Carl Hermann Voss, *Rabbi and Minister: The Friendship of Stephen S. Wise and John Haynes Holmes* (Cleveland: World Publishing Co., 1964), p. 316; Halperin, *Political World,* pp. 242-44; AJ Conference, "Bulletin of Activities," Dec. 15, 1944, Jan. 19, 1945; Minutes of Administrative Committee Meeting, Aug. 24, 1944, Zionist Archives, AJ Conference Minutes of meetings.

72. ECSJPE, "A Year in the Service of Humanity," Aug. 1944, p. 29, PSC papers, box 5, folder 22 (and reel 6); CJR (Feb. 1943) 6(1):3-4, (Feb. 1944) 7(1):80-84, (Apr. 1944) 7(2):178; Summary of Position of American Jewish Committee [Nov. 8, 1943], AJC papers, Proskauer, Emergency Committee 1943; *JTA News Bulletin,* Aug. 3, 1939, pp. 3-4, Dec. 15, 1943, p. 2; CW (May 28, 1943) 10(21):3; Halperin, *Political World,* pp. 164-165.

73. CW (Oct. 8, 1943) 10(28):2; Minutes Executive Committee AECZA, Sept.

20, 1943, Minutes AECZA, Sept. 20, 1943, Silver papers, 4-2, AZEC 1943-44; Halperin, *Political World,* p. 247; Minutes of Executive Committee, Oct. 17, 1943, Interim Committee Minutes, Oct. 17, 1943, Zionist Archives, AJ Conference Minutes of meetings. Rabbi Israel Goldstein was president of the Synagogue Council of America.

74. Alexander Kohanski, ed., *The American Jewish Conference: Proceedings of the Second Session, December 3 to 5, 1944* (New York: AJ Conference, 1945), pp. 42-52, 209-20; attachment to Digest of Minutes of the Interim Committee, Dec. 15, 1943, Minutes of Executive Committee, Jan. 18, 1945, Jan. 25, 1945, Mar. 1, 1945, Zionist Archives, AJ Conference Minutes of meetings; "The Rescue Committee of the American Jewish Conference . . . December 4, 1944," pp. 33, 90-94, AJHS, AJ Conference papers, box 4; Digest of Minutes of the Interim Committee, May 12, 1944, p. 5, AJHS, AJ Conference papers, Published Material, box 6; AJ Conference, *Report of the Interim Committee and the Commission on Rescue, Commission on Palestine, Commission on Post-War* (New York: AJ Conference, 1944), 16; Hyman to Warburg, Apr. 6, 1944, JDC papers, Reports, Jan. 1944–Aug. 1945; NYT. Apr. 20, 1944, p. 10, Aug. 1, 1944, p. 17; AJ Conference, "Bulletin of Activities," Aug. 4, 1944. More data may be found in the AJ Conference's executive committee minutes from Oct. 17, 1943, through Aug. 30, 1945, located in the Zionist Archives.

75. Minutes Executive Committee AECZA, Sept. 20, 1943, Minutes AECZA, Sept. 20, 1943, Silver papers, 4-2, AZEC 1943–44; AZEC Minutes, Nov. 15, 1943, AZEC Executive Committee Minutes, May 1, 1944, Zionist Archives; Digest of Minutes of Interim Committee, Nov. 23, 1943, p. 10, AJ Conference Press Release, Nov. 17, 1948, AJHS, AJ Conference papers, box 6, Published Material; CJR, (Aug. 1944) 7(4):430-31; Executive Committee Minutes, Oct. 12, 1943, Oct. 19, 1943, Nov. 2, 1943, AJHS, American Jewish Congress, box 6; Administrative Committee Minutes, Jan. 19, 1943, p. 160, AJHS, American Jewish Congress, box 3; *National Jewish Monthly* (July-Aug. 1944) 58(11):360-61, (Sept. 1944) 59(1):1, (Jan. 1945) 59(5):150-51, 167; Neustadt-Noy, "Unending Task," pp. 347-53; AJ Conference, "Bulletin of Activities," Oct. 27, Nov. 24, Dec. 4, Dec. 15, Dec. 22, Dec. 29 (all in 1944); NYT, Dec. 4, 1944, p. 15, Dec. 6, 1944, p. 6; Minutes of Interim Committee, AJ Conference, Feb. 25, 1945, Silver papers, 4-2-23, AZEC-AJ Conference 1944-45.

76. Halperin, *Political World,* pp. 249-50.

77. *Ibid.,* pp. 183, 185, 246, 260, 270-77, 392 *nn.* 59, 61; Leon Feuer, "The Forgotten Year," *American Zionist* (Nov.-Dec. 1967) 58(3):18; AJ Conference, *Report of the Interim Committee,* p. 66; AJYB, 46: 495; Doreen Bierbrier, "The American Zionist Emergency Council: An Analysis of a Pressure Group," *American Jewish Historical Quarterly,* (Sept. 1970) 60(1):87, 98-99; AZEC Minutes, Nov. 15, 1943, AZEC Executive Committee Minutes, Sept. 25, 1944, Zionist Archives.

78. CW (Sept. 24, 1943) 10(27):3; interview with Emanuel Neumann by David Wyman, NY, Nov. 20, 1978; interview with Carl Hermann Voss by David Wyman, NY, Feb. 11, 1978.

79. CW (Nov. 28, 1941) 8(39):5-6, (June 5, 1942) 9(21):6-8; Voss, *Wise: Servant,* pp. 249-50; address by Nahum Goldmann, "Transactions 45th Annual Convention Zionist Organization of America," Oct. 1942, pp. 479-504; Noah Lucas, *The Modern History of Israel* (New York: Praeger, 1975), p. 187; Silver, *Vision and Victory,* pp. 41, 48, 63-64.

80. AECZA Minutes, May 3, 1943, AZEC Executive Committee Minutes, Nov. 29, 1943, Zionist Archives.

81. Silver, *Vision and Victory,* pp. 14-21, 48-52. Also reflected in AZEC Minutes, May 1, 1944 (attached to AZEC Executive Committee Minutes, May 1, 1944), Zionist Archives.

82. NYT, Mar. 10, 1943, p. 12; *JTA News Bulletin,* Mar. 10, 1943; *Liberal Judaism* (June 1943) 11(2):63.

83. NYT, Mar. 10, 1943, p. 12, Apr. 13, 1943, p. 17; PSC papers, folio 6, scrapbooks 13 and 16, and reels 18 and 20; "We Will Never Die" (pamphlet) [nd], PSC papers, box 10, folder 15; *Answer* (May 1943) 1(2):9; *Miami Herald,* Apr. 17, 1943, p. 10A; Boris Smolar column, Mar. 19, 1943, *Jewish Chronicle* (Chicago), Apr. 2, 1943, PSC papers, reel 18; Hecht to Waldman, Jan. 26, 1943, Trager to Rosenblum, Feb. 1, 1943, AJC papers, Emergency Committee 1943-44; Voss, *Wise: Servant,* p. 257; Report on Attempts to Stage "We Will Never Die" [early 1944], PSC papers, box 13, folder 57; Merlin to Ziff, Apr. 23, 1943, PSC papers, box 1, folder 8; Dec. 29, 1942, Planning Committee Meeting Minutes, WJC papers, U-185/2; I. I. Taslitt in *Jewish Review and Observer* (Cleveland), Apr. 23, 1943, PSC papers, reel 18.

84. NYT, May 4, 1943, p. 17; *Congressional Record,* 89:4044-47, 4140-41; *Answer* (Aug. 1943) 1(7-8):4.

85. Perlzweig to Wise, June 16, 1943, Wise papers, American Jewish Congress, Perlzweig; Tucker to Wise, June 17, 1943, AJC papers, Proskauer, Emergency Committee 1943; Bromfield to Taylor, June 21, 1943, Taylor to Welles, June 23, 1943, Welles to Taylor, June 23, 1943, Taylor to Bromfield, June 24, 1943, Myron C. Taylor papers, box 5, Correspondence 1938-1954; Hyman to Pickett, July 13, 1943, American Friends Service Committee papers, Refugee Services 1943, Committees and Organizations, American Jewish Joint Distribution Committee; Hyman to Wiley, July 27, 1943, JDC papers, Reports, Jan. 43-May 45; *Answer* (July 5, 1943) 1(5):10, (Aug. 1943) 1(7-8):14, (Feb. 1946) 4(2):18; NYT, July 13, 1943, p. 12, July 21, 1943, p. 13; *NY Post,* July 22, 1943, p. 6; MD 688I/66; *NY Herald Tribune,* July 26, 1943, p. 14; William to Thomas, Aug. 2, 1943, Elbert Thomas papers, box 56, E General (E-1).

86. *Answer,* (Aug. 1943) 1(7-8):22-23.

87. MD 688I/35; Lerner to FDR, July 31, 1943, Watson to Lerner, Aug. 10, 1943, Early to Lerner, Aug. 22, 1943, FDR papers, OF 76-C; ECSJPE, "A Year in the Service of Humanity," Aug. 1944, pp. 5-6, 8, PSC papers, box 5, folder 22 (and reel 6); Bergson to Eleanor Roosevelt, Aug. 11, 1943, with attachments, Eleanor Roosevelt papers, box 2899, file 190 Miscellaneous; "My Day," Aug. 13, 1943,

Eleanor Roosevelt papers, box 3148; Bergson to Eleanor Roosevelt, Oct. 13, 1943, Secy to Mrs. Roosevelt to Bergson, Oct. 18, 1943, Eleanor Roosevelt papers, box 297, file 30.9; Bergson to Thompson, Oct. 19, 1943, Thompson to Bergson, Oct. 29, 1943, with enclosure, Bergson to Thompson, Nov. 3, 1943, Eleanor Roosevelt papers, box 84, file 30.1; NYT, Aug. 19, 1943, p. 7; *Answer* (Nov. 1, 1943) 1(12):5; Long, Memo of conversation with Bergson and Hirschmann, Sept. 1, 1943, Breckinridge Long papers, box 202, Refugees 1943–44; MD 688I/31-32, 36-38.

88. NYT, Aug. 12, 1943, p. 10, Aug. 30, p. 10, Sept. 7, p. 16, Oct. 5, p. 29, Oct. 17, p. 14; ECSJPE, "A Year in the Service of Humanity," Aug. 1944, p. 9, PSC papers, box 5, folder 22 (and reel 6); Eri Jabotinsky to Altman, Oct. 12, 1943, PSC papers, box 1, folder 10; *Washington Post,* Oct. 7, 1943, p. 1; *Washington Times-Herald,* Oct. 6, 1943, p. 25, Oct. 7, 1943, p. 3; *NY Post,* Oct. 6, 1943, p. 5; *Time,* (Oct. 18, 1943) 42(16):21; *Morning Journal* (NY), Oct. 7, 1943, pp. 1, 2, Oct. 8, 1943, p. 3; *Forward* (NY), Oct. 7, 1943, pp. 1, 9; *JTA News Bulletin,* Oct. 7, 1943, p. 4; *Washington Star,* Oct. 7, 1943, p. 6; *Answer* (Nov. 1, 1943) 1(12):4, 11.

89. Watson to Lerner, Aug. 30, 1943, AW to RR [nd], TOI to MHM, Sept. 29, 1943, Lerner to McIntyre, Sept. 29, 1943, Levovitz to Early, Oct. 3, 1943, MHM to Watson, Oct. 4, 1943, Watson to Levovitz, Oct. 5, 1943, FDR papers, OF 76-C; President's Appointment Diaries, Oct. 6, 1943, FDR papers, PPF 1-0 (1), box 186; Diary of the President 1943, FDR papers, PPF 1-0 (3), box 195; *Washington Times-Herald,* Oct. 7, 1943, p. 3; NYT, Oct. 7, 1943, p. 9.

90. "A Proclamation by the Union of Orthodox Rabbis" [nd], "A Proclamation by the Union of Grand Rabbis" [nd], FDR papers, OF 76-C. The rabbis' pilgrimage received front page coverage in only one major New York or Washington newspaper, the *Washington Post* (Oct. 7, 1943). Among major news magazines, only *Time* reported the event (Oct. 18, 1943, p. 21). Gillette to Thomas, Jan. 24, 1944, Elbert Thomas papers, box 80, C-5 Congress; Thomas to Secy of State, Oct. 1, 1943, SD file 840.48 Refugees/4521; *Congressional Record,* 89:8125; *Washington Post,* Nov. 24, 1943, p. 12; NYT, Nov. 10, 1943; p. 19, Dec. 21, 1943, p. 10; U.S. House of Representatives, *Problems of World War II and Its Aftermath: Part 2, The Palestine Question* (Washington: GPO, 1976,) p. 16.

91. MD 693/198, 694/88; *Interpreter Releases,* (Jan. 10, 1944) 21(1):14; Gillette to Thomas, Jan. 24, 1944, Elbert Thomas papers, box 80, C-5 Congress; interview with Peter Bergson by David Wyman, NY, Jan. 10, 1974; NYT, Dec. 21, 1943, p. 10; *JTA News Bulletin,* Dec. 13, 1943, p. 2, Dec. 22, 1943, p. 2; Long to Thomas, Oct. 27, 1943, SD file 840.48 Refugees/4521; U.S. House of Representatives, *Problems of World War II,* pp. 36-40, 77-139, 161-210; N. Goldmann, Minute of conversation with Congressman Sol Bloom, Dec. 8, 1943, Silver papers, Manson I-80, Sol Bloom; House Resolution 352, 78th Congress, 1st session, National Archives, Legislative branch, box 16432 (2 folders); Emanuel Celler, address at Jewish Historical Society of NY, Oct. 23, 1975.

92. Union of Orthodox Rabbis to Gillette, Ellender, et al., Nov. 14, 1943, Union

of Orthodox Rabbis to Wagner, Mead, Nov. 14, 1943, Vaad Hahatzala papers, box 24; Silver to Bloom, Nov. 25, 1943, National Archives, Legislative branch, box 16432; ECSJPE, *The Work is Still Ahead* [Dec. 1944], p. 11, Senator Guy M. Gillette, address at Commodore Hotel, Dec. 20, 1944, pp. 5-6, PSC papers, box 6, folder 27; AP dispatch, *Oakland Tribune,* Jan. 3, 1944, under cover Keane to McCrillis, Jan. 27, 1944, Harold Ickes papers, Secy of Interior files, Associations 1944 Jan.-Aug.; Minutes of Interview with Senator Guy M. Gillette, Jan. 17, 1944, Silver papers, Manson II-35, Sen. Guy M. Gillette.

93. Digest of Minutes of Interim Committee, Dec. 15, 1943, p. 5, AJ Conference Press Release, Dec. 2, 1943, form letter from Goldstein, Monsky, and Wise, Dec. 27, 1943, AJHS, AJ Conference papers, box 6, Published Material; AJ Conference Press Release, Dec. 2, 1943 (2d version), National Archives, Legislative branch, box 16432; NYT, Dec. 3, 1943, p. 4, Dec. 31, 1943, p. 10; U.S. House of Representatives, *Problems of World War II,* pp. 217-43; memorandum issued by Interim Committee of AJ Conference, Dec. 29, 1943, pp. 6-7, SD file 840.48 Refugees/5025 (also in PSC papers, box 4, folder 14); CW (Jan. 7, 1944) 11(1):15-16.

94. *Conference Record* (AJ Conference) (Jan. 15, 1944) 1(6):3; Executive Committee Meeting, AJ Conference, Nov. 6, 1943, p. 2, Digest of Minutes of Interim Committee, Nov. 23, 1943, pp. 4-7, Dec. 15, 1943, pp. 4-5, AJHS, AJ Conference papers, box 6, Published Material; CW (Dec. 10, 1943) 10(35):3; Minutes of Interview with Senator Guy M. Gillette, Jan. 17, 1944, Silver papers, Manson II-35, Sen. Guy M. Gillette.

95. E.g., Minutes of Executive Committee of AZEC, Oct. 18, 1943, p. 3, Nov. 29, 1943, pp. 4-5, Jan. 3, 1944, pp. 4-5, Apr. 17, 1944, pp. 3-4, May 1, 1944, p. 4, May 15, 1944, p. 3, June 5, 1944, p. 5, Zionist Archives; Neumann to Wise, Oct. 7, 1942, Wise papers, World Affairs, Israel Goldstein; interview with Dean Alfange by David Wyman, NY, Mar. 22, 1979; Minute of a Meeting with John W. Pehle, Feb. 10, 1944, p. 4, Silver papers, Manson II-90, WRB; Meyer Weisgal, *Meyer Weisgal . . . So Far: An Autobiography* (New York: Random House, 1971), p. 188.

96. *San Francisco Examiner,* Dec. 22, 1943, p. 12; *NY Post,* Dec. 20, 1943, p. 3; N. Goldmann, Minute of conversation with Congressman Sol Bloom, Dec. 8, 1943, Silver papers, Manson I-80, Sol Bloom; MD 688II/138, 693/198, 694/88-89, 97; House Resolution 350, 78th Congress, 1st session, National Archives, Legislative branch, box 16431, including, e.g., Celler to Bloom, Jan. 14, 1944; *Washington Post,* Jan. 25, 1944, p. 10; [Eri Jabotinsky] to Ben Eliezer, Jan. 11, 1944, PSC papers, box 1, folder 11; Dorothy Detzer, *Appointment on the Hill* (New York: Henry Holt, 1948), p. 242.

97. Morse, *While Six Million Died,* pp. 74-89.

98. MD 688II/240-1, 692/25, 287-92, 693/82-91, 188-210, 212-29, 694/80-110, 190-202; Detzer, *Appointment,* 242-43; *Washington Post,* Jan. 25, 1944, p. 10; M. E. Jones to Foreign Service Executive Staff, Jan. 11, 1944, American Friends Service Committee papers, Foreign Service 1944, Foreign Service (General); [Eri

Jabotinsky] to Ben Eliezer, Jan. 11, 1944, PSC papers, box 1, folder 11; NYT, Jan. 23, 1944, p. 11.

99. *Conference Record* (AJ Conference) (Feb. 15, 1944) 1(7):6-7; NP (Feb. 4, 1944) 34(10):227, 235; "The Rescue Committee of the American Jewish Conference" (typescript), Dec. 4, 1944, pp. 14-16, 140, AJHS, AJ Conference papers, box 4; MD 693/235-36, 694/59-60, 89, 707/220-21, 710/194, 735/24, 26, 77; Detzer, *Appointment,* pp. 242-43; interview with Dorothy Detzer Denny by David Wyman, Washington, D.C., May 11, 1965; *Washington Post,* Jan. 25, 1944, p. 10; *Answer* (Feb. 12, 1944) 2(3):7, 11, 13, 16, 18; NYT, Jan. 27, 1944, p. 4; *Interpreter Releases* (Mar. 27, 1944) 21(14):126; printed, untitled brochure on activities of ECSJPE [early 1945], p. 9, copy in PSC papers, box 9, folder 69; Wilson, Memo of conversation with Goldmann, May 19, 1944, SD file 867N.01/2347; Gillette to Thomas, Jan. 24, 1944, Elbert Thomas papers, box 80, C-5 Congress.

100. "Action Taken" memo, Jan. 18, 1944, McCormack to Executive Director, Feb. 19, 1944 [actually 1945], WRB papers, box 28, WRB vol. 3; Stewart to Pehle, Feb. 8, 1944, WRB papers, box 50, Other Government Agencies (Treasury Department); Pehle to Heller, Rosenwald, Wise, Apr. 7, 1944, WRB papers, box 26, United Jewish Appeal; Montor, Minute of a Meeting on the Subject of the WRB, Feb. 4, 1944, Minute of a Meeting with John W. Pehle, Feb. 10, 1944, Coons to Voorsanger, July 10, 1944, JDC papers, WRB 1944; MD 694/207, 696/150-63, 709/27, 711/136, 716/178; "History of the WRB," pp. 6-7, 356-60, WRB papers, box 110; "Final Summary Report of the Executive Director, War Refugee Board" [Washington, 1945], pp. 13-15; *NY Post,* Jan. 24, 1944, p. 23; Henry Morgenthau Jr., "The Morgenthau Diaries: The Refugee Run-Around," *Colliers,* Nov. 1, 1947, pp. 22ff. The figure of 100,000 to 200,000 is based on a large amount of research to be incorporated in my forthcoming book on the American response to the Holocaust. In brief, the WRB helped evacuate about 25,000 Jews from Axis territory, played a crucial role in the safeguarding of 48,000 Jews in danger in Transnistria, and contributed significantly to keeping the Budapest Jews from being deported to Auschwitz. Raoul Wallenberg, a WRB agent, was actively involved in protecting at least 20,000 (and probably many thousands more than that) of the 120,000 Budapest Jews who survived.

101. ECSJPE, "A Year in the Service of Humanity," Aug. 1944, pp. 31-41, PSC papers, box 5, folder 22; NYT, June 18, p. 24, July 10, p. 9, Aug. 25, p. 6, Aug. 30, p. 15 (all in 1944); *Answer,* (Aug. 29, 1944) 2(8-9):22, 2 (supplement), Sept. 12, 1944, p. 2; *NY Post,* Feb. 10, 1944, pp. 20-21, Apr. 10, 1944, p. 16; CJR (Oct. 1944) 7(5):571; Silver and Wise to Scott, Sept. 8, 1944, Silver papers, 4-2-50 AZEC 1944-45; AJ Conference, *Report of the Interim Committee,* pp. 24-34, 79; Silver and Wise to Taft, Sept. 8, 1944, Robert Taft papers, box 818; Lipsky to Taft, Sept. 13, 1944, Taft papers, box 819; Tenenbaum to Wagner, Sept. 1, 1944, Wagner papers, Palestine files, box 2, folder 28; Aaron Berman, "American Zionism and the Rescue of European Jewry: An Ideological Perspective," *American Jewish History,* (Mar. 1981) 70(3):322-23; Council of Jewish Federations and Welfare

Funds, Budgeting Bulletin, #B-16, June 1944, Vaad Hahatzala papers, box 17; Kalmanowitz to Sternbuch, Dec. 5, 1944, Office Report to Committee Members and Patrons [Aug. 1945], Vaad Hahatzala papers, box 8; Lewin, *Polish Review* (1977) 22(4):17; Isaac Lewin, "Attempts at Rescuing European Jews with the Help of Polish Diplomatic Missions during World War II: Part II," *Polish Review* (1979) 24(1):59; Vaad Hahatzala, memorandum, Jan. 10, 1945, Vaad Hahatzala to O'Dwyer, Feb. 5, 1945, WRB papers, box 27, Vaad Hahatzala Emergency Committee; MD 718/92, 106-110, 172, 192, 225, 719/158, 180; Clattenburg to Foster, Feb. 26, 1945, SD file 840.48 Refugees/2-2645.

Chapter 2

1. Chaim Bermant, *The Cousinhood: The Anglo-Jewish Gentry* (London: Eyre & Spottiswoode, 1971).

2. Andrew Sharf, *The British Press and Jews under Nazi Rule* (London: Oxford University Press 1964), esp. pp. 10-11.

3. Archives of the Board of Deputies of British Jews, London, C11/2/35/3.

4. *Ibid.,* C11/2/37/1.

5. Bernard Wasserstein, *Britain and the Jews of Europe 1939-1945* (London: Oxford University Press 1979), pp. 168-69.

6. Archives of the World Jewish Congress, London.

7. Lichtheim to Linton, September 26, 1942, Central Zionist Archives, Jerusalem, L22/134.

8. Lichtheim to Linton, September 29, 1942, *ibid.*

9. A. J. Sherman, *Island Refuge: Britain and Refugees from the Third Reich 1933-1939* (London: Paul Elek 1973), p. 30.

10. Walter Laqueur, *The Terrible Secret* (London: Weidenfeld and Nicolson 1980); and Martin Gilbert, *Auschwitz and the Allies* (London: Michael Joseph, 1981).

11. Minutes of meeting on November 25, 1942, Central Zionist Archives, Z4/302/26.

12. Jacob Katz, "Was the Holocaust Predictable?", *Commentary,* May 1975, pp. 41-48.

13. "Proposals of the Jewish Community as regards Jewish refugees from Germany," April 1939, Public Record Office, London, CAB 24/239. See Sherman, *Island Refuge,* pp. 30-31.

14. Memorandum dated April 7, 1933, Public Record Office, London, CAB 24/239.

15. "Memorandum on the Refugee Question in the United Kingdom," September 11, 1935, Public Record Office, London, FO 371/19678/452.

16. Sherman, *Island Refuge* and Norman Bentwich, *They Found Refuge,* (London: Cresset Press, 1956).

17. Norman Bentwich, *My Seventy-Seven Years* (London: Routledge and Kegan Paul, 1962), p. 41.

18. David Wyman, *Paper Walls: America and the Refugee Crisis 1938-1941,* (Amherst: University of Massachusetts Press, 1968), pp. 75-93.

19. Sherman, *Island Refuge,* p. 265.

20. Wasserstein, *Britain and the Jews of Europe,* pp. 82-83.

21. *Ibid.*

22. *Ibid.,* p. 132.

23. R.T.E. Latham minute, December 24, 1940, Public Record Office, London, FO 371/25254/487.

24. Minutes of Cabinet Committee on the Reception and Accommodation of Jewish Refugees, December 31, 1942, Public Record Office, London, CAB 95/15.

25. M. Gordon Liverman to A. G. Brotman, May 14, 1940, Board of Deputies of British Jews Archives, London C2/3/3/10/2.

26. N. Laski to A. G. Brotman, *ibid.,* C2/3/5/10/5.

27. N. Laski to Winston Churchill, August 9, 1940, *ibid.,* C2/3/3/10/2.

28. Sir A. McFadyean to N. Laski, August 29, 1940, *ibid.,* C2/3/5/40/5.

29. Minutes of meeting, *ibid.,* C11/7/2/6 (emphases in original).

30. Selig Brodetsky, *Memoirs: From Ghetto to Israel* (London: Weidenfeld and Nicolson 1960), p. 220.

31. The Earl of Avon (Sir Anthony Eden), *The Eden Memoirs: The Reckoning* (London: Cassell 1965), p. 358.

32. Wasserstein, *Britain and the Jews of Europe,* p. 190.

33. Lady Reading to Winston Churchill, January 16, 1943, Public Record Office, London, PREM 4/51/8/556.

34. Hansard, House of Lords, March 23, 1943.

35. Memorandum dated February 12, 1943, Board of Deputies of British Jews Archives, London, C11/7/1/5.

36. Minute (signature not identified), June 14, 1941, Public Record Office, London, FO 371/26172.

37. Quoted in Paul Addison, *The Road to 1945: British Politics and the Second World War* (London: Cape 1975), p. 253.

38. Minute dated May 6, 1941, Public Record Office, London, CO 733/449/P1/0/20.

39. Norman Bentwich, *My Seventy-Seven Years,* pp. 191-92.

40. Quoted in Chaim Bermant, *Troubled Eden: An Anatomy of British Jewry* (London: Vallentine Mitchell 1969), p. 194.

41. *Kol Kitve Ahad Ha-am,* Tel Aviv: Dvir 5721 (1961), p. 71.

Chapter 3

1. Labour Party Archives (hereafter: LPA), minutes of a meeting of the Mapai Center, December 7, 1938.

2. Rich documentation about the topic in Nathanel Katzburg's *Mediniut b'Mavoch Mediniut Britania b'Eretz Israel, 1940-1945* (The Palestine Problem in British Policy, 1940-45), (Jerusalem: Yad Yitzhak Ben-Zvi, 1976).

3. *The Letters and Papers of Chaim Weizmann* (Ed. by Aaron Kleiman), vol. 18 series A (January 1937-December 1938) (Jerusalem, 1979, Transaction Books), no. 326 (Dr. Weizmann to Sir Warren Fisher, April 19, 1938).

4. Dr. Weizmann to Blanche Dugdale, July 7, 1938 (*Ibid.,* no. 337).

5. Ben Gurion at the 4th Mapai Conference, May 7, 1938 (David Ben Gurion, *B'Maaraha,* Tel Aviv, 1941, 2:47-48).

6. "[I] didn't know then that not concentration but death camps awaited the refugees whom no one wanted. If I had known that, I couldn't have gone on sitting there silently hour after hour being disciplined and polite." (Golda Meir, *My Life* [London, 1974], p. 127).

7. Ben Gurion at the meeting of the Mapai Center on December 7, 1938 (LPA).

8. *Davar* (Tel Aviv), July 3, 1938.

9. Minutes of the Jewish Agency Executive (hereafter: JAE), June 26, 1938 (Central Zionist Archives (hereafter: CZA), S 25/9817.

10. Minutes (LPA) of the 4th Mapai Conference, May 8th, 1938.

11. A. J. Kochavi, *The Attitude of the Jewish Agency Executive to the Distress of the Jews of Europe from the Anschluss to the Outbreak of the Second World War* (in Hebrew) (M.A. thesis, Haifa University, 1981, pp. 151 ff.) For Kaplan's later views see Minutes of the JAE, June 27, 1943.

12. E.g. the so called "Siah B" (B faction) struggle; a split between the Mapai and the Ahdut Avoda occurred in 1944.

13. Anita Schapira, *Berl Katznelson.* A Biography (in Hebrew) (Tel Aviv: Am Oved, 1980), 2:605.

14. *Ibid.,* p. 606.

15. One of the early authoritative works about the "Mossad" is Shaul Avigur's *Im Dor ha'Hagana* (With the Hagana Generation) (Tel Aviv: Ma'arachot, 1970). Reliable is Ehud Avriel's *Pithu et ha'Shearim* (The Gates Have Been Opened) (Tel Aviv: Sifriat Ma'ariv, 1976); a fictionalization of the "Mossad's" early activities 1938-1940 is Peggy Mann and Ruth Klüger's *The Last Escape* (New York: Pinnacle Books, 1974).

16. See Y. Gelber, "Ha'Itonut ha'Ivrit b'Eretz Israel al Hashmadat Yehudei Europa, 1941-1942" (The Hebrew Press in Israel about the Extermination of European Jewry), in *"Dapim le'Heker ha'Shoah ve-ha 'Mered",* new series, Vol. 1., (Tel Aviv, 1969), pp. 30-34. Yoav Gelber's later writing on "Zionist Policy and the Fate of European Jewry (1939-1942)" (in *Yad Vashem Studies,* 13:169-210), based almost entirely on primary source material, is the best analysis of the Yishuv leaders' attitude toward the fate of European Jewry in the first years of the war.

17. E.g. J. P. Perk (signed for J. M. Martin) to Dr. Weizmann, February 12, 1941 and Lord Moyne's reply to Dr. Weizmann, February 19, 1941 (CZA, S 25/2518).

18. J. H. Peck (on behalf of Churchill) to Dr. Weizmann, February 12, 1941 *(ibid).*

19. Minutes of the JAE Meeting, October 19, 1941.

20. *Ibid.,* November 9, 1941.

21. *Ibid.,* November 16, 1941.

22. *Ibid.*

23. *Ibid.,* December 14, 1941.

24. The Executive of the Zionist Organization. Organization Department, Jerusalem, September 28, 1942, no. 848 to Lichtheim (Geneva) (CZA, L 22/3).

25. *Ibid.* The best comprehensive work about when and how the news of the mass murders reached the western world is Walter Laqueur's *The Terrible Secret* (London: Weidenfeld and Nicolson, 1980); however, the book treats only marginally the Yishuv's information and its reaction.

26. Lichtheim (Geneva) to Y. Grünbaum, October 8, 1942, no. 845 (CZA L 22/3).

27. Sharet to Linton (London), November 20, 1942 (CZA S 25/5183).

28. *Ibid.*

29. Anita Schapira, *Katznelson,* 2:666-667.

30. Dr. Weizmann to Halifax, February 16, 1943 (CZA S 25/2492).

31. *Ibid.*

32. E.g. the correspondence between Weizmann and Churchill (February 7 and 19, 1941) /CZA S 25/2518/, Sharet on behalf of Romanian Jewry (May 15, 1942, CZA S/25/2492), Dov Josef (Bernard Joseph) on behalf of Jewish refugees from the Balkans (February 9, 1943, CZA S 6/3602) and Weizmann to Halifax on behalf of Romanian Jews (March 4, 1943, CZA S 25/2492).

33. Neima Barzel, *The "Working Group" and the Zionist Leadership in Slovakia, 1941-1944* (M.A. thesis (in Hebrew), Haifa University, 1981, p. 75.

34. About the activity of the Rescue Committee see Arieh Morgenstern, "Vaad ha'Hatzala ha'Meuhad shel ha'Sochnut ha'Yehudit upeulotav b'shanim 1943-1945" (The Rescue Committee of the Jewish Agency and its Activity During 1943-1945) (in "Yalkut Moreshet," June 1971, pp. 60-97).

35. A cross-section of the group's activity in the *Archion Lishkat ha'Kesher b'Kushta* (the register of the Archives of the Yishuv's Rescue Board in Istanbul), vol. 1., Hungary, Haifa University, 1977.

36. About the group's activity see Dalia Ofer, "Peulot ha'Mishlahat ha'Eretz Israelit b'Kushta—1943" (The Activity of the Eretz Israel Delegation in Istanbul), in *Rescue Attempts During the Holocaust,* (Yad Vashem, Jerusalem, 1976), pp. 360-370.

37. Minutes of a meeting of the JAE, June 27, 1943 (CZA S 25/295).

38. Minutes of a meeting of the Rescue Committee, March 23, 1943 (CZA S 26/1239).

39. *Ibid.*

40. *Ibid.*

41. Memorandum by A. Hartglass (CZA S 26/1239).

42. *Ibid.*

43. *Ibid.*

44. There is no evidence about the echoes of the memorandum; the immigrant organizations, mainly those representing immigrants from Romania, addressed sharply-worded letters and notes to the Yishuv leadership, criticizing their lack of efficiency.

45. Letter to the JA, the Rescue Committee and to the Histadrut Executive (Istanbul, August 3, 1943, CZA S 26/1240).

46. Minutes of a meeting of the JAE, November 29, 1942.

47. E.g. at the meeting of the Zionist Executive Committee, July 5, 1943 (CZA S 25/299) and at the meeting of the inner Council of the Zionist Executive Committee, September 1, 1943 (CZA S 25/301).

48. Minutes of the Mapai Center, August 24, 1943. (LPA)

49. *Idem,* August 28, 1943.

50. Minutes of a meeting of the JAE, August 22, 1943.

51. Minutes of a meeting of the Secretariat of the Histadrut Executive Committee, November 18, 1943.

52. Minutes of a meeting of the Zionist Executive Committee, May 18, 1943 (CZA S 25/297).

53. Minutes of a meeting of the inner Council of the Zionist Executive Committee, September 1, 1943 (CZA, S 25/301, pp. 4., 8.).

54. *Ibid.,* p. 10.

55. *Ibid.,* p. 15.

56. Historical Documentation Center, Haifa University, H3C 59.5.

57. *Ibid.*

58. Yoel Palgi, *'Ruach g'dola ba'ah* (And Behold, A Great Wind Came) Tel Aviv: Am Oved, 1977, p. 17.

59. Chaim Hermesh, *Mivtza Amsterdam* (Operation Amsterdam) (Tel Aviv: Ma'arachot, 1971), p. 7.

60. *Ibid.,* p. 8.

61. *Ibid.,* p. 57.

62. About the circumstances prevailing in Budapest see Rafi Ben-Shalom, *Ne'evaknu le'maan ha'chayim* (We fought for Life) (Tel Aviv: Moreshet, 1977); see also note 59 (Haifa University, p. 15, Ben Shalom's remarks).

63. About the echo of the Hungarian events see Raphael Vago, "The Destruction of Hungarian Jewry as Reflected in the Palestine Press" (reprinted from Randolph L. Braham, ed. *Hungarian-Jewish Studies,* (New York: World Federation of Hungarian Jews, 1973), 3:291-324).

64. Inter alia see *Archion Lishkat ha'Kesher b'Kushta,* pp. 105-117.

65. Shaul Avigur to Sharet, June 4, 1944 and J. M. Martin to Dr. Weizmann, April 24, 1944 (CZA S 25/5205).

66. Minutes of a meeting of the Secretariat of the Histadrut Executive Committee, December 29, 1943 (LPA, The Meetings of the (Histadrut) Executive Committee, 1939-1945).

67. The leaders of the immigrants from Romania contended that the Yishuv

leadership was not alert and efficient in the practical questions of the immigration (e.g. financing, the problem of the repatriation from Transnistria, etc.). E.g. the Association of Immigrants from Romania to Sharet, January 11, 1944, and to the JA, March 29, 1944 (CZA S 25/5743). See also Dr. M. Landau to Ben Gurion, September 21 and October 3, 1944 (S 25/5743).

68. Brand's version in Alex Weissberg, *Advocate to the Dead. The Story of Joel Brand* (London: Deutsch, 1956).

69. Sharet's reaction to Brand's accusations in his *post scriptum* to the Hebrew edition of Weissberg's book (Tel Aviv, 1957, pp. 232-237). S. B. Beit-Zvi's *Post-Ugandian Zionism in the Crucible of the Holocaust* (in Hebrew) (Tel Aviv: Bronfmann, 1977), is a scathingly critical appraisal of the Yishuv leadership's role during the Holocaust. The book includes a number of postwar letters of Ben Gurion and Sharet written to the author.

70. Eliezer Livne, "Sihot Ahronot im Berl Katznelson" (Last Talks with Berl Katznelson) *"Haaretz,"* July 31, 1964.

71. *Ibid.* I am indebted to Professor Leni Yahil who made available to me her MS of a comprehensive work about the Holocaust. I have used chapter 20, pp. 125-129 of her MS.

72. Berl Katznelson launched a pretentious literary enterprise publishing dozens of novels during the last war years.

73. Livne, "Sihot Ahronot."

Chapter 4

1. *Ludwig Report,* p. 118/9.

2. *Ibid.,* p. 125.

3. "Strictly racial refugees, e.g., Jews, are not to be considered as political refugees." *Ibid.,* p. 205.

4. *Ibid.,* p. 192.

5. The composition of the Board was changed somewhat on November 2, 1941; further changes occurred, notably on March 25, 1942, and on March 28, 1943.

6. Minutes, SIG Assembly of Delegates, 25 May 1941.

7. Minutes, Central Committee, SIG, November 2, 1941.

8. Files of the "Ludwig Report dossier" in the archives of the SIG.

9. The letter was quoted in full in the Swiss parliamentary debate of June 8, 1954, on the origins of the introduction of the regulations requiring the marking of passports of German Jews with the letter *J.* It was obviously intended to show the close association of the Swiss Jews with the authorities. The *Ludwig Report* mentions in this connection an article published in the Swiss Jewish paper *Schweizerisches Israelitisches Wochenblatt* (Swiss-Jewish Weekly) on the parliamentary debate. It stated that the attitude of the representative of Swiss Jewry at that time and now deceased to whom Rothmund had referred was not approved in large circles of Swiss

Jewry. This had led to internal differences and finally to the resignation of the person in question. (*Ludwig Report,* p. 150)

10. Ludwig Report, p. 318.

11. Edgar Bonjour, *Geschichte der Schweizerischen Neutralität,* 6:39-40.

Chapter 5

1. Harry O. Sandberg, "The Jews of Latin-America." *American Jewish Yearbook,* New York, (1917–1918) 19:35-105.

2. Louis Sobel, Jewish community Life and Organization in Latin America, *The Jewish Social Service Quarterly,* (June 1944) 20(4):179-190.

3. Ira Rosenswaike, "The Jewish Population of Argentina," *Jewish Social Studies,* (Oct. 1960) 22:195-214; U. O. Schmelz, and Sergio Della Pergola, *Ha-Demografia shel ha-Yehudim be-Argentina ube-aratzot aherot shel America ha-latinit* (The Demography of the Jews in Argentina and in Other Countries of Latin America) (Tel Aviv: Hebrew University of Jerusalem and Tel Aviv University, 1974).

4. Harry O. Sandberg, "Jews of Latin America," p. 41.

5. Haim Avni, *Mi-Bitul ha-Inquizitzia Ve-ad hok ha-shevut—Toldot ha-hagira va-yehudit le-Argentina (The History of Jewish Immigration to Argentina, 1810-1950)* (Jerusalem, The Hebrew University of Jerusalem, 1982), p. 184.

6. *Ibid.,* pp. 248-49.

7. *Ibid.,* pp. 270-75.

8. *Di Idische Zeitung,* Buenos Aires, Nov. 28, 1932. Editorial.

9. Municipalidad de la Ciudad de Buenos Aires, *Cuarto Censo General, 1936,* vol. 3 (Buenos Aires, 1939) as quoted by Ira Rosenswaike, "Jewish Population of Argentina," p. 203.

10. Jaime Favelukes, "La asistencia social en nuestra colectividad." *Mundo Israelita,* Buenos Aires, Oct. 11, 1930, p. 3.

11. *AJC* (American Jewish Committee Arhives) RG1-EX0-29, Mexico 1911, 1931–1939 Ziegfrid Lifschitz Report, June 1931.

12. *AJA* (American Jewish Archives, Cincinnati), Morris D. Waldman Papers, *Report on Visit to Latin America* by Morris D. Waldman, Nov. 1944, p. 8; Nathan Bistritzky, *Al ha-yahadut veha-tzionut be-America ha-Latinit* (On Judaism and Zionism in Latin America) (Jerusalem: The Jewish National Fund, 5707 1946–47), p. 17.

13. *JCA/LON* (Jewish Colonization Association, Archive, London) material for Oct. 1936 Session, B. Mellibowsky, Mission au Perou, Mar. 24, 1936.

14. Avni, Jewish Immigration to Argentina, p. 282.

15. Judith Laikin Elkin, *Jews of Latin American Republics* (Chapel Hill: The University of North Carolina Press, 1980), pp. 46-47; Mellibowsky, Mission au Perou.

16. *AJA* Rhodes Collection Box no. 2249, Friedrich Borchardt and David Glick, reports on Ecuador, Bolivia, Paraguay, July 20, 1939.

17. Margalit Bejarano-Bachi, *Ha-kehilah ha-sefaradit shel Buenos-Aires* [The Sephardi Community of Buenos-Aires] (M.A. Thesis, The Institute of Contemporary Jewry, The Hebrew University of Jerusalem) Jerusalem, 1974.

18. *Ibid.,* p. 64.

19. *Ibid.,* pp. 89, 143-147.

20. Haim Avni, "Argentine Jewry: Its Socio-Political Status and Organizational Patterns" *Dispersion and Unity,* (1971) 12:128-62; (1971-72) 13-14:161-208; (1972-73) 15:158-215.

21. Zvi Schechner, *Bi-drahim lo makbilot, hashvaat toldot ha-hitargenut ha-kehilatit ba-yahadut ha-Ashkenazit shel Mexico ve-Argentina, 1930-1957* [In Unparallel Ways—A Comparison of the History of Ashkenazi Communal Organization in Argentina and Mexico], (M.A. Thesis, The Institute of Contemporary Jewry, The Hebrew University of Jerusalem) 1978, pp. 22-67.

22. A. Margolin, *Vegn un Ziln fun Kampf* (Ways and Aims of the Struggle) (Buenos Aires: Ediciones Alerta, 1943).

23. Zionist Organization, *Report of the Executive of the Zionist Organization* submitted to the XVI Zionist Congress 1929, p. 140.

24. *CZA* (Central Zionist Archives, Jerusalem) File no. S53/468, A. S. Juris to N. Goldman and L. Lauterbach, Sept. 27, 1941; S25/3027, A. Milbashan, "Report on the Development of Zionism in South America in 1940" (Hebrew) Apr. 14, 1940.

25. Bistritzky, On Judaism and Zionism, pp. 57-58.

26. Bejarano-Bachi, Sephardi of Buenos Aires, pp. 132-42.

27. Avni, *Jewish Immigration,* pp. 199-201, 268-69.

28. *CZA* S5/519, M. Kostrinsky, to Zionist Executive, London, Aug. 6, 1938.

29. *WJC* (World Jewish Congress Archives, New York), LA4, Memorandum Submitted to the First Secretary of the Brazilian Embassy, Washington June 1, 1943.

30. *WJC* LA14, B. Zuckerman, Report, July 20, 1943; LA2 J. Hellman to N. Goldman, Aug. 17, 1940; *CZA* S25/3027, A. Mibashan, Report Apr. 14, 1940, p. 3.

31. Boris Sapir, *The Jewish Community of Cuba* (New York 1948); *CZA* S5/473, E. Sourasky to L. Tov, Nov. 13 1939; *Ibid.,* Victor Mitrani to Zionist Executive, Nov. 16, 1940.

32. Zvi Schechner, Unparallel Ways, pp. 107-13; *CZA* A346/49, J. Tchornitzki to M. Graiver, Nov. 19, 1938.

33. Moshe Nes-El, *Yahadut Chile 1930-1950,* [Chilean Jewry 1930-1950] (M.A. Thesis, The Institute of Contemporary Jewry, The Hebrew University of Jerusalem) Jerusalem, 1974, pp. 95-115. *CZA* S53/299 L. Yaffe to K. Blumenfeld, Nov. 7, 1942.

34. *CZA* S53/468, A. S. Juris to N. Goldman and L. Lauterbach, Sept. 27, 1941.

35. *AJA* Morris Waldman Papers, Report on a Visit to Latin America by M. Waldman, Nov. 1944, p. 12; *AJC* RG1-EXO 29, Latin America 1943-50, Muts to J. Slawson, Sept. 22, 1944.

36. Avni, op. cit., 1982, various chapters about JCA's work and HICEM's relationship with SOPROTIMIS.

37. A curious product of the support offered in Mexico and in Cuba are two basic volumes on the history of the communities there. See Sapir, *Jewish Community of Cuba,* and Leon Sourasky, *Historia de la Comunidad Israelita de Mexico* (Mexico: The Author, 1965).

38. *AJA,* Rhodes Collection, Box 2249, F. Borchardt and D. Glick to JDC, July 20, 1939; *Ibid.,* Misc. file, D. Glick "Some Were Rescued." Reprinted from *Harvard Law School Bulletin,* Dec. 1960, pp. 6-20.

39. Sobel, "Jewish Community Life," pp. 184-85; for fuller contemporary reports on the settlement of German-speaking Jews, see Asociacion Filantropica Israelita, *Diez Años* de Obra Constructiva en America del Sur, 1933-1943, (Buenos Aires: Asociacion Filantropica Israelita, 1943).

40. *CZA* S5/389, Z. Nijenson and J. Bronfman to World Zionist Executive, Dec. 30, 1938.

41. Among many others see *CZA* S53/468, Reports from A. S. Juris, Sept. and Oct. 1941; Z4/10224, United Zionist Organization of Mexico to Head Office of Keren Ha-Yesod, Sept. 18, 1941. Report on Jaffe's activities.

42. *CZA* 25/2037 N. Bistritzky, to L. Lauterbach, Nov. 25, 1943; "Summary of My Activity in Latin America," 1946.

43. *WJC* LA 14, Report of Baruch Zuckerman, July 20, 1943.

44. *WJC* LA 18 Report on Mexico and Central America by Mrs. Kate Knopfmacher, Feb. 1, 1944.

45. *CZA* A 346/49 Manuel Graiver's correspondence on stationery of "Campaña de Pasajes, colecta Nacional de Pidion Shebuim para Trasladar Refugiados a Palestina" (National Campaign for the Redemption of Prisoners [and] for the Shipment of Refugees to Palestine)—that was the name he gave to the 1940 Keren Ha-Yesod Campaign in Mexico of which he was director.

46. *CZA* S53/316, L. Yaffe to Keren Ha-Yesod in New York, July 23, 1941; S5/389 A. Mibashan to K. I. Blumenfeld, Nov. 17 1940.

47. *AJC* RG1 EXO-29, Argentina 1937-44, J. Schwartz to M. Waldman, Mar. 13, 1940; *WJC* LA1 J. Hellman to N. Goldman, Dec. 30, 1939.

48. *Mundo Israelita,* Buenos Aires, Feb. 28, p. 4, Mar. 7, p. 6, July 25, 1942. (The encounter and interchange of declarations of the *DAIA* and the Comité Central Israelita de Ayuda.)

49. *WJC* LA15 A. Tartakower to J. Hellman, Mar. 31, 1944; J. Hellman to Tartakower Apr. 11, 1944.

50. *AJC* EXO 29, Latin America 1943-50, M. Gottschalk to M. Waldman, July 9th 1943.

51. *Ibid.,* Latin America 1936-38, M. Waldman to J. N. Rosenberg, Memo Mar. 4, 1937; M. Waldman to C. Adler Apr. 21, 1937; *Ibid.,* Latin America 1943-50, J. Landau to J. Slawson, Dec. 16, 1943. In Apr. 1944 the AJC approached A. Dorfman

from Buenos Aires to assume the Committee's representation. In 1945, Maximo Yagupsky, an educator was engaged.

52. *AJA* Morris D. Waldman Papers, Report Nov. 1944, pp. 19, 23, 24.

53. *Ibid.,* pp. 25, 26.

54. Isaac Kaplan, *Idische Kolonies in Argentine, Zihroines fun a agrar cooperativist* (Jewish Colonies in Argentina, Memoirs of an Agrarian Cooperativist) (Buenos Aires: Friends of the Author, 1966). Kaplan was also many years member of the board and vice president of the DAIA as well as a Keren Kayemet leader.

55. Benjamin Mellibowsky, "Meine 51 yor zu dinst bei der JCA, HICEM-HIAS un SOPROTIMIS" (My 51 Years of Service with JCA, HICEM-HIAS and SOPROTIMIS), *Argentiner YIVO Schriftn,* (Buenos Aires, 1957) no. 7, pp. 91-167.

56. *CZA* A346/49, J. Tchornitzki to M. Graiver, Nov. 19, 1938; S25/2037, A. Mibashan to L. Lauterbach, Dec. 6, 1939.

57. Moshe Davis, *Beit Israel Be-America* (The Jewish Experience in America) (Jerusalem: The Hebrew University of Jerusalem, 1970), pp. 299-304; 336-42. Contains an analysis of Rabbi Sithon's ban; Benjamin Benzaquen, *La Colectividad Sefaradi de Beunos Aires* (The Sephardic Community of Beunos Aires). (Beunos Aires: The Author 1929).

58. *OHD* (Oral History Division, Institute of Contemporary Jewry, Hebrew University of Jerusalem), Testimony of E. Lowenstein.

59. Schechner, Unparallel Ways, pp. 18-22.

60. Nicolas Rapoport, *Desde Lejos Hasta Ayer* (From Far Away to Yesterday). (Buenos Aires: The Author, 1957). Contains autobiographical traits of a pathetic Jewish Argentinian. See Avni, *op. cit.* 1971-1973 regarding the DAIA.

61. *OHD,* Testimonies of Haim Finkelstein and Elias Sourasky.

62. Jacobo Palatizki, Di Yidische yugentd un sport bawegung in 1942 (The Jewish Youth and Sport Movements in 1942) *Argentiner Yivo Schriftn,* (1945), no. 3, pp. 131-49.

63. *CZA* S5/519, L. Lauterbach to Poalei-Zion, Oct. 1939; S5/473 L. Dulzin to the Zionist Executive, June 2, 1940.

64. *AJA* Morris Waldman Papers, Report on Visit etc. p. 17; *WJC* LA15 World Jewish Congress and American Jewish Congress, Statement of receipts and disbursements for the fiscal year ending Sept. 30, 1944.

65. Haim Avni, "Mul Shearim Neulim, 1933-1950" ("Facing Locked Gates"). *The History of Jewish Immigration to Argentina,* 1982, pp. 279-355.

66. Henry L. Feingold, *The Politics of Rescue,* (New Brunswick, N.J.: Rutgers University Press, 1970), pp. 22-44, 99-102.

67. James G. McDonald, Draft of an Interim Report on the Mission to South and Central America of Dr. Samuel Guy Inman and the High Commissioner, March–June 1935 (Geneva) 1935.

68. Statements by Helio Lobo, Le Breton A. Gastalú, representatives of Brazil, Argentina, Ecuador, respectively, *Proceedings of the Intergovernmental Committee,*

Evian July 6th to 15th 1938, pp. 17-18, 21-22, 28.

69. Haim Avni, pp. 281, 288-289, 301 and Table 4 "Jewish Immigration to Argentina During the Holocaust Era," p. 372.

70. *Ibid.,* pp. 350-351.

71. See Arnold Ebel, *Das Dritte Reich und Argentinien 1933-39,* (Cologne, Vienna: Bohlau Verlag, 1971); Reiner Pommerin, *Das Dritte Reich und Latinamerika 1933-1942* (Dusseldorf: Droste Verlag, 1977).

72. S. Adler-Rudel, "The Evian Conference on the Refugee Question," *Leo Baeck Institute Yearbook,* (1968) 13:235-38.